ESSENTIAL CARE IN THE FIELD

Other books by Jackie Drakeford and Mark Elliott and published by Swan Hill Press

ESSENTIAL CARE FOR DOGS

Other books by Jackie Drakeford and published by Swan Hill Press

WORKING FERRETS
RABBIT CONTROL
THE HOUSE LURCHER
THE WORKING LURCHER

ESSENTIAL CARE
IN THE FIELD

A FITNESS MANUAL FOR
WORKING DOGS

Jackie Drakeford
and
Mark Elliott
BVSC VetMFHom MRCVS MIPsiMED PCH DSH RSHom

SWAN·HILL
PRESS

Copyright © 2007 Jackie Drakeford and Mark Elliott

First published in the UK in 2007
by Swan Hill Press, an imprint of Quiller Publishing Ltd

British Library Cataloguing-in-Publication Data
A catalogue record for this book is available from the British Library

ISBN 978 1 84689 014 7

The right of Jackie Drakeford and Mark Elliott to be identified as the authors of this work has
been asserted in accordance with the Copyright, Design and Patent Act 1988.

Printed in Malta by Gutenberg Press Limited

Swan Hill Press

An imprint of Quiller Publishing Ltd
Wykey House, Wykey, Shrewsbury, SY4 1JA
tel: 01939 261616 Fax: 01939 261606
E-mail: info@quillerbooks.com
Website: www.countrybooksdirect.com

CONTENTS

Authors' Note

This book has been written to offer owners first aid advice when dealing with emergencies and minor ailments involving dogs. Whilst written using veterinary knowledge and from experience, it should never be used as a substitute for professional (veterinary) assessment, advice and treatment. It should be noted that on occasion the provision of first aid, however well intentioned, has the potential to cause harm to the patient and to the provider. It is the responsibility of the reader to consider these risks when deciding on a course of action in any given situation. It should also be noted that even in the hands of professionals, with all the facilities of modern medicine, a successful outcome from treating illness or emergency cannot be guaranteed, and permanent debility or even loss of life can occur. In the field results can be expected to be even less successful. Any illustrations and photographs are provided as a guide and are in no way intended to be complete, or step-by-step instructions.

The authors and publisher cannot be held responsible for any loss or personal injury caused by the application of any advice provided in this book.

In all cases where there is any doubt, contact your nearest veterinary surgeon immediately.

INTRODUCTION

The 'Golden Thread' is that invisible link which exists between working dogs and their handlers. The rapport between dog and human is at its strongest and most profound when the dog is fulfilling its working instincts under human guidance. It is deeply moving when seen at its best, blurring the lines between canine and human, almost spiritual in its harmony. There are many ways in which dogs work with us, far exceeding anything that they would do for themselves, and often in danger of

The Golden Thread

compromising their own welfare on the way. Dogs are infinitely generous with using their health and strength, their particular skills and instincts, under our instruction to help us. Inevitably, there are accidents and illnesses which can occur as a direct result of this willingness. We in our turn can do our best to keep risks to a minimum, and give the most appropriate care for that particular dog working in that particular discipline, whatever difficulties arise.

Working dogs now have the potential to be better cared for than in any time in history, and to live longer in health, but we still have gaps in our husbandry. Closed gene pools in pedigree dogs, and inherited defects in pure and cross-breeds, can make choosing a pup a minefield. Improved veterinary knowledge can sometimes risk leaning into over-medication or unnecessary surgery, and a less clear-cut decision over when a dog still has quality of life or if it is time for a merciful end. More available food gives more opportunity to feed badly, more toxins in the environment can mean more challenges to health. Human fitness regimes are not necessarily suitable for dogs, nor can dogs have any concept of winning or losing working competitions held by and for humans. And some risks never change, some diseases are never conquered, some parasites are never eradicated. In these pages, we discuss how best to source your dog and how to pick the best one for your job, how to feed it and get it fit, how to avoid many health problems and how to cope with those that cannot be avoided, and then how this care translates into the working day and night.

The majority of working dogs in the UK nowadays lead a life of happiness and fulfilment such as other dogs could only dream of, but work itself is a risk, just as indolence, overweight and lack of stimulation can bring ill-health too. This book shows how to choose the right working dog in the first place, how to then create the best environment for it, whatever its discipline, and how to achieve optimum health. The healthy dog gets fitter, works harder, recovers faster, heals better and lives longer than the unhealthy dog. The sheer shine and bounce and joie de vivre of a fit, fulfilled dog doing the job it was bred for is a joy to behold. There is no better way for a working dog to spend its life than by working, and we have written this book to enable working dogs and their owners to access the very best of care tailored specifically for the working dog in the field.

1. Choosing the Right Dog
HOUNDS FOR GROUNDS

C aring for your dog starts with getting the right one in the first place, whatever its purpose is destined to be. That means looking very hard at what you want from the dog, and, equally importantly, what you do not want. Look at how you intend to keep the dog, how, where and under what conditions you will work it, whether it has another role as a family pet, show dog, competition dog or all of them. Consider which flaws you could, at a pinch, tolerate, and which you could not. Then you will need to be honest with yourself about what you can offer the dog, what you are not prepared to give the dog, whether and how you are prepared to change your lifestyle to accommodate the dog, and if you can meet it halfway with any of these. Before you choose the dog, remind yourself about your own personality traits and flaws, and be honest. Often our own faults are the very ones we find least attractive in others. There is nothing to be gained by getting a dog that annoys you without it even having to do anything, and everything is improved if you can enjoy your dog no matter what it does. There will be hard work and storms to ride out which are no fault of anyone, just part of a dog growing up and then growing into its career. If this all seems too much trouble, reflect that a little trouble now can save years of discord. A good working dog is a joy, and a bad one a constant irritation. One person's useless dog is another's paragon, and a lot of misery can be saved on either side if you choose the best dog for you. That is, not the best dog for anyone else except yourself: not the one that your partner likes, your children fall in love with, your friend would pick or the breeder has left over and is offering a discount on. You are the person who will be training and working the dog, and it has to have a personality with which you can gel. You work the dog however often you work it, but you live with and care for it every day of its life. This means that it is not sufficient for the dog to be good at its work: you have to like it as well. And the dog needs to like you, which it won't if you are always finding fault with it. Too many people get wrapped up in what a dog can do physically without ever considering its mindset, and indeed their own. If you choose your dog with as much care as you choose your job, your partner or your car, you will start with a huge advantage, especially considering the length of time you expect to live together, and the level of performance you will be expecting.

PHYSICAL

Let us take a look at the physical side of the dog, both as a breed and an individual. You choose a dog well if you have some knowledge of its parents. Certain breeds are prone to certain physical problems, some of which do not manifest themselves until several years of work later, which means that if you do not pick a dog from working stock, these faults may lie dormant and unknown in either parent. Similarly with young dogs, which may show a great deal of promise in the field but have not yet been so well tested that hidden unsoundnesses have appeared. Neither can this be avoided by breeding only from mature well-tested stock, for while this is good in theory, there is often less opportunity to breed from older animals for health reasons. Older bitches can present a higher risk of birthing difficulties, or be reluctant to mate, less fertile, or have problems with carrying the litter because their legs and backs are weaker. Older male dogs can be reluctant to mate if they have always been stopped from so doing, or they can be too weak in the hindlegs for the actual mating, have reduced sperm count or even undiagnosed prostate troubles. I had a stud dog that I did not breed from at all until he was six, because I wanted him thoroughly proven in his work and soundness. At nine, after only siring a few litters, he developed prostate trouble and had to be castrated. He threw beautiful puppies that went on to be excellent workers, and I have always regretted not breeding from him sooner.

There may be dogs which are superb workers but are not physically sound, which can be kept going with a mixture of luck and skill, and which will be used for breeding because their working abilities are too good to lose. If bred to a sound partner, and the pups are well-reared, the risk may be worthwhile, and the unsoundness buried – but you have to be aware that it might reappear in later generations if you are unlucky and the progeny of two dogs carrying the same latent defect are mated. Some physical defects can be brought out by careless rearing, or kept dormant by good husbandry. The more that you know of the breed in question, and the more that you know about the parents of the puppies that you go to see, the better will be your chances of owning a sound and capable dog. Some breeds are scanned for hip and eye problems, and breeders will advertise the puppies from parents that have been tested. Do not be afraid to ask to see the results, for I know more than one breeder who had the parents scanned with an unacceptably high score resulting, and went ahead and bred anyway, advertising the pups as having come from parents which had been 'hip and eye scored' which indeed they were. The dog with a high score on one side of the breeding may get away with it, but a high score on both sides is odds-on to develop the same unsoundness, though there is some evidence that careful rearing and a natural diet can make a difference. If you buy the pup from a position of knowledge, then there are physical conditions where you might take the calculated risk if everything else fits – and there might be conditions that you will not entertain no matter how good the rest of the dog. The racehorse people say: 'Breed the best to the best and hope for the best' and that is a good maxim to follow.

MENTAL

Some breeds are known to be hard-going, some almost always laid-back, and some contain the whole spectrum. If you have a choice of several breeds that will do your job, then consider the different personalities – are you happy with the high-speed pzazz of a cocker spaniel, or would you feel better with the bonhomie of a good labrador? Are you a strong enough character to earn the respect of one of the German HPR (hunt, point, retrieve) breeds, or will it walk all over you? Do you favour the sassy, up-for-it terrier, and will you mind breaking up the inevitable skirmishes? Does the border collie fervour light up your soul or drive you to distraction? Can you keep up with a beagle? Whatever the job that you have in mind for the dog, consider not only the mental attributes needed for that job, but the character inherent in each breed. There are tasks that can be well done by several different breeds and crosses between breeds, but each is done in the manner of that particular breed or cross, and while one or more will suit you, another may not. You cannot choose your relatives but you can choose your dog, yes, even the size, sex, colour and mindset.

Certain jobs can only be done by certain breeds, but there are still wide personality variations within those breeds. For instance, a pack of Welsh foxhounds hunts differently from a Modern English, and an Old English pack will need different handling from either. You will not change the working personality of a hound or dog, but you can adapt your own ways if you wish. If you do not wish, stay away from that type of canine, for there is no need to make both your lives a misery.

Lowland Foxhounds

REARING

Breeding is not purely a matter of genetics, but involves rearing as well, and rearing starts even before conception. Healthy parents breed healthy litters, and a bitch that is well looked after during her pregnancy will have more chance of bringing forth healthy pups than one that is not. There is usually little harm in a bitch being lightly worked during the first few weeks of her pregnancy, depending on her job. Steady sustained work such as produced by a gundog can be carried on, but the short, all-out sprints of a running dog need to be curtailed. Greyhound breeders believe that bitches should be let down from their usual fitness before the mating, for field-fit bitches may not conceive so easily, and super-fit bitches may not even come into season. This is also a problem in lurchers, and other sighthounds. Usually there is a rush of pups being born three months or so after the work season ends, which has

A well reared litter

given the bitches enough time to let down and come on heat. Disciplines in which bitches do not need to be so very fit tend not to show any problems here, and some used in the shooting sports can irritatingly come on heat right in the middle of the season. None of this is a consideration for the stud dog, however, which will be ready to mate at any time, and the fitter he is, the better.

Once the litter is on the ground, the prospective purchaser should be satisfied that the pups are well fed and housed, and present a picture of lively health. We are lucky if we can visit a litter one or more times before we choose our pup: a lot of breeders will allow this, myself included, because it is so important that the pup goes to the right person. However, do be considerate of a breeder's time, make proper appointments and do not stay too long. Do not go from seeing one litter straight to another because of the risk of carrying infection.

GENDER

Dog or bitch? This choice will depend on a lot of external factors. Do you have dogs already, with which the new one will have to fit in? If your dogs are kennelled separately, it will not matter too much, but if they live together in the house, it will. Some breeds are more fiery than others, some more tolerant. Adding a dog to a group of bitches can have a steadying influence: the male will usually be hopelessly henpecked and always at the bottom of the status pile, but generally speaking it is a happy arrangement. One bitch in a group of dogs, however, can have the same effect as the sudden arrival of a woman into a group of men. Whatever earnest discussions had been taking place previously in perfect male bonding, the group immediately collapses into disarray and posturing, and previous 'best mates' can fall out permanently. All-bitch groups and all-dog groups will have their status grumblings, especially if there is no clearly-defined 'boss' or if a strong character has been removed from the pack, and the astute human will supervise any uneasiness and make sure that it does not develop into bloodshed. Bitch fights tend to be worse than dog fights, but this is breed-dependent, and some male dogs will fight to the point of doing each other damage as well. The best preventative for any of this is a strong, authoritative human in charge and a clear canine second-in-command, who, as sergeant, will keep the troops in order, knowing that he or she can count on human backup in case of insurgency. If in doubt, keep the main antagonists separate any time they are not under direct supervision.

The other certain issue with a mixed pack is that bitches will come into season and males will become agitated over it – how much again depends on the individual and the breed. Obvious solutions include having key players neutered, or sending one away for the duration of the season. If you take the second option, it is less risky to send the dog away, for many a litter has been born as the result of an on-heat bitch and a moment of human inattention in the boarding-kennel environment. You have a much stronger interest in keeping your bitch unmated than the staff of a boarding kennel, who are unlikely to make any other redress than an apology. You can keep entire dogs and bitches together at home – I have for years – but it takes a certain amount of dedication at season time, and you must be able to trust everybody in the house to shut doors. There may also be a certain amount of howling. Bitches tend to cycle close together so with several bitches you can be dealing with seasons for weeks at a stretch, though at least it gets it all over with in one go. One advantage of this is that if you want a particular bitch to come on heat, kennelling her near another on-heat bitch may well bring her into oestrus sooner. Coursing and racing people do this a lot to get the seasons out of the way early. It is inadvisable, however, to kennel the two together unless they get on really well at all stages of their cycles, because the on-heat bitch changes to a higher status during her season, and this can precipitate fights.

I have heard it said that bitches are more faithful and less likely to stray, but I do not agree. Any dog, especially one with a high working drive, will stray, and the way to stop that is with a fence or a pen. As for faithfulness – that is something you have to earn. A broad generalisation is that male dogs bond closer to female people and vice versa. However, it is perfectly possible to keep the same gender as yourself, and work closely with a lovely bond between you. If you get the dog that suits you, the gender will be of secondary importance if you live with just the one dog, but if you already have a settled pack at home, consider very carefully the impact of a new arrival of either sex.

BITCHES

Seasons

If you are keeping one or more bitches, you need to be completely au fait with the process of the bitch coming into season. It is normal for a bitch to have her first season any time from six months old onwards. Some will then cycle every six months, but others, especially the more ancient breeds, may only come on heat once every year. Some, especially sighthound breeds, have infrequent seasons, and I know of several who only come into season every few years, it being quite common among this type not to have the first season until three or four years old. Interestingly, once bred from, these will often revert to an annual cycle. Your bitch's season is therefore peculiar to her, and she will need at least two seasons before she settles down into a routine. I had one that cycled alternately every seven months, then ten months; curiously, her granddaughter seems to be displaying the same pattern so far.

Most bitches give plenty of warning prior to their season. The extra hormone activity makes their coats softer and shinier, they urinate more often, and some scent-mark like male dogs. Many will show a marked change in temperament. The start of the season is known as 'showing colour' when red fluid drips from the vulva, and the season is timed from the first day that colour is seen. The vulva will swell and soften over the next few days, size varying with the bitch, some being very discreet and others glaringly obvious.

During the season, the colour of the discharge sometimes changes from red to straw-coloured at the time the bitch is ready to mate, but with my own bitches it has always stayed red throughout the season. Some bitches are very neat about keeping themselves and their surroundings clean, while others are less fastidious and lavish their condition everywhere. The bitch is usually ready to mate (known as 'ready to stand') between ten and fourteen days, but I have known pups conceived on the fourth day, and my current youngster was the result of a mating at nineteen days. The average length of a season is twenty-one days, but bitches that do not cycle very often can go on for another week when they finally get around to it. They can also be ready to stand early and for longer. A few bitches do not show colour at all, but the enlarged vulva will give the game away, the other warning signs are apparent, and the bitch will be just as ready to mate. Owners of entire bitches need to be aware of any changes in their animals, and simple observation will ensure that the season does not come as a surprise.

False pregnancy

After the season, many bitches, even maiden ones, will exhibit signs of pregnancy, which can be very convincing. Nipples will swell and stand proud, the abdomen will swell, and the bitch may well become secretive or uncooperative. At around the time that she would have given birth, she may develop nesting behaviour, and in extreme cases, behave as if she has whelped. She may come into milk, hide herself away and not want to come on walks, amass a collection of soft toys to 'nurse' and even defend the phantom litter to the point of attacking strange dogs or people. A similar number of bitches will never exhibit any of this behaviour, or only after some seasons, or show a much more diluted form of it, just appearing off-colour or subdued, and many owners will never notice. The false pregnancy is a natural condition, evolved to help raise litters in a pack environment, and nothing to worry about at all. In three weeks, the phantom pups will be 'weaned' and the bitch will dry up her milk and become her old self. Extremes of physical and mental symptoms can be alleviated using natural remedies, treating the dog holistically (see Chapter 5). There are dog behaviourists that become incredibly exercised about false pregnancy, trying to treat it with drugs, depriving the bitch of her toys and generally getting very heavy about the whole issue, but it is better treated sympathetically and as the temporary condition it is. Hormones are deep and powerful, and better worked with than against. Probably the best way to react to a false pregnancy is to let the bitch get on with it, but give her less food and more exercise. This will mimic the circumstances of a bitch that has lost her litter, which is a natural occurrence too, and so will help her to return to her non-breeding state more quickly.

Be aware that the bitch with the phantom litter may be the only household member who knows where it is, and keep visitors and especially children, who might inadvertently trespass on her 'nest', right away from her. Bitches that display maternal aggression are not aggressive per se, it is the hormones talking, but the bite hurts just as much, and can lead to trauma and permanent damage on both sides. Best to avoid the problem for the very short time that it may be an issue.

Working the on-heat bitch

Some wryly say that the bitch is in season twice a year, and the dog is in season all the year. If you have a bitch, you may lose a considerable part of the working year when she is on heat, depending on the job she does. The coursing or racing greyhound is at her peak a few days before her season, but is traditionally never run in season or for three months afterwards because of false pregnancy issues and the idea that fat builds up around her heart and lungs at this time. This may not be an anatomical fact, but in truth it is difficult to get a bitch conditioned for really hard work until she is past the false pregnancy state and her hormones have adjusted.

Those that work alone, or with other bitches, and under close control, can pretty much continue as normal during the season, and it is much better for them to get plenty of exercise which has a cleansing effect, preventing stagnation. However, for animals that are only sexually available for a short time each year, the need is correspondingly greater, and some bitches will not concentrate on the job in hand, instead trying to make a break for freedom and the finding of male dogs. Some bitches are very much more highly-sexed than others, and it is a matter of knowing how yours is and not taking any risks. Some will bolt at the first opportunity, some will only lose discipline when ready to stand, and some will prefer their work in any case. Do not underestimate the ability of male dogs to detect a bitch on heat, either. I can remember ferreting on private land with an on-heat bitch, and emerging from a hedge to find a labrador and a terrier running towards us. Fortunately the bitch in question was the ultimate professional, and saw the pair of them off in no uncertain terms. Another year, when I chose to breed from her, she and her suitor were just getting acquainted in what we thought was a secure compound when a golden retriever appeared, having scaled the high wall.

Bitches worked in packs with other bitches may have to be pulled out temporarily, not just from the straying point of view but because of the status change enjoyed by the on-heat bitch, and consequent risk of fights. The bitch worked solo, however, can become a furious hunter, because the hormone changes at this time prepare her not just for breeding a family but for raising and protecting it.

Working through false pregnancy

If the bitch will work – and a few will hole-up and refuse to come out – then work her if you can, for the reasons already mentioned. Even if she cannot do her proper job, being out and about will speed up her return to normal. It is a traditional way of stopping bitches producing milk to cut their feed rations and work the socks off them. Be careful in the presence of other dogs, because she may be rather sparky, and do not let strangers pet her, because she may be sore from her swollen teats. A lot of bitches will be delighted to continue working, and show no different behaviour at all.

Working through real pregnancy

Light work only is the best way once the bitch has been mated, depending on her normal discipline, and that only for the first four to six weeks depending on how strenuous her workload is. Sod's Law will see the accidental litter held and produced no matter how hard the bitch is worked, while the carefully planned litter might be lost through tragic accident. I have known many bitches worked through the first weeks of pregnancy without problems, particularly if the dog is lightly tasked and the owner can stop working her at any time. I do not work my own dogs at all through a pregnancy because their job is unpredictable and might involve more than I would want a pregnant bitch to do, but they all get plenty of steady exercise until they are heavy enough to find it uncomfortable. If your dogs normally play and rough-house together, take your pregnant bitch out on her own.

Spaying

In certain working disciplines, bitches are almost always spayed, so that there is no working time lost during seasons under conditions where the bitch would risk pregnancy. The most obvious downside is that if the bitch proves an exceptional worker, her line cannot then be carried on. There are also many health drawbacks to spaying bitches, especially if they are spayed too young, one

CHOOSING THE RIGHT DOG

of the most distressing of which is urinary incontinence, reckoned by the makers of one of the drugs used to treat it to occur in 20% of spayed animals. Some of the available drugs to treat incontinence can have unacceptable side-effects in some of the bitches, too. I have lived with a bitch made incontinent through spaying, and it is a nightmare, believe me: seasons are so little trouble compared with that. Mentally and emotionally, spaying before the first season is now thought by many trainers to leave the bitch immature, as if stuck permanently in her pre-teens, which can mean that she is less likely to take to training and work properly. If a bitch must be spayed, it is better for her to have at least one season first, so that her hormones are in order and her mind and body is mature. Spaying about halfway between seasons will be best for her.

MALE DOGS

There exists a mindset that a male dog will take any opportunity to stray, fight other male dogs, cock its leg anywhere and everywhere, behave unacceptably in front of the vicar, and travel miles in search of bitches. A very few will, and certain breeds are more prone to this than others, just as other breeds are not highly-sexed at all. Serious Lotharios need serious training and confinement, and much as I dislike neutering for neutering's sake, castration of a very highly-sexed and troublesome male dog is sometimes justifiable. However, it is not a decision to be taken until all other solutions have been tried, not a total panacea for all cases, and certainly is never ideal before the dog is mature. Adolescent male anythings go through an oversexed phase, and most grow out of it in due course. Many a good dog has been castrated when patience and training would have seen him through the phase and out at the other side as a useful animal still with the potential for breeding other useful workers. Castration can also have other considerations. Dogs castrated very young may become permanent puppies in their outlook, which can give problems in their interaction with other dogs. There can also be undesirable effects on skin and hair, heavier-coated breeds sometimes developing a long fluffy pelt that needs regular trimming and thinning. All in all, entire dogs of either sex are seen by many to be healthier, happier, and more responsive to training.

BREEDING

You may never wish to breed from your dog, or you might have something so good that it would be a pity not to pass those genes on to future generations. There is passionate argument from those who dedicate so much time and effort to saving and rehoming unwanted dogs that all dogs should be neutered. Such is the volume of neglected and abandoned dogs that you can see why they think that way. However, taken to its ultimate conclusion, if good responsible people are prevented from breeding out of healthy stock, then all you have left is irresponsible people breeding from inferior stock. It could be argued that few puppies are unwanted at the time they are purchased: most become that way because people have not been willing to put the time into them that they need, or have had a major lifestyle change that the dog has fallen out of, or that they never realised how much time, effort and expense it takes to raise a dog properly. In the case of working dogs, most are bred for the job from tried and tested working stock, and to see the parents and grandparents is to know the pups. Many working dog people like to keep their dogs entire if they possibly can, not only for better health but to keep their options open in case this time they have something extra special from which they would like to breed. Some people feel that there is something lacking in neutered dogs for certain jobs, while others think that there is no difference at all. It is a matter of individual choice, but there need be no rush to make that choice, and dogs of either sex can be 'run on' in their entire state until such time as they either prove neutering would be a good idea, or that it would not. Neutering does tend to be done in the pet world for social convenience, but the 'slash and burn' style of dog care is not so readily seen in the working world.

Health questions

Veterinary argument is that neutering brings health benefits: there is often a lot of pressure on owners to get this done, but the long-term downsides have not been adequately studied. Neutered dogs allegedly live longer, and there is a range of health issues that neutering supposedly protects against. Let's take a look.

Although there are breed averages for age, you cannot tell how long a dog *might* live, but only how long it *has* lived. Working dogs might not live as long as pet or show dogs because of the working environment – cold, wet, hot, the stress on their limbs from the miles covered, accident or injury. Or they might live longer in health because they are kept lean, fit and fulfilled. Dogs of either sex that are neutered too young may not grow to the same pattern as if they had been allowed to mature naturally. This can have significant repercussions in working dogs, which perform best and remain soundest when kept within the optimum size for their job. Entire male dogs may or may not develop prostate or testicular problems. It seems odd to argue the case for neutering on the basis of preventing something that might not in any case occur, and is easily dealt with if it does. For example, castrating a dog to prevent prostate problems is rather drastic when castration IF those problems occur will resolve the issue. Castration is also often seen as a first resort in addressing certain behaviour issues that could in truth be worked through using less drastic means in the majority of cases. Similarly, the case for spaying a bitch to prevent a womb infection (pyometra) fails to consider that most bitches would not develop this condition, and the downsides of spaying are seldom adequately discussed. Both spayed and unspayed bitches develop mammary tumours; though it is considered that spaying before the first season tends to reduce that risk, you might well be left with the other problems discussed above.

If you have to respond to pressure to have your dog neutered, remember that lack of evidence for resultant problems does not mean they have been looked for: absence of evidence is not evidence of absence. However, keeping dogs as Nature made them is not without its responsibilities, and for those who, for one reason or another, risk breeding accidental litters, neutering their dogs can seem preferable.

BUYING A PUPPY

Price

Rearing a litter of puppies properly is very expensive, not just on money spent but on the reduced potential for whoever looks after them to earn money while the litter is being cared for. It is not simply a matter of shutting bitch and pups in a shed for twelve weeks and adding food and water at intervals. Puppies need to be kept clean and warm, but not too warm, well handled and socialised, accustomed to domestic noise varying from washing machines to playing children, allowed outside to romp freely, fed the best possible food and perhaps taken for rides in the car so that the journey to their new home is not such a shock. To the stud fee and massive amounts of food for the bitch and pups you can add any veterinary bills, endless bedding, Kennel Club (KC) registration if the litter is pedigree, pre-mating health scans, and advertising costs. In comes a buyer wanting the moon for sixpence. We all know someone who boasts of how little his dogs cost to buy. Yes, it is possible to get a good puppy cheaply, but you are far more likely to get a good puppy if you pay a fair price. Usually the price reflects the amount of care that the breeder has taken with the dam and litter, and I have seen a lot of puppies reared 'on the cheap' that have cost a fortune in veterinary bills after they change hands, and sometimes for the lifetime of the dog. 'Cheap' may mean that the pups and bitch have had poor food, not enough heating, limited human contact or all of these. It might seem only a few weeks out of a dog's life, but in those few weeks the pup is laying the foundations of its second teeth, its joints, bones, limbs, even its nails, all of which will be expensive to maintain if not right in the first place. A pup riddled with worms can sustain such intestinal damage that it will have a sensitive stomach for ever after, and there is not much pup to feed a host of fleas, from which illness may result. While pups will always have a few worms and fleas, you are going to have a much healthier prospect from a breeder who has taken the trouble to get on top of these.

Well socialised with people

Mental issues exist here as well, because an inadequately socialised pup can be very difficult for the new owner to bond with, or may be fine with its immediate human 'family' but never at ease with strangers, or other dogs, or dogs of certain breeds. Puppies that have been exposed to noise as whelps are far more likely to take in their stride such occurrences as the sound of gunfire, fireworks, applause, shouting and all the other everyday sounds that we take for granted. Some breeds are particularly noise sensitive and it does not take much for such sensitivity to flip over into phobia, which is extremely hard to deal with. Dogs that are destined to live in the house will need to be unfazed by television and radio noise, and household appliances (does your dog have its bed in the kitchen? Does it freak out when the washing machine goes into its spin cycle?). Can it cope with a household of humans at the rowdy ages? Take your pup if possible from a similar environment to the one you live in, but if you cannot do that and the pup is perfect in every other way, do try to

… and other dogs

introduce it gently to a noisier life, remembering how much more sensitive a dog's hearing is than yours. Even a car radio can be purgatory to the dog that is unused to noise and has its travelling box right next to the speakers. I have to be extra careful about this because we lead a quiet life with little in the way of electronic sound, and I have to make a conscious effort to accustom my pups to noise. We do have one dog that was bred in a noisy household full of children, televisions on in every room, and blaring music, and she is absolutely bombproof with everything; I remain forever grateful to her breeder.

Some sources condemn the litter raised outside and recommend that pups are only ever bought from litters raised in the house, but this is not as clear-cut as it might seem. With large litters, large breeds, or the unholy combination of both, the only way to survive is to move the pups outside at about three weeks old. Pups born outside will not automatically be lacking in care and attention, either. It depends on the breeder, and you can get a pretty good idea of how much time has been spent on the pups by how well the breeder knows them. Puppies show their individual personalities very early, and by the time they are ready to go to their new homes, the breeder should know each by its character. I have heard a well-known breeder comment that 'they are all the same at eight weeks old' and that is one person from whom I would not be keen to buy a pup.

There are breeders whose expenses are less perhaps because they own both dog and bitch, have access to free dog food, or are professionals with all the equipment and staff on hand, but they still have to pay veterinary and registration expenses, and even one episode of veterinary intervention with either bitch or pups can be very expensive. Consider the cost of a well reared pup to be an investment, and seen over the ten or so years of working life and companionship that you will have from that animal, and it will not seem so very expensive at all. Consider the 'saving' of buying a cheap pup against the extra veterinary bills and maybe the behavioural and training problems that can arise in the under-socialised or poorly developed dog, and it will not seem so cheap. Some people have the skills to make a good dog out of a pup that has had a poor start, but for most of us, we are better to start with the brightest, healthiest pup in the first place.

Colour

While it is true enough that 'a good dog is never a bad colour', colour can be important. Is there a colour that you particularly dislike? You are going to be looking at that dog for a long time, so you may as well choose something that you find pleasant to gaze upon. There is a lot of prejudice against white or pied dogs in some activities, while in others, the light-coloured dog is more valued because it can be seen better. Thus the pied coursing greyhound could be seen more clearly over a long distance, which is precisely why the poaching lurcher would be more likely to be fawn, grey or brindle. In working terriers, the rough-coated white frequently has its origins in white lakeland stock, bringing with it skin sensitivity and often poor nails, which are not so often seen in the smooth-coated white. Pied, white or black terriers are ideal for working in cover because they show up much better, and are not at risk of being mistaken for a fox, which can happen with red, fawn and grizzle terriers. A dog that has to sit for long spells in concealment, such as while wildfowling or pigeon-shooting, is better to be in the yellow and brown spectrum, for black shows up as much as white. Mottled colour groupings such as those found in spinonis, German pointers and some spaniels are good camouflage, whereas the black and white of the collie stands out among the

Yellow labrador for Wildfowling

sheep. Red and white collies were seldom favoured on the hills because they can look like foxes, even quite close up. Some collie experts reckon that the different colours carry different temperaments, too, those with the red genes being more difficult to handle than the plain black and white. If colour matters to you for whatever reason, then it is important enough to take into account when you decide on your pup. If the 'perfect' pup is the wrong colour, however, you need to decide just how important that colour is, and whether it is a matter of life or death – as with the russet dog driving cover for shooting and risking being mistaken for a fox – or mere inconvenience, such as the dog showing up in the hide.

Choosing which pup

This has to be one of the most pleasant 'tasks' for the prospective owner. There you are with a litter of round, healthy pups tumbling over each other to reach you, harass your shoelaces and snuggle into your hands. After eliminating candidates because of gender and colour preferences, you may have only one pup left, but what if there are two or three to choose from, or if it does not matter to you whether you have one or another?

The shy pup

Received wisdom always used to be to pick the pup that runs up to you first. In every litter there is a mix of personalities, and the first pup out is not necessarily the right one for every buyer. Bold pups grow into bold dogs, and if you are choosing from a bold breed as well, you are going to have a very strong character inside that velvet pelt. This might suit you very well, and so this is your pup and off you go. If you do not have the personality that relishes keeping upsides of this little being, consider the others. There may be a very shy pup that comes out last and approaches you carefully. These pups, once given confidence in and by their owners, can be the most dedicated of canine partners, but they will not suit the loud and hasty personality. Consider the breed: if it is a strong-minded breed, then the shy pup will still be plenty bold enough for most people, but if it is a breed that tends to nerviness, then this pup might need more confidence than many owners wish to give. Note I say 'wish' rather than 'can' because plenty of people have the ability to cope with either end of the personality spectrum, but do not choose to have the hassle. There is often a pup that sits apart from the others, and this is the thinker. Thinkers make cracking working dogs, but they are very demanding of their owners, needing one at least as intelligent as they are themselves. If you need

The thinker

to work your dogs as part of a group, or even a pack, if you like to be Boss, this is not the dog for you, because it will work for itself unless it finds you worthy. If smartass people really annoy you, this dog will annoy you as well. If you are as solitary in your ways as this pup, if you are flexible enough to throw the book away and adapt your training to the huge challenges that this animal will present, then you will have a soulmate working with you as an equal partner.

In between these extremes, there will be one or more pleasant, seemingly unremarkable puppies. Any of these will make fine workers. Once they are away from their littermates, each will blossom, particularly if there was one very strong pup in the litter that was overshadowing them. Which to choose? Rather than opt for the first pup to reach you, take the last one to leave you. I am often left with one little soul asleep on my foot or my lap once the others have greeted me, sussed me out, and gone back to puppy games. Even a tiny pup can be a shrewd judge of compatibility, and I can honestly say that, although some have been harder work than others, I have never had a dog that did not suit.

Second-hand dogs

You can, of course, get a dog from someone who has to part with theirs for one reason or another, or you want to rescue a dog. If you have a good eye for a dog and a fair bit of experience, know what you like and are prepared to put in the commitment, it is possible to get a very good dog this way. It is also possible to make a big mistake and take on a heap of trouble wrapped up in a dogskin. You may know the whole story – well-bred dog, well raised, started training, owner taken job abroad/divorcing/taken ill, just a series of circumstances that lead to the dog being in need of a new home. You may be told a tissue of lies, or some of those vague excuses – moving house (oh, and you all forgot you had a dog), partner/children suddenly allergic to dog (quite a catch-all, this one), job involves longer hours, dog does not get on with new partner's cat/dog/gerbil. Or the dog may have committed some 'crime' which is just part of being a dog e.g. dug holes in the garden, left unsightly patches from peeing on the lawn, barked when left all day, disembowelled the sofa (what fun!), or else it has been owned by someone who does not realise that dogs need to be trained. Sometimes the cute puppy has simply grown into a gangly, bolshie adolescent, and no-one can be bothered with it any more. There may just be a huge personality clash. Most of these can be made into good dogs, and also good working dogs, if they change homes young enough, for often it is the working instinct which makes the dog a challenging pet. Taken at any time up to their second birthday, most of these dogs can be trained, and as they often change homes after puppy cuteness has been replaced by adolescent turmoil, they are usually worth the effort. Breeders of working dogs will try hard to place their pups in working homes, but sometimes they do go as pets. This can still work out as long as the new owners are aware of the working instinct and prepared to cope with it. Even dogs from non-working strains will work, but the drive is far higher in dogs that have been bred for generations to do a particular job, and it takes skill to adapt that to pet life. Many otherwise good dog owners simply cannot handle the hardwired worker, and lucky are those animals that find a second home where they are allowed to fulfil their instincts. The advantages for the second owner are that there is a clear picture of the dog's physical and mental attributes, and that, while there might be training mistakes to undo, the basics are often in place.

Failed pets

There are also failed pets which will never make decent workers given a million years and sheer genius in dog training, and these are offered eagerly and in huge numbers to the working-dog owner by people who know in their heart of hearts that euthanasia is the only solution for that particular animal but have not the bottle to see their responsibilities through. Into this category slink a host of troubled, untrained, unsocialised dogs, neurotic, numb or just plain nasty. You are told that if you do not take the dog it will be put down, and the only answer to this type of emotional blackmail is unemotional agreement that it is the better decision. At four years old, the working dog is at the peak of its abilities; though it can continue working in health for maybe another four to six years, this is as good as it gets. The four-year-old disastrous pet is not worth the time it would take to get it even halfway useful, because it does not have that time. Certainly if anyone wanted to take it on as a project, or there is something about the beast that appeals, why not, but realistically it will be an old dog before it could be trusted to work in the field rather than leaving embarrassment or carnage in its wake. Because the working dog spends so much time either under close control or working on its own initiative, it must be obedient, and it is rare for a dog taken on as a troublesome adult to be able to have its problems ironed out to the extent that it can be trusted either to obey instantly or to maintain its decorum when out of sight.

There is a misunderstanding with many pet owners that a working dog is a lesser being than a pet one, when in fact it needs to be far more. They think that the working world is a dustbin for failed dogs, or more usually dogs that have been failed by their owners, whereas in truth it is the cream of the crop that works best. Most of the people who could make something decent out of such animals already have plenty of better dogs.

Breed rescues

These are organisations that specialise in one particular breed, and most are extremely knowledgeable about it. Where the multi-dog or even multi-animal type of rescue organisation usually has little knowledge of breed differences or even working instincts, the breed rescues know their type of dog to the inch. If it is a pedigree dog that you want, and you prefer to give a home to a 'rescue' then you can rely on the breed rescues to find you what you need and steer you away from what you think you need but do not. Breed rescues are more likely to have a full background to each dog, and will want yours as well. They will offer aftercare and advice if needed, and can be a good source of working dogs so long as you meet their criteria. Give them as decent a donation as you can spare, for they do an incredible job, and are often overlooked by larger animal rescue organisations which might do well to draw upon their expertise.

Names

New owners sometimes find that a change of name is politic, either because the dog has bad memories of the old name, or because the old name is something no sane adult wants to utter in public. Sometimes the old name is too similar to a command, or to the name of an existing dog, or too inviting of malapropism under stress (try saying 'Shane – sit' and see where it gets you). If you take a dog from a dog rescue organisation, the chances are that it has only had that name for a few weeks anyway, and will be perfectly happy to be called something else. Rescue staff have to call the dogs something, and the same old favourites get recycled indefinitely, so do not feel bad, or even that it is 'unlucky' to change a dog's name. Call it whatever you want, for it is sure to collect at least one other name along the way, to each of which it will answer. It is very easy to change a dog's name: tack the new one on the end of the old one and use it often, especially for nice events such as food and exercise, and then phase out the unwanted name. Always use the dog's name to call it for pleasant experiences such as food, affection and walks; when you need to give it eye drops or trim its nails, go and get it. A sound recall is vital, and you dilute its power every time you associate the name in the dog's mind with something it will not like. Similarly if you scold a dog, use any other words but its name. I am sure you will find plenty of suitable alternatives.

INTRODUCTIONS

When you come home with the new dog, make the introductions to the home pack in a place where each has plenty of space to display appeasement and superiority signals, advancing and retreating as circumstances dictate. I keep the dogs shut in so that I can release one at a time into that open space, introducing them one by one with the highest-ranking dog first. Once the top dog has seen and approved the newcomer, bring in each of the others in order of seniority, until they are all together. Allow plenty of time with this, so that each meeting takes place in an unhurried manner, and each of the dogs is settled with the new one before you release the next.

SETTLING IN

A new dog will take time to settle into a new home, whatever its age. Very young puppies seem to make the transition most easily, so long as they have plenty of company, whether canine or human. Some adult dogs find puppies irksome, so do make sure they can find refuge from the needle teeth and over-exuberance if that is the case. Most adult dogs are very tolerant of puppies, but you should not assume that it will automatically be all right, and however good the relationship, every dog deserves some peace and quiet. A few adult dogs will not tolerate puppies at all, so you will need to keep them separate if so. An adult dog telling a puppy to mind its manners can be noisy, with a great deal of snarl and snap to it, but an adult dog that truly wants a puppy out of the way can do the job quietly and efficiently, and you might walk in on a tragedy. Beware of kennelling an adult and a pup together until you are sure that they will be happy in a confined space – I do know of a bitch that climbed up the weldmesh of the kennel to avoid a pestering pup.

A few dogs – of either sex – will 'mother' a small pup, and the puppy's transition to new ownership will be much smoother for it. Very maternal bitches can even come into milk. Just let this happen: it will stop soon enough,

Bitch mothering new pup

and if it soothes the puppy, why not? If a pup joins the household at the same time as a bitch would have had a litter if she had been mated during her season, the two will often bond deeply. This is a bond to which you will need to give due attention when training, being sure to separate them then, but it is otherwise a good thing to happen.

If you do not have other dogs, then be prepared to spend as much time as possible with your puppy while it adjusts to its new life, and indeed afterwards. You should not expect a pup – or a grown dog - to spend hours shut away, bored and lonely.

Settling an adult dog into its new home is usually straightforward, so long as you appreciate that there may be a 'honeymoon' period when the dog does not put a foot wrong, followed by a difficult time while it establishes your boundaries and strength of character. So long as you are just and consistent, this should soon pass. If other adult dogs are involved, the new dog will also be testing the other dogs, to see where it can fit in. There are ways of helping both adult dogs and puppies to settle. One is the DAP (Dog Appeasement Pheromone) available from your vet in spray and diffuser form. It emits a scent said to replicate that of a suckling bitch, and many dogs find it soothing. It smells a little musty to the human nose, but is not offensive. Bach flower remedy Walnut helps for adjustment to changes of circumstance, or you can use their Rescue Remedy. Flower remedies work on the emotions and so are safe to give with whatever else you use. If a dog is having a tricky time changing households then the best treatment is spending as much time as you can with it and giving it lots of work and exercise so that it is tired in body and mind. Schedule your life so that you can spend plenty of time with the dog, getting it used to your going out and coming back at random times. Avoid the use of psychotropic drugs, which are recommended by a surprising amount of so-called behaviourists, because a dog is unable to learn while in a drugged state, and while it may seem to have settled, in reality it could be very distressed but unable to express it.

PUPPIES TOGETHER

Every dog book you have ever read will tell you not to get two pups of the same age together, and this one is no exception. Whether littermates, from different litters, or even different breeds, two pups together are far more than twice the work and hassle of one. There are dog experts who can make a

Two pups will bond with each other

good fist of raising and training two puppies from whatever background, but these are people with many years of experience and, critically, the time to work on each pup separately. Two puppies will bond with each other rather than you, and you will never be able to train them to any sort of standard unless they are exercised and preferably housed separately. Of course, the whole idea of getting two together was that they would amuse themselves while you got on with something else, wasn't it? Even that might not be the case, because pups similar in age and temperament might grow into dogs that vie with each other for superior status, and those cute chubby pups rolling around and making baby growls might one day have the kind of fight that does serious damage. This can be a particular problem with bitches. However, it is not invariably the case, and you could just as easily end up with two dogs that are best buddies and form a pack whenever they are out together. Either way, you will not have a controllable pair of dogs.

If you need to have two dogs available to work, the easiest way is to get one and train it to the standard you require, and then get the second as a pup and do the same with that. Then you can work them together, and at the first whiff of anarchy, separate them until you have brought the miscreant back up to standard. You may have to do this at intervals all through the dogs' lives, or you could only have to correct matters once or twice. I have two dogs with a seven-month age gap who are the best of friends, and, being different breeds, they present different training challenges. Even so, I do very often have to take them out individually to maintain the level of control that I need when I work them together. Seven months is a bit too close in timing: a year would have been better, but the right pup came along a little earlier than ideal, and that first year was rather hectic!

DECISIONS

Some of us get a dog bred to work in a certain discipline, and some of us get a dog of the breed or type that we enjoy and then see what it does best. Whichever it is, we need to do a bit of research beforehand and incorporate a degree of flexibility afterwards. Let's start at ground level.

The body

What sort of terrain do you intend working your dog over? The horse people say 'No foot, no 'oss' and it is the same for dogs. A dog with well-cushioned paws, the 'cat' foot, will perform well on most going, while a long, or 'hare' foot indicates a suitability for fast work over rough terrain. The Scottish deerhound, Fell foxhounds and salukis all favour the longer foot, with long, strong toes for gripping, while lowland types of foxhound, labradors and most HPR breeds show a rounded, fleshy foot. The foot needs good legs and joints above it, lighter bone for rough country and heavy 'timber' for clay. It is not that a particular type of foot cannot function over different ground, but that some feet will absorb more punishment than others. There is also the matter of injury, for flint country is hard on any kind of foot, but a fleshy foot tends to sustain less real damage because the vital tendons are better protected than with the long foot.

Moving up, a longer-limbed dog will find travelling over the coarse heather and steep broken ground associated with high moorland a lot easier than a stumpy low-slung version, which by contrast comes into its own in forestry and estuary. Then you need to consider coat, for some breeds are very much more waterproof than others. The dog designed for frequent immersion demands a different coat from the dog that will be exposed to chill wind and

Frequent immersion

A good size for their job

driving sleet – think labrador and border collie – and the dog working the grouse moors in August needs different care from the one out on the same moors with the stalker in winter. Heavy-coated dogs in lowland bramble country can even need unpicking from thick covert from time to time, and give hours of diversion to their owners afterwards, dematting and combing vegetation from the coat. Some breeds are tough and versatile enough to work hard and well under a widely differing assortment of conditions, and others are more specialist. Some coat types are easier to keep comfortable and free from parasites, though all will need regular grooming, whether it is a matter of a polish with a grooming mitt, a regular teasing-out of tangles, or proper stripping and trimming. Under the coat is the skin: silk-fine on a whippet, rhino-tough for a terrier, and everything in between for the others. Look at the eyes and ears: are the eyes protected by a bony brow and high cheekbones, are the ears likely to shred in thick thorn cover? Are you working barbed-wire country, where a thin skin combined with a gung-ho attitude will result in a dog crisscrossed with scars? Is the breed of choice one that is customarily docked for working and what are the risks if yours is not? If the dog needs to retrieve, is the mouth big enough, the neck strong enough, and the legs long enough to carry the burden easily? Terriers can be first-class gundogs, but a retrieve on a pheasant will have them at the limit of their capabilities purely as a matter of size, whereas springer spaniels will be working well within themselves. That same springer will not find a goose anything like as easy as a labrador will.

The mind

Do you need a degree of independence in your dog, or instant obedience? Should it work on its own initiative, always to your bidding, or have to change in a moment from one to the other? Might it have to work over long distances, even out of sight, or stay close at all times? There is no pleasure in having a hard-going independent individual when what you want is a kind, biddable one. Do you need a dog that will hunt by instinct, and so require steadiness training, or one that would rather stay at heel and need encouragement to go forth and seek whatever you want sought? Every dog has a working distance: some like to stay close and others to range far. Do you prefer to work on reining yours in or sending it out? Do you want a jack-of-all-trades or a master of one? Does the dog need to be sociable with other dogs, will it be jovial and laid-back about being bundled into the beaters' wagon with a pack of strange dogs and humans, will it panic, might it fight? How do you want the dog to be with strangers, shy and skulking like the lurcher, or happy to go off with whoever takes the leash? Most of all, how would you like it to fit into your own mindset, whether as a servant or a colleague? Every dog is a little different from every other, tackles the same tasks in an individual manner, and each one will teach you something new just when you may have thought there was nothing new to learn. Choose carefully, rear and train with the final objectives always in mind, and you will have every chance of a long and enjoyable relationship with your canine helper.

2. FIT FOR ANYTHING
BODYWORK MAINTENANCE AND ENGINE TUNING

FIT FOR WHAT?

There are two degrees of fitness: fit for life and fit for work. The first is straightforward and as necessary for a pet dog as a working dog, for it refers to the level of fitness that goes with optimum health. This kind of fitness is achieved by correct feeding (which includes water as well), exercise and rest, plus physical care, mental stimululation and emotional harmony. A dog that is cared for in this way has the best chance of its immune system firing on all cylinders, which will help it resist infection and recover quickly from injury. It is astonishing how fast a healthy dog will heal. The system of keeping fit for life involves adjusting your dog care in relation to the health needs of the individual dog at any specific time, and in particular to its age, for very young and very old dogs have different needs from each other and from the dog in its prime. This is the essence of stockmanship, of looking at the dog and really seeing what is before you, and then adjusting the dog's schedule to suit its own requirements. Under the aegis of 'fitness' comes regular care of coat and feet, and a quick response to any signs of 'dis-ease'. If you know how your dog is when well, you will know when it is not quite right, not something as obvious as (for instance) lameness, but a slight difference in gait, or appetite, coat, skin, eyes or temperament. Dogs are great stoics and can hide pain until it becomes really severe. Their wild ancestors would risk death at the mouths of other pack members if they showed weakness, and very often our own domestic dogs will still try to hide early symptoms of illness. It is up to us to be observant.

WORKING FIT

Fit for work covers the particular work for which that dog is bred and used, which are not necessarily the same, for some disciplines take on dogs that are bred for a different task, for instance springer spaniels being used to detect drugs or explosives. Although the dogs can mostly adapt and even excel in such employment, their minds and bodies are genetically predisposed to other work, and so their handlers need to be extra aware of where the differences lie. Training and working within the genetic mindset equals a happy, fulfilled dog that will work well for years, but if the inborn needs are ignored (such as when a dog with a natural quartering pattern is retrained to track only on ground-scent and in straight lines) sooner or later the mental stress is likely to reappear in the form of behavioural or even physical illness. Working fit also means fine-tuning the physical body for optimum performance, which is different in various disciplines. For instance, working foxhounds can easily cover fifty or more miles across country on a hunting day (this refers to real hunting not artificial scent-trailing), coursing greyhounds may need to run at top speed for two to three hundred yards up to four times during one competition, while the equivalent for coursing lurchers can be eight six-minute runs that day. The shepherding collie will be working literally from dawn to dusk almost every day of its working life, the pack hounds go out

Working Foxhounds

Shepherding collie

twice a week, the greyhounds run hard once a month and the coursing lurchers every week. The rough shooter's dog will work one or two days a week, the picker-up's dog might be out four times a week in the season, the peg dog once a week. All these times are approximations, for every dog should be worked and rested according to its individual needs within that discipline. It takes different preparation for a dog to give its all on one day than to work close to its limits every day, or every week, and many dogs are required to perform in several different disciplines, for instance the shooting dog that goes rough shooting, driven shooting and wildfowling all through the season, or the 'jobbing' lurcher that is required to go ferreting, lamping, bushing or coursing to an erratic pattern. Temperature plays its own part, for the dog worked on bitter cold days will need different care from the dog working in summer temperatures or high humidity. There is, too, an art in getting a dog fit for a particular day, and then allowing its system to relax and recuperate by gradually reducing that fitness, a system known as 'letting down' and which racehorse trainers have honed to near perfection. If the event for which a dog has been prepared is cancelled, then the super-fit dog needs special care to drop down its fitness to maintenance level without compromising its ability to be brought to peak again at a later date. Very fit dogs can become sharp, sparky and reactive in temperament, just like any other athlete: they cannot help it and allowances need to be made. Some disciplines, such as Search and Rescue (SAR), cannot be predicted, and so the dog needs to be ticking-over fit rather than at peak fitness, for it will need to produce a good performance at short notice and in varying and often hostile conditions. If such a dog has been working abroad and then has to go into quarantine, it is going from one type of stress for which it has been trained to another for which it will have had no preparation, and in addition is going from hard work and great fitness to little or no exercise of any kind and a radical change of diet. As SAR dogs tend to be of the highly reactive and intelligent breeds, they need extra care in this kind of situation if they are to survive in mental and physical health.

CORNERSTONES OF FITNESS

Feeding is critical for fitness, and such a large subject that it is dealt with separately in Chapter 3, along with some discussion on supplements. Rest, both everyday and recuperation from specific activity, is so important but often overlooked, as is mental care. Stress can have an enormous effect on general health and thus on fitness. Mostly, when we think of fitness, we think of exercise, so let us look at that first.

Everyday exercise

This really does mean every day for a healthy dog, whether kept in house or kennel, whether worked professionally or as a hobby companion. Before you prepare your dog for any task, its needs are ideally for two daily walks, each of around one hour, which should include as much free running as possible. These times can be adjusted to suit the owner: for instance, a ten-minute spell of training is tiring for a dog, and so can follow a ten-minute run around and precede a twenty-minute relaxing walk which is the reward for the intensive obedience. Some people prefer to incorporate the training into the walk, and I do this myself, but others like to stick to a specific training time, in which case the dog should be allowed sufficient winding-down after the training before it goes back to kennel or house. The other walk can then be more of an exercising one. Training is hard work for dogs because we are essentially

A pheasant retrieved

interrupting their natural instincts at a stage that suits us, for instance by wanting a pheasant retrieved rather than eaten, or a rabbit chased and caught, but not a deer. Thus dogs need to be in a calmer state of mind preceding the period when we want them to rest, for a short training spell followed by a resting time consolidates training in the animal mind much better than a long training session, which gives a dog time to get tired and maybe confused or bored, in which circumstances it will revert to the instinctive behaviour that we do not want (such as refusing to recall for the umpteenth time). Always end on a good note, even if it means going back to a previous exercise, stop a session that is going wrong and have some fun instead, and never train when you are short of time or temper, or feeling under the weather.

Walks are very stimulating for dogs, but in a totally different way from training, as they are working within their natural instincts. As we see the world primarily visually, so they examine by scent, and dogs return from their exercise period refreshed in mind and body. They should be allowed plenty of time to empty bowels and bladder, which needs to happen several times

A rabbit caught and retrieved

along the walk. The owner is not at liberty to ignore this either, for by watching what and how a dog eliminates, health issues can be detected. For instance, a bitch moving into her oestrus period will give plenty of warning because she will urinate more frequently than normal, and she will specifically scent-mark, sometimes even 'scratting' up the ground with her back legs more in the manner of a male dog. The newly-broken ground attracts the scenting of other dogs, who then learn that there is a most interesting event likely to take place in the near future. Within a day or two of her season, she may well show a looseness of the bowels. A dog having difficulty in urinating is showing you that it needs a visit to the vet (take a urine sample when you go there) and a dog that is urinating more than usual needs its water intake monitored, as it may be doing something as simple as fighting off a fever, or something as serious as developing an illness such as diabetes. Whichever it is, you will need to know, the dog will need its bowl refilling more often, and it will also need access to outside more frequently if a house dog or one that likes to be clean in its kennel. Bowel movements give detailed information of a dog's health, and any dog owner should be familiar with what is normal and so able to spot what is not. Of course, what comes out will vary with what goes in, and so it is perfectly normal for a dog fed a varied diet to show varied bowel movements, and again the owner needs to know what is typical of that particular dog. You can't beat a showing of lively tapeworm segments first thing in the morning to alert you to a necessary course of action, but a lot of signs are far less obvious and the astute owner will need to tune into the dog on a more subtle level as well.

Dogs from young adult to late middle-age will easily handle this kind of steady exercise regime, and although they can survive on very much less, they will not be fit on it. For instance, if bladder and bowels are not sufficiently stimulated to empty by regular walking, toxins can build up inside the dog, which can show in skin conditions, digestive upsets, depression, or even early joint or muscular aches and pains. Exercise increases the blood circulation and also lymphatic drainage, each of which brings cleansing, keeps the immune system healthy and increases healing of injuries. A bitch just off her season particularly needs this for optimum health. It is relatively unusual for healthy dogs to show loss of appetite, but if this happens, more exercise will usually activate that appetite. The natural internal cleansing will show externally with a shiny coat and loose-fitting clear skin, under which muscles will slide, contracting and extending without exaggeration. In attitude, the dog will be interested in the world around it, and able to accept direction with good humour.

Play

Some dog behaviourists encourage owners to remain the focal point of their dog's attention by encouraging play with balls, Frisbees and other toys while out on walks. While there is a place for this, some dogs are extra toy-oriented and become over-excited with this type of interaction. Too much stimulation may result in a dog that is so high on stress hormones that instead of resting when it comes home, it is ricocheting off the walls with excitement, and may take several hours to wind down. With two walks daily, such dogs can be almost permanently in a state of agitation, which can precipitate health as well as behaviour problems. Such dogs can often benefit from Bach and other flower remedies, or from homeopathic consultation with a professional, as treatment would need to be constitutional and individual to that particular animal. Sensible play with dogs that enjoy it is a different matter, and this is best undertaken at a particular place on the walk which leaves the dog

Typical dog play

sufficient recovery time to wind down afterwards. Dogs taken out in groups will often play with each other, which, because it is within the normal span of a dog's behaviour, will not create that degree of frenetic excitement that artificial play can. It is normal for dogs to spar with each other, chase and rough-and-tumble, which is all stylised hunting behaviour. It can look and sound really savage, but well-socialised dogs will be pulling their punches and backing off as soon as one says 'enough'. Precautions are necessary to avoid damage to the vulnerable: for instance, puppies need to play with other puppies of the same size and at the same stage of development, and can sustain damage playing with bigger, stronger dogs, just as elderly dogs that are not as steady on their limbs as they once were will not be improved by being cannoned into by a rumbustious teenage pup. Very young pups and elderly dogs will sometimes enjoy playing together, with the older dog being wonderfully tolerant but at the same time teaching the pup manners and demarcation lines. When it works, it works well, but some older dogs cannot be fussed with pups at all, and so should be allowed their chosen peace and quiet rather than being made to suffer the attentions of the young.

Safe dog toy

Source your dog toys with care. There are no regulations covering safety or suitability for dog toys, so you need to take charge of what you use. Buy toys that will feel good in the dog's mouth (not highly-coloured slippery fabric designed to appeal to the human eye instead of the dog) big enough not to be swallowed or block the back of the throat, and not too heavy. Above all, try not to let your dog play with sticks because there is enormous potential for injury if your dog stumbles while running with a stick. Some dogs are very good at finding sticks out on walks, and astute owners carry a safe toy or two either to distract them before they find their stick, or to effect a swap if they already have one. Be considerate of other dogs while you are playing with yours: it can be exasperating for someone trying to train their own dog to have another person throw a toy right in front of it. This is written by the owner of a dog that brought the village cricket match to a standstill with a terrific retrieve of the ball in play over three hundred yards, for which I was seen to praise him lavishly as I had spent a lot of time establishing his retrieving.

Discourage playing with sticks

Some dogs don't play with toys, and tend to give the human that tries to interest them in such trivia the kind of look that makes you wonder just who is the more intelligent. There is nothing wrong with the dog that has no interest in toys, and you might as well accept it rather than trying to cultivate something that may not exist within the dog at all. Dogs that are very driven in their work are often totally disinterested in anything outside it: this is perfectly normal for that dog and nothing about which to be concerned.

Aftercare

After daily exercise, a dog should be ready for rest. Food should not be given immediately the dog returns, but at least an hour later, though water should be available at all times. A brief check of feet and coat is all that is needed now, with time set aside for grooming after the dog has slept. Different breeds have different coat care needs, but a swift brush down is good for any dog, again stimulating circulation, removing dead coat, revealing the presence of parasites, lumps, bumps, thorns and other unwanted beasties, and also being a close bonding experience between handler and dog, provided such handling is gentle and patient. This is the time to put in groundwork which your vet may one day bless you for: see that the dog is used to being inspected all over, feet, mouth, ears, eyes, teeth and genitals. On a regular basis, trim or strip hair that is otherwise likely to be soiled, note unusual signs such as watering eyes or smelly ears, and while dog breath is not the sweetest, unhealthy breath smells foul and is telling you that something is wrong either in the mouth itself or further back in the digestive system. Likewise a healthy dog does not smell any more than slightly 'doggy' and a coat that stinks belongs to a dog with an internal cleansing problem that needs your urgent attention.

AGE AND EXERCISE

It is so important for health to give the right amount and the right type of exercise at either end of the dog's life. Pups under a year old benefit from short, frequent exercise spells, which can actually be very time-consuming

Socialising

48

for the owner, as no sooner is the pup home and settled, it seems to be time to take it out again. Rather than going to the same place every time, drive the pup short distances to different places so that it can enjoy a change of smells and environment. Ten minutes outside the school, the recreation ground or the shopping centre will accustom the pup to noise and traffic without overwhelming it, and equally it should be introduced to livestock and country smells. Big-boned pups and fast-growing breeds especially should not have their joints and limbs stressed by being asked to jump out of cars or go down flights of stairs, but all pups need to learn to scramble through woodland and be introduced to such hazards as barbed wire and electric fencing before they are big and strong enough to go sufficiently fast to hurt themselves. A pup should not be asked to jump before it is a year old, though many will teach themselves, and my last pup would float over the baby-gate I used to keep her out of some rooms, or suddenly arrive on the table, from a very early age. Try to keep these events to a minimum, for the pup has the rest of its life to be jumping, once its limbs are strong enough. There is a great fashion among some branches of working dogdom to have tiny pups leaping barriers, even retrieving over obstacles, but it really is not necessary. They can learn to jump perfectly satisfactorily later in life, and at far less risk to their development.

Between nine months and a year old, most pups will be building up to half an hour of exercise twice daily, and after a year old, unless the pup is of a slow-growing or giant breed, an hour each time will be safe. Let the pup have the final say, though: if there is any sign of lameness, cut back on the walking. Much as pups love to run and bounce, this is also not a good time to be throwing balls etc. for them, as the twisting and jumping can strain growing limbs and joints. Retrieving can be more safely taught to the very young by rolling the ball away from you both and then encouraging its return. Pups by themselves will twist and leap enough, but that is different from the owner making them do so, and possibly missing the first signs of tiredness or soreness which can indicate a problem. Pups that repeatedly show signs of soreness may have growth problems affecting their bones. A useful homeopathic remedy is Calc fluor, which seems to get them over this and prevent further damage.

At the other end of life, it is all too easy for the owner to miss signs of pain from ageing. The trouble is that the senior dog has so much experience and is so good at its job that it knows all the short cuts to doing that job well, and so the owner is less likely to notice problems developing at first. "First they get good and then they get old" is such a sad truism. However, awareness is

Old dogs can still enjoy a day out

than denial, and the old dog can be worked for a long time after its body starts to deteriorate, if we only pick up on the early signs and treat them.

There is no need to miss out on the experience of older dogs, and indeed they get so much fulfilment from their work that they can suffer emotionally if their working life is cut short. They may need to be switched to different tasks, or work shorter hours, but they can still enjoy going out. More care needs to be taken with keeping them warm, ensuring that they are dry and comfortable after work, and stopping before they become exhausted, for these old warriors are so dedicated that they will literally work themselves to a standstill if allowed. Long days in the heat, wet or bitter cold need to stay in the past now, but half a day in temperate conditions will rejuvenate an old dog. Some types of work do not allow for slowing down, but there are still ways for the older dog to carry on, and before the hunting ban it was normal for foxhounds and beagles that were losing their speed and endurance to be drafted to slower packs, or those that only hunted half a day, or even sent on to hunt with the minkhounds. Many a bobbery pack, hunting mixed vermin, would have the odd beagle or foxhound, and I well remember a lovely old beagle, Watchful, who left her hare-hunting days at nine years old to work with a mixed pack of crossbred French bassets and terriers kept by a gamekeeper. She was finally put down at sixteen years old, when blindness and other infirmities had overtaken her, after living a happy fulfilled life in a pack environment and doing what she loved best. Working lurchers can switch from coursing and lamping to ferreting and bushing, in the latter case often operating on a consultancy basis, letting the younger dogs do the hard work and just stepping in when needed. Gundogs can do half a day's driven shooting or picking-up and be tucked up in a coat in the car at lunchtime, or taken home if the shoot is near enough and someone kind will come out and collect them. It is up to the owner to find ways of keeping older dogs stimulated and happy, rather than left behind grieving and forlorn while the younger ones have all the fun. Mental health is very important for physical health, and old dogs who still have some interest in life will last longer than those which are retired and forgotten. There will come a time when the old warrior will just manage a few slaps of the tail when it hears the gun cabinet being opened or the ferret-locators being tested, and then life becomes much quieter for them, though they all enjoy being taken out for a sniff and potter around and a bit of one-to-one attention.

FINE-TUNING

A dog can stay within the fitness levels described above for all of its life, and be healthy, but some disciplines require extreme fitness for optimum performance. Equally, some do not. The sharpness required in a working foxhound would be disastrous in the confines of a driven shoot. For those dogs that need to produce high performance, there is a division with most disciplines between speed and endurance. Foxhounds, staghounds and beagles need to be able to travel fast, but no faster than the scent that they are following permits. They need to be able to work for hours at a time, maintain high levels of concentration, remain biddable, and hold staunch to their quarry. Contrast this with a coursing sighthound, which has to perform for a short time right at the edge of its physical limits, sprinting, twisting and turning. Catch or miss, it must at once allow itself to be handled, and calm down completely so that it gets maximum rest in the time that elapses before its next course. The ratting terrier may have to work all day in a variety of

Ratting terriers

temperatures, whether in the cover-crops in winter or the chicken-sheds in summer, while the sheepdog must work in whatever conditions exist, and in some that test it to its physical limits, whether finding sheep in snowdrifts or driving flocks in a heatwave. Crucial to this kind of fitness is correct feeding and exercise combined, bolstering the stamina of the stayer and the speed of the sprinter by developing to its fullest extent the inborn capacity to do either. It is very important to bear in mind that most dogs can only develop within the limits of their own genetic blueprint, and while exceptions exist, these are freaks. A dog is born with a certain physical potential, governed by its build, heart and lung capacity, and the very underrated but vital input of its liver. Not only does the dog have to perform, it has to display a fast recovery rate after supreme effort. If the dog has to offer both speed and endurance, then the astute trainer does not just bring on the ability that is easiest for the dog – because it will shine naturally at one or the other – but puts in extra work to develop the maximum potential of the lesser attribute. It is logical to think that a sprinter is brought to a peak by short bursts of fast work and that a stayer develops more endurance by long steady work, but there is progress on from this by adding gradient to distance for either type, remembering that it is just as testing to go downhill as uphill. Next, consider interval training. Human athletes first took this up, and trainers of eventing horses were quick to follow suit. Many racehorse trainers use interval training to get work into the horse while keeping it sweet, for performance horses are usually given unnatural amounts of high-octane feed, and as their fitness enters the final degree so their tempers often become edgy. Changing their routine is a good way of maintaining both interest and effort. So it is with working dogs, who appreciate variety and will put greater effort into a new task; natural feeding keeps the temper equable as well.

Interval training at its purest involves precise work incorporating specific distance and speed tasks which operate to a pre-planned programme: so many minutes at this pace, so many minutes at that, with precise rest and extra exertion built in. The working dog does not need quite such exact science as long as its exercise incorporates differing speeds and distances over a period of days. Some dog work creates this quite naturally. For instance, hunting packs of hounds will trot steadily to the first covert, draw slowly through it until they pick up the right scent, then follow that scent at whatever speed the scenting conditions allow, which can be slow and steady in puzzling conditions or fast in good scenting, but which most often is a fast burst followed by a check and slow work, then on to the next sprint. There will be times between hunts

Foxhunting – natural interval training

where hounds will rest for a few minutes, and then they will be off again at a smart trot to the next piece of land. Hounds start their fitness training many weeks before the season opens, by trotting steadily along roads and lanes, with short halts to refresh themselves in water, grazing on greenery and windfall fruit, and then back home again at a steady pace. As their fitness increases, their exercise periods will get faster and longer, strengthening their limbs and hardening their feet for their real job. They will ease into their real work starting with short days in the autumn, working up to the full hunting day and distance very quickly. You can prepare any dog for its job this way, but there comes a time when their fitness for their job will only be increased by doing that particular job. This is especially true of very fast work that places strong demands on heart and lungs. You test how fit the dog is by checking recovery rate, or how long it takes the dog to return to normal breathing and heart rate after exertion: the fitter the dog, the faster it will recover. People who compete endurance horses are very good at this, having only a very short time to get their horse's breathing and heart rate down within acceptable limits during one of the compulsory veterinary checks during a competition. Where dogs are concerned, it is not sufficient to wait until the dog stops panting and has its tongue back in its mouth: you need to monitor the heart rate by resting a finger on the ribcage until the heartbeats slow to normal. Incidentally, a dog does not have a heartbeat rhythm like a human's at peak fitness, so get used to how your dog's resting heartbeat feels and then you will not be startled by what seems to be irregularity. Dogs when fit have a natural varying beat, called a sinus arrhythmia, such that the rate seems to ebb and flow. In humans, this would indicate problems, but it is normal for your dog. There is a very fine line between having the dog ready for a particular event, and 'leaving the race on the gallops' as the racehorse trainers say of an animal which has had too much fast work. Another useful phrase from this source is 'needing the race' as in using a race to bring the horse or dog on in a way that exercise, however fast, will never do, because it lacks that final adrenaline rush of the competition atmosphere. Although animals do not understand competition per se, they are very sensitive at picking up the excitement engendered in their humans during a competition, and will react to that excitement.

REST

Rest is every bit as important as exercise and feeding, but is often neglected when we work on our dogs' fitness. Perhaps we have a streak of puritanism in us that sees rest as indolence, and the sleeping dog as 'lazy'. However, dogs were designed to sleep for most of each 24-hour period, and if we work them so that they have not had the opportunity to rest, then we need to ensure that the rest periods they do get are comfortable and peaceful as well as of an appropriate length of time. After a hard spell of work, the dog should be made physically comfortable, i.e. dried if it is wet, coated if it is chilled, cooled down and allowed several opportunities to drink if it is hot, but not fed straight away. At least an hour should elapse after severe physical exertion before the dog is fed to allow the appropriate changes in metabolism to occur, and then the first meal should be small, the main meal being given after the dog has rested.

The dog's sleeping area should be draught free, and its bed on a surface that does not chill, for instance raised on wood not directly on a concrete floor. The bed should be made of material that is not subject to condensation – I have seen dogs bedded in cut-down plastic barrels, which might be cheap and convenient for the owner but do not provide the best surface for the dog to lie within. The dog has no foreknowledge of arthritis, and some will sleep apparently happily on damp, hard or otherwise unpleasant surfaces, but all this

The importance of rest

stores up health problems for the future, and sometimes not so far in the future as all that. 'Kennel rash' i.e. abrasions or even bursas on elbows and hocks from lying on the wrong surfaces is best avoided, though some dogs seem to be hell-bent on eschewing their soft bedding in favour of precisely the kind of place that will cause damage. Think dog: is the bedding too hot or itchy, does it build up static, is the sleeping area stuffy or draughty, does the dog feel insecure enough to want to see all around it, or is it sharing accommodation with a dog that is intimidating it? I heard of a dog that shared its quarters with a terrier that chose to wet and mess in the bed, and the more fastidious animal preferred to lie outside. Sometimes there are no reasons that a human can see for the dog to lie on a harsh or abrasive surface, but the results are obvious. Even tails can be damaged, if the dog habitually lies with its tail under the kennel door.

A double layer of wire mesh ensures that dogs cannot reach others in adjacent kennels, and is an expense well worth having. Bizarre injuries and even unwanted matings can occur when bits of one dog are accessible to its neighbour. Whether dogs are kennelled solo or in pairs depends very much on the individual: some gain a great deal of comfort from the physical presence of another dog and others start or endure a campaign of intimidation. Personally, I prefer dogs to be in sight but not reach of each other, for as well as canine politics, there is a real prospect of the dogs bonding with each other rather than their human handler, and thus being much more difficult to train. As for more than two dogs together, there is an old saying: 'kennel three, bury one'. Three is a dodgy number where any livestock are concerned, for two will often gang up on one, sometimes terminally. As for keeping larger numbers of dogs together, well, it can certainly be done without huge problems, and is the normal way to kennel hounds that are worked in packs. The fine-tuning of it depends on the kennel-huntsman. Some keep dogs and bitches separately, and others keep both sexes together and separate any bitches about to come into season. The demeanour of the doghounds gives ample warning of this even if the bitch's signs have been missed. One huntsman I know says that the doghounds are far better behaved if they live all the time with the bitches rather than if they only meet them on exercise or out working, when they can become protective or combative. Others feel differently and keep their hounds separated by gender all the time. Kennel fights do occur whatever the regime, and it is part of the kennel-huntsman's skills to anticipate trouble and deal suitably with individuals who look as if they might precipitate an incident as well as having the authority to end skirmishes quickly.

To get the most out of its rest, the dog should be confident enough for deep sleep as well as light dozing, both of which are necessary. Some are very much more sensitive to outside influences than others; some feel most secure when screened away from the outside world and some need to be able to see what is going on. Favoured sleeping areas can be raised for a good view, or else dark and den-like. The trick is to know the dog and give it whichever it needs. Sleep can seem such a trivial thing compared with food and exercise, but it is every bit as important, as anyone who has worked shifts will assure you.

REST AND EXERCISE

Rest periods incorporated into a fitness programme are often neglected, too. That every period of sustained work should ideally be followed by sufficient rest is generally known, but rest as part of getting a dog fit for athletic effort can be poorly understood. Maximum possible fitness is not achieved by increasing work steadily to the highest level the dog can take, but by pausing in a series of plateaux with each spell of levelling-off allowing the dog's system to adjust to the work that it has been doing. These short breaks are so important, not just for muscles and joints to rest and repair themselves, but for allowing the more mysterious interactions between organs to function without being under constant duress. The dog is stronger for the break from serious work, which need only be a few days to begin with, but ideally ten days to a fortnight before the big event.

Similarly with a dog that has accomplished its work and is being prepared for rest and recovery. It is unwise to stop a fit animal's training abruptly. The dog should rather be let down by degrees, being allowed progressively more and longer rest periods synchronised with less demanding exercise. Some exercise is always desirable for keeping the dog's mind sweet, for boredom leads to dogs finding their own entertainment, which is generally of a kind that irritates humans.

MIND AND BODY

The mind is often seen as a separate entity from the body, but there is no doubt that dis-ease in one usually has an effect on the other. Thus for best health, we try to keep both in good order. As well as the refreshing changes of routine already mentioned, a dog should not have too much pressure put on it to succeed. Dogs love to please, and most will try their hardest, but they have off days in the same way that we do. Ultra-competitive owners can affect the dog, which will sense their disappointment if it has been outclassed by another on the day. A dog can only do its best, and if it falls short of what it can normally do, or despite giving its all is beaten by a better performance, it is not only good sportsmanship that demands a gracious acceptance of the result. Sensitive dogs can become bewildered and demotivated if their handler reacts sourly to the result of their efforts. Dogs do not understand cups and ribbons, or their names on a roll of honour. They do understand when their handler is unhappy with them. Intrinsic in the psyche of the predator is the

Dogs don't understand about winning

capacity to accept 'failure' and be ready to try again, and we would do well to develop this in ourselves.

Also important to the dog's mental health are its comfort and security, and the astute owner always has an eye to this. Dogs love leadership, someone to take the responsibility for decision-making and personal safety. Dogs like precision in their commands and stability in their day-to-day dealings. A dog that needs to use its own initiative while working is far more likely to do this well and return to human control as soon as required if it does not have to make its own decisions in any other sphere.

BODYWORK

Do what you will with the 'engine', if the bodywork is in poor repair, the dog cannot perform adequately, and many honest dogs will injure themselves in trying. Just a few minutes each day is all that you need to keep your dog's physique up to the mark, and half of those minutes consist of observation. You see that your dog is the right weight, that its coat may need attention, that a nail might need trimming, that its gait is not quite as fluent as it should be. These might seem small issues, but a piece of grit in your shoe is small, and you know just how much that irritates.

Stroking

This is where the house dog scores over the kennelled dog, because if a dog sits next to you and you have a free hand, chances are that you will stroke it. Not only does stroking bond owner and dog, it will tell you a lot about the dog. Does your hand stink after you have touched your dog? Your dog is unwell, and is trying to eliminate toxins through its coat and skin. Dogs smell of dog, but they should not reek. Does your hand travel freely through the coat, or is the coat a mass of tangles and dead underfur? This must be attended to so that coat and skin can cleanse properly. Does the dog flinch away from you when you touch a certain area? Is one area hotter than the rest of the dog? Can you feel lumps that might be anything from ticks to tumours? Are there thorns or grass seeds that need to come out? Is that a cyst between those toes? Your hands are so sensitive that you can detect a single grain of salt on a smooth surface, and your hands will tell you as much about your dog as your eyes. So will your sense of smell, even though it is poor compared with a dog's. A bad smell means trouble that needs to be investigated. Conversely, a clean dog that is happy to be touched

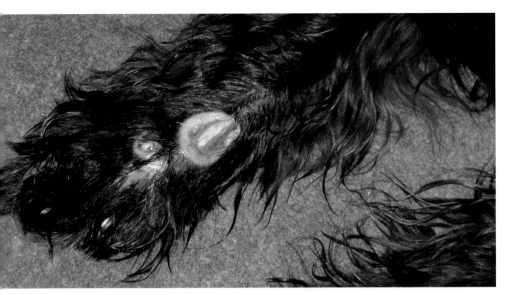

Grass seed injury

all over will gain enormous benefit from your caresses, and may well elect to groom you in return. This can be in the form of appreciative licks, hard grooming licks such as a bitch gives her pups, and most intimate of all, those scratching nibbles from the small incisor teeth. How much of this you tolerate is up to you, but be aware that your dog is offering you a huge compliment, so if you turn away the grooming gesture, please do so gently and politely.

Brushing and combing

How much of this you do, and with what, depends on the coat of your dog, but such treatment needs to be considerate. Take care brushing out tangles, and always support the area that you are grooming, for example with a hand under the belly when you brush the back. If you prefer to take the dog to a professional groomer for stripping out of undercoat for instance, this is a good course of action, but do not leave things until the dog is a dreadlocked mat. As with much dog maintenance, a few minutes each day is preferable to one grand de-coking effort every now and then.

Even light or smooth-coated dogs benefit from a good brushing, and they enjoy it too (mine come running when they hear the word 'brush'). I also comb them through with a flea comb, which as well as finding little hoppers, removes dead hair and plant life such as cleavers or grass seeds. Flea dirt shows up as small black specks which, when wetted, make red-brown streaks, which are dried blood, and often you will see flea dirt before you ever find fleas.

Massage

This is very beneficial for working dogs, both before and after sustained effort, especially if their work requires a fast response. Though many canine working disciplines do not have a tradition of massage, there is no doubt that it does a lot of good. Massage stimulates blood flow, oxygenating the muscles and carrying away the detritus of hard work. Animals massaged before work have less chance of muscle injury, and massaging after work helps to remove the build-up of lactic acid and other substances that otherwise result in stiffness. By massaging, you can detect tiny changes in the muscle structure, which usually show up as hardness where the muscle ought to be uniformly smooth. Small changes indicate small tears or strains; large changes mean significant damage and the need to see an experienced professional as soon as possible, for muscle damage does not improve for waiting.

The best way to learn to massage is to have someone else show you, and also to have massage treatment yourself. You will quickly see what benefits you and what does not, and understand the right amount of pressure to use. Familiarise yourself with the main muscles on your dog, for you are massaging muscle not bone, and gently stretch the dog's limbs, including the tail, through their natural planes of movement. Do not do this until you are absolutely sure of the right way, and preferably get someone who knows the job to demonstrate what is needed. Do not massage the abdomen, as this can cause vomiting if done the wrong way. Massage is not difficult, but it is easy to do it badly, and it is much better not to massage at all than to get it wrong.

Dogs will show you where they need extra massage by leaning into your hands and sometimes crooning with appreciation. They will also show you if they have any tender spots, and you may need to consult a professional about these. A dog that has been massaged prior to resting is much less likely to get up stiff and pottery, and the older the dog, the more it will benefit.

VACCINATION

Working dogs should be vaccinated, and then should be given annual boosters, shouldn't they? After all, they come into contact with many diseases through their activities.

Contact with disease

Initial vaccination we would argue is certainly advisable in working dogs, but the need for boosting the immunity to all the diseases for which vaccine is available annually, after the recommended first one at fourteen months old is a matter of much polarised debate in both the veterinary and dog worlds. Views on this topic are changing rapidly as more knowledge comes into the open. Some manufacturers of vaccines seem to be responding positively to the debate and are researching their products in more depth, and many are now recommending increased intervals between some vaccines. This situation is evolving rapidly and is likely to have changed further by the time you read this, so please take the following only as a guide, and be prepared to do your own research and base your decision to give subsequent boosters on the information that you have.

It used to be the practice for young puppies to have two injections of multiple live vaccines, given two to four weeks apart. Start and finish times varied with different vets and vaccine manufacturers, but eight weeks and twelve weeks would be about average. After that, an annual booster for all was advised. This has long puzzled many thinking dog owners, who reason that annual boosters are not required for human vaccinations, so why for pets? At the same time, immune-system illnesses are seemingly on the increase in dogs and other animals, and some openly blame the vaccination programme. Concerned vets query this as well, but are between the proverbial rock and hard place, as both regulatory frameworks and the vaccine manufacturers (who mostly provide their own evidence) control the mainstream information on which vets have to base their advice. It is a fact that the minimum duration of immunity is the basis for many of the arguments used in the UK, rather than the maximum duration, and this supports the position of those who profit from increased sales.

Some time ago an organisation called Canine Health Concern (see Useful Websites and Addresses) sent out questionnaires to large numbers of dog owners, analysed the results, and put some force behind the argument that annual boosters were not only unnecessary, they were actually harmful to susceptible animals. Some enlightened vets had already started offering annual blood titre tests for distemper, parvovirus and infectious hepatitis (any of which can be fatal to the dog that contracts them), which indicated that immunity to some of the diseases vaccinated against lasted a lot longer than previously thought. The results of these titre tests began to enable dog owners to make an informed decision on the need to boost their dog's immunity for those diseases that year or not.

Parallel to this debate, many parents, as well as lobbying groups, are actively querying the possible ill-effects of multiple vaccinations of live viruses in very young children, but as they mostly only receive a fob-off from the authorities, public confidence and uptake of multiple live-virus vaccination programmes has plummeted. Many of those refusing vaccines for their children are opting also to do the same for their dogs and this is reducing the overall level of 'herd' immunity in the dog population which, it is claimed, will lead to disease outbreaks.

Radical reformers who refuse to vaccinate at all rely on keeping the dog's immune system as strong as possible as defence against disease – but we live in an artificial world and we must remember that diseases such as distemper, hepatitis and parvovirus killed huge numbers of dogs before vaccines were found to combat them. This debate is not helped either by cynics on either side, and while opposing groups face each other across a line in the sand, caring vets and worried owners cast about for the most up to date information on what to do for the best.

Some good news arrived in recent research published in the USA by the

FIT FOR ANYTHING

American Animal Hospital Association. This found that vaccine-induced immunity lasts a lot longer than initially thought, and that vaccinating after the first booster at approximately fourteen months of age probably does not stimulate further immunity in a dog.

It seems, therefore, that a later puppy vaccination (finishing at or after twelve weeks of age rather than earlier when the intended immunity may not be fully established) followed by a booster at fourteen months of age, and further vaccination only if indicated by low immunity levels in blood titres, may well be the best way to go for now.

It is a good topic to discuss with your vet at your dog's annual check-up, as new evidence emerges and competing manufacturers respond to the debate with increased durations of efficacy for their products. However, experience suggests that not every vet has kept abreast of the changing protocols in the vaccination debate, and some put extreme pressure on their clients to administer boosters, even threatening them with barring them from the practice if they refuse. It is therefore up to the wise owner to keep as up-to-date with continuing research as possible, and to find a vet who is happy to discuss these important healthcare issues. This way the owner and vet together can take an informed decision about whether or not to vaccinate further.

PARASITES

Parasites, both internal and external, have evolved to live together with the host, and therefore the need to break the cycle is a continual process. While most healthy dogs can cope with a light parasite load (with the exception of mange, a constant risk in working dogs but thankfully fairly easily treated nowadays), we humans prefer to have as few on and in our dogs as possible, especially if they are the kind that we share. Although good feeding and general husbandry are important in reducing parasites, not all of them will be repelled, and as the unnatural environment we offer with domestication is so ideal for their proliferation, we almost always have to use chemicals to kill them. People often ask if homeopathy can kill fleas, to which the reply has to be that it can only make them healthier! The best products have always been those previously only obtainable from your vet, but new legislation now allows good products and appropriate advice from pet stores and similar outlets. It is worth remembering that your dog will not have problems such as fleas all the time; as it is always best to keep chemical exposure to a minimum, there is little need to treat until the problem arises. (see Chapter 5).

65

Worms

All dogs have worms of various sorts. They are born with them, no matter how well-kept the bitch, and they acquire more simply by being dogs, sniffing around in the great outdoors and eating dubious savouries. A straightforward worming programme three or four times a year, using a veterinary-approved wormer, will cover most eventualities. Do not be tempted to use cheap pet-shop remedies as they are simply not man enough for the job and some can have unpleasant side-effects. Feeding garlic and brewer's yeast in tablet form (odourless types of capsules as well as fresh garlic are not good for dogs and can cause colitis), a few pumpkin seeds daily and plenty of green vegetables will help create a hostile gut environment for worms, but you will still need to worm your dog.

Fleas

Most of the fleas found on dogs are in fact cat fleas, and these will happily bite humans as well. The dog will also pick up fleas from a variety of other animals, such as rabbits. A daily going-over with a flea comb will keep fleas at bay, but at certain times of year, the outdoors is hopping with fleas, and you will probably need to do more. Fleas are difficult to repel, though adding a few drops of lavender and rosemary essential oils to water and dipping your flea comb in before you use it will help. Because dogs have such a sensitive sense of smell, essential oils should not be used on a daily or too-frequent basis (see Chapter 4). There is a number of flea treatments available, some of which are better than others. Generally, products that require anything put in food or applied to the coat which needs a flea to bite before it takes on the chemical, are less than ideal as it is the bite of the flea that causes problems, and the chemicals must hang around in the animal's system to be effective. Many therefore prefer products applied to the coat which kill the flea before it bites. You do not have to cover the whole dog. Instead, treat those areas which are most popular with fleas, such as the tail root, groin and 'armpits', behind the ears and along the hackle line the length of the back. If cats are kept, they must be treated too, as cats tend to be flea reservoirs and can harbour huge numbers, often without any outward sign of discomfort.

Received wisdom is that, without treating the house, you are doing no good treating the animal. Though houses do harbour fleas, your house can be pristine and your dog will still bring fleas back from every walk at certain times of year. Most of the chemicals recommended for treating house infestations are very toxic to people and animals as well as to fleas, and we all get enough exposure to chemicals as it is. Some houses do need treatment and this is better done when the usual inhabitants can go away for a few days to let the chemical odour clear. Central heating and carpets are blamed for house infestations, but I have never seen either in a rabbit warren, and these are alive with fleas. A reasonable halfway measure is to place a flea collar inside your vacuum cleaner and vacuum often. Those fleas that are taken in will die, and the whole household is not exposed to unnecessary chemicals.

Ticks

Ticks loiter in long grass and woodlands, waiting for a passing dog, and then crawl aboard. They are small spider-like creatures, and easily missed when uninflated, but once they have found a host, they bury their heads under the skin, take aboard blood, and swell up. We then see the tick body, which can sometimes be mistaken for a wart if you are not used to them. Areas frequented by deer and sheep carry a particularly heavy tick population, and we need to check ourselves as well as our dogs on a daily basis if in tick country. You cannot actually feel a tick on you, though it does hurt when you pull them off. Many flea treatments tackle ticks as well, or you can grasp them as close to the skin as possible, give a half-turn anticlockwise (some old wives' tales have a lot of legitimacy, and it really must be anticlockwise) and pull them off, which usually brings the head out too, or coat the tick with something that stops it breathing, such as Vaseline, butter or nail varnish, or something that stings and makes it back out, such as alcohol. You can also buy a useful plastic hook device for hooking ticks out if you do not have fingernails. There are various alarming old kennelmen's tick removal methods, such as holding a lighted cigarette to the creature. This is not a good idea as it can burn the dog as well as the tick, and in any case it is not worth starting smoking on the off chance you will find some ticks to remove. You will also hear horror stories of infections and abscesses resulting from pulling a tick off and leaving its mouth parts behind. Sometimes you do leave the tick head in, but so long as you dab the site of the wound with something antiseptic – I use tea tree or lavender oil – it will not do anything dramatic. A healthy body will simply annex the tick remains by forming a small pimple and carrying them to the surface in the scab at the top. After a day or two, the scab falls off with the foreign body contained within.

What if you don't do anything? The tick will eventually fall off when engorged, and crawl away. However, too many ticks will have a debilitating effect on the host, and some ticks also carry diseases such as Lyme's disease, which can be very nasty indeed. They are therefore best removed and killed as soon as detected, and any human or dog tick victim developing a red rash circle at the site of the bite, or flu-like symptoms, is best advised to visit a GP or vet, explain the circumstances, and in humans get a blood test for Lyme's along with appropriate treatment.

Foreign parasites

Ticks are becoming a major problem in some areas, and these can carry several diseases, some of which are life threatening. In these circumstances it is worth considering preventative treatment, especially as we are now seeing tick-borne diseases in the UK that have been brought back by people who have taken their dogs overseas 'on holiday'. Given the risks, especially with the parasite-borne diseases endemic in certain foreign areas, can it really be worth the expense, hassle and real danger involved in taking the dog abroad for a week or two? Once brought home, these parasites can flourish and spread disease to other dogs, which will have little resistance to them and could become seriously ill or even die. It is a high price to pay for human selfishness: the dogs themselves would be far happier being spared the journey, the heat and the risks, and looked after in kennels or at home.

If you really have to travel abroad with your dog, do some research on the areas to which you are going, and obtain extra protection if necessary. This is not just a matter of your own dog's health, but the health of others too. If your dog has been abroad and develops any disquieting symptoms, be sure to advise your vet that you have been away and to which countries, so that he or she will have a better idea of what to look for and treat.

This is the fit dog, in all its power and beauty. Once you have seen a fit dog, once you have seen how your own dog looks and performs at optimum fitness, nothing else will do. From the dog's point of view, it has simply reached its physical and mental potential, and it feels good.

3. FEEDING FOR WORK
HEALTH IN, HEALTH OUT

At a time when human nutrition is attracting a lot of study – and a lot of mythology – we are at last beginning to understand the truth about canine nutrition. The dog is primarily a predator, a scavenger and a carnivore: every tooth in its head is pointed. That does not mean, however, that dogs only eat meat, and an all-meat diet lacks essential nutrients. What it does mean is that dogs are designed to eat the bodies of other animals, and in as natural a state as possible. Hide, hooves, hair, feathers, bones and offal, fresh-killed or decomposing carrion is what the dog will choose to eat, given the option. Just as with dog training we humans step in and interfere so that the dog does as we wish, so with feeding we change the intake of the natural dog to suit our lifestyles and prejudices. Just as with training we sometimes take matters too far and make the dog do things that are detrimental to its well-being, so with feeding we humans have tended to ignore the obvious and fed our dogs on things that are cheap and convenient to us rather than valuable to the dog. Then, as humans will, we have attempted to justify our actions. Thankfully, many of us have since had second thoughts, and now we have the potential to feed our dogs better than dogs have ever been fed since they stopped hunting for themselves and started scrounging from settlement middens.

The natural dog has a digestive system which is designed to extract nutrients from bones and skins as well as from meat, and a short gut which propels waste matter out quickly. Thus the dog can survive eating carrion that would make a human ill, because the bacteria do not get as much chance to multiply within its digestive tract to the point where they would overwhelm the dog's immune system. Dogs can also survive on relatively little food, or the wrong food, for long spells. This last has given many so-say dog nutritionists the opening for claiming that dogs are really omnivores, because they can survive on low-meat or even meat-free diets, and the more illogical among them will even offer the wisdom that dogs can really be vegetarian. Certainly, dogs in the natural state will seek out and eat vegetable matter, needing either

Carnivore teeth

the nutrients within or the healing and cleansing properties of a particular herb or root. The canine digestive system, so ferociously efficient with hide and bone, is less good at extracting nutrients from vegetable sources in their natural state. This is why wild canids will eat the partly-digested gut contents of prey animals. They are selective about this, too, some parts of the gut being eaten straight away while others are left scattered until exposure to air and bacteria takes the 'sting' out of the digestive fluids. With smaller prey, such as voles or baby rabbits, the whole animal is swallowed, initial digestion in the dog being a matter conducted more in the stomach than in the mouth. Dogs feeding off a large animal will be vulnerable to larger predators, so will tear off large lumps of meat and swallow them, to regurgitate later either for pups left at the den, or for themselves. Domestic dogs which have never even seen a wildlife programme will still attempt to carry their food away from their bowls to eat in a different place, and this is why. If your dog does this at every meal, it might not be eating in what it considers to be a safe place. Is the dog being fed in an open area where people or other animals can approach while it is eating? Many dogs will retreat to their beds with food, so perhaps you should feed there.

Enter the human, who for various reasons finds it inconvenient to feed the dog on whole raw carcases and carrion. Until relatively recently, meat was far too expensive and scarce for most people to feed to dogs, and even bones would have all the goodness cooked out of them before a dog came anywhere near them. Dogs would be fed on stale bread, kitchen scraps, sour milk slops, porridge and the like. Dogs also – and this is critical – had the freedom to roam, scavenging fruit and vegetable matter, eggs, carrion, farm and stableyard muck, stealing from human habitation (remember the cartoon dog running out of the butcher's shop with the string of sausages or a joint of meat?) and with plenty of opportunity to catch wild animals and birds. Dogs kept confined to the Master's kennels, with less chance to find their own food, tended to be better fed from those results of their professional hunting and shooting careers that were less acceptable as human food, as well as unsaleable produce from the farms. In days before refrigeration, high meat often became available for dog food. Many areas were served by 'the cats'-meat man' hawking mainly horsemeat for the luckier pets. This should not be taken as a model of good dog husbandry: sometimes it was, sometimes it was not. Dogs succumbed to a variety of diseases and parasites, not to mention dangers ranging from traffic, traps, and irate landowners, to other dogs, and fewer lived into old age.

Times have changed for the dog, and responsible owners now keep their dogs away from scavenging opportunities and do not allow them to roam. This puts feeding wholly into the hands of the dog owner, and for much of the last hundred years, the pet-food manufacturer. If you asked most people what they fed their dogs, even now, the answer would still be a puzzled 'dog food'.

Commercial dog food has seen several incarnations. Tinned meat and biscuit was the old-fashioned way, with the odd 'treat' of butcher's meat such as boiled lights (lungs and trachea). The main drawback to this from a human point of view was the stink of the meat, and the fact that feeding it often caused loose bowels and flatulence in the dog. When dogs were kept outside in kennels it was not such a problem, but when pet dogs started moving indoors, and being transported by car, it certainly became one. Then we became more responsible about cleaning up after our dogs, which is not so easy with the typical sloppy tinned-meat stool. Enter the era of dried food: easily stored in sacks, taking seconds to prepare, and with the end result being much easier to bag and bin. It looked less appetising, so some versions were made in a variety of shapes and with coloured pieces added, so that it seemed as if we were feeding our dogs something less monotonous. A meat-smelling additive was added just before packaging. Extra comfort was gained by pictures of smiling scientists, and assurances that the food contained every known nutrient needed by every dog. Usually there was a veiled threat in the form of ordering the dog owner not to add even one tiny extra to the 'complete food' because that would unbalance its careful scientific nutritional formula, and nameless horrors, it was implied, would be the result.

Reading the list of contents on both tin and sack was a puzzler to the thinking dog owner. Tinned 'meat' seemed to be almost all water, though there was a textured cellulose option along with something like 'meat protein', 'meat derivatives' and similar meaty mentions. Dried food appeared to involve rather a lot of cereal, and components such as 'residue' as well as those meat derivatives again. But the nutritional breakdown figures were more familiar and encouraging, split into 'protein', 'carbohydrates' and 'vitamins' among others. There had to be preservatives and antioxidants as well, and usually 'permitted colour'. The smell from the sack, once opened, was reassuringly 'meaty' and dogs found it attractive, though by the time the bottom of the sack was reached, the smell seemed to have evaporated. Some dried foods were made more appetising by the addition of molasses or caramel.

People fed generations of dogs by one or more of these methods, apparently without harm. After all, what was there to compare them with, except for other dogs fed on commercial pet food? Many veterinary practices found these foods to be a lucrative sideline, easy to store and with a captive audience to sell them to. Some even gave away free samples as inducements, and the ethos was enhanced by the development of special diets for particular health problems or as part of post-operative care. Dog trainers and boarding kennels also capitalised on the growing market for dried food.

Then there came the 'moist' foods, vacuum packed, selling themselves on being full of natural ingredients, and as the organic market burgeoned in human food, so dog-food manufacturers brought out 'holistic' and 'organic' dried and moist food options that they claimed were better than their previously supposedly excellent diets. Not only were these extremely convenient to buy, store and use, they salved the consciences of the more food-aware because they cost rather a lot more, and were clearly a healthy option, at least until the owner paused to wonder just how holistic and organic highly-processed matter could be.

Meanwhile, veterinary practices see more and more dogs with immune-system related illnesses, dreadful teeth, bad skins, bad breath, and most of all, seriously overweight. Dog trainers have become 'behaviourists' dealing with rising levels of psychological problems in dogs. That they did not have to look far for the reasons behind this did not mean that many of them looked at all. This should not be grounds for condemnation, for how many people live their own lives fuelled by processed food, and feed their children on it? Perversely, the dogs fed on vegetarian diets to fit in with their owners' prejudices probably have the better deal at this point, if only because those diets are fresh and largely organic.

Some kennels and some individuals never moved away from fresh meat and some form of cereal, whether the porridge, flesh and broth commonly served to some packs of hounds or the meat and biscuit on which many dogs were fed before commercial food became the norm. Few people fed raw meat because there was a widespread idea that it made dogs vicious or sick, and most food was thoroughly boiled. Sometimes vegetable matter was boiled along with it. Dogs did well on this so long as they had access to some fresh raw food, and many would eagerly devour windfall fruit or new shoots of grass and herbs in the appropriate season. Table scraps were the salvation of many a pet dog that was otherwise fed on food with much of the nutritional value boiled away, as was the odd rabbit carcase bolted down before the owner could stop it. Manure from large herbivores was eagerly sought and devoured, providing pre-digested vegetable nutrients in a form easily utilised by the canine digestive system, and for many dogs, this is still the case.

During these decades of feeding dogs specially-prepared pet food, a swell of unease was growing with many dog owners. They did not like the listings, protein levels and strange ingredients on the sacks and tins. They didn't feel comfortable with the glib assurances about balanced diets and the one-size-fits-all school of nutritional thinking. They did not believe that adding something to a commercial dinner was going to make their dog ill through unbalancing its diet, and they could not see why the thinking among human nutritionists was that we should eat a wide variety of fresh foods while the dog food manufacturers insisted that dogs should be fed exactly the same highly-processed food day in day out. Caring vets were puzzled about the growing incidence of certain canine illnesses, physical and psychological, that had previously been rare. As often happens in the field of scientific discovery, several people in different parts of the world reached the same conclusions at roughly the same time – we were giving our dogs the wrong food, and this was making them ill. So what could be the right food? Obviously, we needed to 'ask' the natural dog, and observe results.

The natural dog replied that it ate whole raw carcases, fresh and rotting, dung, fruit, vegetation that it chose for itself, eggs when it could get them and very little else. The natural dog neither ate nor needed cereal-based starch, molasses, sugar beet, textured cellulose, artificial flavourings, colourings, or preservatives dressed up as chemical antioxidants. It obtained real vitamins from its chosen diet and so did not need the synthetic ones found in dog food, the heat from processing having destroyed the natural vitamins. The natural dog ate a very varied diet, depending on whatever it could find or hunt and kill, and the vegetable matter it ingested varied with the season of the year, and so conditioned deficiencies from eating exactly the same food day in day out never occurred.

The breakthrough book was *Give Your Dog a Bone* by Australian vet Dr Ian Billinghurst, which appeared in 1993. Slightly different in recommendation was the work of another Australian vet, Tom Lonsdale's, *Raw Meaty Bones*. Where Ian Billinghurst considered that it was vital for the dog to be fed vegetable matter, crushed so that the dog could digest it, Tom Lonsdale simply advised feeding raw meat still attached to its bones. These feeding regimes were cautiously tried by many people, and named the BARF diet – either 'Bones And Raw Food' or 'Biologically Appropriate Raw Food'. Cautious we may have been to start with, but the astonishing change in our

Lean fit terrier

dogs, physically and mentally, welded us to the 'new' method of feeding that was in fact the very oldest and most nearly correct diet. A few people, such as those who cared for certain kennels of working hounds, had never fed any differently, but most of the rest of us had been seduced by the weasel words of that smiling scientist at least some of the time, and fretted needlessly when we sneaked our dogs some real food instead of the 'complete diet' in the sack. A very short time into BARF feeding, dog owners found that tartar-encrusted teeth became clean, breath became inoffensive, skin conditions cleared up, along with mucky ears and nail bed infections, the dogs' coats shone and their body shape changed to a fitter-looking outline, lean along the ribs, with a tight tuck-up and a strong topline. Behaviourally, dogs became calmer and more receptive to training, because of course they were receiving better quality protein (which produces fewer waste metabolites that stress body and mind) and nothing in the way of artificial additives. Just think of the problems in children that are attributed to additives and you wonder that the connection has not been made before. The vitamins in the processed food had of necessity to be synthetic, but now our dogs were getting natural vitamins and minerals. Not surprisingly, those of us who had made the changeover became somewhat evangelical about it, which tended to frighten many dog owners back into the arms of that friendly scientist. It is a very hard thing to do to take back the responsibility for your dog's well-being when it could so easily be left with the dog food manufacturers. And after all, as well as running their businesses, surely they had our dogs' welfare at heart – didn't they?

Canine Health Concern (CHC) again is chiefly responsible for raising awareness of what exactly did go into pet food, and the link between the pet food industry and giants of human food manufacturing was revealed in a popular television documentary. This showed waste products from processed food factories, restaurants and the like being recycled as pet food, despite in some cases being so rancid or decaying that high-temperature processing was essential. At around the same time, a crime was uncovered whereby condemned meat destined for the pet food industry had been reprocessed and redirected into the human food chain. Far from being the 'prime cuts of fresh meat' advertised, it seemed that some of the meat in some of the pet food was rotting.

Let us stop and take stock here. Dogs themselves would be unconcerned at eating decomposing meat, most waste from human food outlets, or even other dogs. The potential for causing ill-health chiefly comes from the high cereal content, rancid fat, sugars, the processing and the artificial additives. Since CHC's exposure, the pet food industry has cleaned its act up a lot, and a few manufacturers had never in any case linked their product to the worst excesses of the human food industry. However, the regulations concerning what may be used in pet food, and what it may be called (did you know that chicken feathers are among the substances that can be classified as protein?) are broad, and the widespread use of cereal, chemicals and synthetics continues. It has to – the food would not keep otherwise. But, I hear you say, feeding fresh raw food is a big step, you do not have time, you are afraid that you will feed an unbalanced diet and so harm your dog, or you just plain do not want to. You choose to feed your dogs exactly as you please, but it is not really so daunting to feed them what is best for them in terms of health, work output and maintaining a strong immune system, so before you finally decide, come a little further with us, and look at what is really involved and what compromises can be achieved.

BONES

Even the word is frightening. Many people have been told that bones are dangerous for dogs and should never be fed, or else that bones make dogs aggressive. There is, as ever, a little grain of truth here and there. Cooked bones are certainly dangerous for dogs, yes, even the cooked bones you can buy at pet shops, and should never be fed. You may well have given your dogs cooked bones for years, and never had any problems, but there is considerable risk involved in feeding cooked bones nevertheless. Cooking alters the chemistry of the bones, making them liable to splinter, and changing their structure so that they become almost indigestible and so can cause intestinal blockage. Vets deal with this kind of emergency over and over, which probably accounts for many of them being totally opposed to the feeding of bones. Pieces of raw bones, however, are what the dog has been designed to digest, and the dog's awesome stomach capabilities will process raw bones into firm stools that cleanse the gut of mucus on the way through, and as a bonus, squeeze out the anal glands on the way out. These stools are easy to clear up, and while dog mess can never be described as sweet violets, they do not stink as horribly as the output of dogs on processed food.

Raw bones should not be fed just as bones however. They need a good wrapping of meat attached for best dog value. The dog tears at the meat and crunches the bones, so the bones are not bolted down in lumps by greedy dogs, and are padded by the raw meat eaten at the same time. Aim for feeding the sort of bones that can be crunched right up, such as chicken wings and boned-out carcases, lamb or veal ribs, and breast of lamb. Even small dogs can annihilate large bones, as you see with this small terrier enjoying lamb ribs (see overleaf). It takes some time for a dog to eat raw meaty bones, thus the dog is having occupation and enjoyable exercise without even realising it.

Certain bones are better not fed, such as the marrow bones beloved of cartoonists. Dogs go mad for the marrow, and narrow-muzzled dogs can damage themselves trying to get it out of a bone sawn in half by a helpful butcher. Though the cartilaginous round ends of marrow bones are very nutritious, some dogs might chew off big lumps and swallow them whole, and big bones in general can cause wear on the dog's teeth. Vertebrae of large animals can cause problems with some small dogs, or with greedy ones

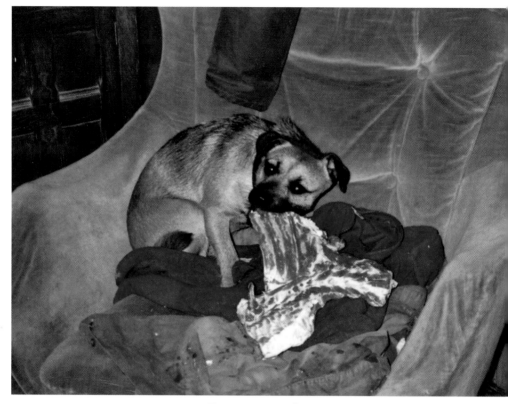

Eating raw meaty bone

that might swallow them in lumps rather than crunching them up, and are generally better avoided. Steer clear of bones from mature animals: if you give bones from animals raised for human consumption, these are killed while still immature, and all but the largest bones and vertebrae will be suitable for dogs.

Chicken bones are one area that raises a shocked response because we have all been on the end of received wisdom that chicken bones are very bad for dogs. It is cooked chicken bones that are bad – very bad – never feed these. Meaty raw chicken bones are fed by many people without causing problems, and I have weaned generations of puppies on whole chicken wings. If you are still nervous of feeding bones, you can start by pulverising small bones e.g. those in chicken wings (which are softer than most kibble) by hitting them with a hammer, or putting them through a mincer. An industrial mincer is a very good investment for committed BARF feeders who have access to a lot of carcase meat: we get a lot of rabbits and squirrels, and can reduce the (paunched and beheaded) cadavers to mince, hide, bones and all, which then stores easily in a freezer.

The mineral constituents of the bones should all be balanced in ratio, therefore are ideal nutritionally for providing a dog's needs, and especially those of a lactating bitch. However, intensively-reared meat can sometimes be lacking or unbalanced in certain minerals, especially phosphorus, so it is important to provide a variety of meaty bones and not just feed those from one type of animal.

After the dogs have enjoyed their bones, it is wise to clear up thoroughly. There may be pieces of bone left which, while quite harmless when wrapped in meat, may become sharp once dried out. There may be the odd bone buried for later as well, which, if you have more than one dog, may well become an object 'of contention'. Bones are a valuable resource as far as dogs are concerned. If a dog has behavioural issues which have not yet been sorted out and which centre on resource guarding, it is better not to give whole bones but instead crush or mince them as described earlier, and feed a little at a time so that nothing is left over to guard. Some dogs are better fed separately from other dogs, and many like to have a human companion present when they eat, presumably because they then feel protected. Personally, I always supervise my dogs at feeding times because you can see so much of what is going on about the dog by watching it eat. The astute owner can home in on poor general appetite, pain in the mouth, and status changes within the dog group, the last of which can be the first signs of illness. Also, it is important to see that each dog eats its own ration and does not try to steal another's. Low-status dogs can sometimes be intimidated into leaving their food even if the bullying dog does not actually take it.

That is really all there is to the feeding of bones. No mystery at all. Watching the unalloyed pleasure dogs get from chewing up raw bones, not to mention the exercise, is every bit as rewarding as knowing that you are feeding them correctly.

Furthermore, each dog only has so much chewing in it, even at teething-time, when it sometimes seems as if you are living with a furry chainsaw, and if it gets most of the chewing-need out of its system by eating bones, there is less likelihood of your possessions being gnawed instead. Processed dog food seems in comparison to be more inhaled than eaten – there is even small kibble made for smaller dogs! Kibble does not get rid of the itch in the jaws that makes a dog want to chew. If your dog, in the course of its work, is expected to retrieve game, it is far more likely to be happy to hand this over, even if there is the exciting taste of blood, if the dog enjoys plenty of meat and bones in its daily diet, and is not craving either. By contrast, the dog that eats the first pheasant of the day, or swallows a young rabbit in cover, might not just be disobedient – it might be trying to tell the owner that it has unfulfilled nutritional needs.

MEAT

As with bones, the 'chew' of raw meat is as important as its nutritional value, and the tooth-cleaning aspect is enhanced when the dog has to tear at its meat. Sometimes, for our own convenience in storage, we do mince meat, but as much as possible should be fed in a lump or attached to the bones we feed. Minced meat, especially with minced bone matter within it, is excellent, however, for feeding with vegetables, of which more shortly. But what meat should be fed, and how do we source it?

There are times when I think that every time I find a good source of raw meat, some Government directive or other appears to stop it. Certainly, it is much harder to get raw meat for dogs than it used to be, when any abattoir or hunt kennels would guarantee a regular cheap supply, and in due season, farmers would have livestock carcases available. Luckily, there are now several companies that supply frozen raw meat for pet food in blocks or bags that are easy to store. Butchers will supply their own pet mince, which can be variable in quality, or if you only have one or two dogs, it is little more expensive to buy people-quality meat from the butcher than it is to buy processed food for the dog, and far better nutritional value. If you live in a country area, you might be able to get surplus rabbit, hare, venison and so on from people who shoot it, though there are regulations concerning this with which it is wise to be familiar. Any meat is suitable for dogs, though most of us steer clear of pork, which can be rather too rich and can cause diarrhoea in dogs with sensitive digestions.

Wild meat has stronger bones than the young animals killed for human consumption, which is another good reason for mincing it with the bones in if you have the equipment. Wild meat also carries its share of parasites, but freezing any meat for a minimum of four weeks in temperatures of minus 20°C or below is sufficient to kill most of them. Appropriate worming of your dog, which you should do in any case, will get rid of the rest. When I bought the industrial mincer that converts so much game to mince for my dogs, the gamekeeper who sold it to me commented that it would take anything up to deer ribs, which 'did make it whine a bit'. That was all right, I told him, because I had something that dealt very well with deer ribs, and that could whine a bit as well.

FAT

Fat should be left on the meat, as it contains important nutrients. It is also improves the look of skin and coat. Thin dogs will gain weight on fatty meat, such as breast of lamb, and will put the extra flesh on the right places, rather than showing the cereal-fed dog's apparent tendency to layer fat on ribs and abdomen. A very few animals, often closely-bred show dogs, cannot cope well with fat due to digestive abnormalities, so if you have one of these, experiment until you can find out how much fat it can comfortably manage. Dogs metabolise fat for energy, which is what they are designed to do, and so they can process proportionally much larger amounts than we can.

OFFAL

Offal is easily obtained, and dogs love it, but it should not be fed too often, once or twice a week being recommended. Liver, especially from deer, is very rich in vitamin A and too much can cause harm, but it also has a high nutritional value, so should not be neglected as a foodstuff. Dogs adore offal, and a little can often tempt a shy feeder to get started on the rest of its dinner.

REGURGITATION

Dogs will sometimes swallow their meat, then bring it up again. This again is normal dog behaviour, and, queasy though it looks to us, is actually helping the dog by mixing the meat with digestive enzymes. Left alone, the dog will then eat its meat and keep it down the second time. Best not to watch if it upsets you. Dogs eat meat and bones messily, some more so than others, so feed them somewhere this does not matter, for it is all part of how they enjoy their food. If you have indoor dogs, remember the world is their napkin, and you might like to dry their jaws with a towel before they find something expensive to wipe themselves upon.

BACTERIA

What of bacterial nasties such as Salmonella or E.coli that we, in our Health-and-Safety cosseted world live in terror of? Yes, these are capable of causing human and canine illness, though healthy dogs are far less likely to be affected because of their stronger digestive processes and that short gut which processes food very quickly. People opposed to the feeding of a natural diet (usually those with a vested interest in selling commercial dog food) sometimes try to frighten those making the changeover by talking-up the risk of bacterial infection, yet vets have commented that they have come across more cases in dogs fed processed food than they ever have seen in those fed on BARF. Pause and consider the number of humans who handle raw meat frequently, such as farmers, game dealers, abattoir workers and fieldsports followers. You do not hear of them dropping like flies of infections caught from carcase meat, nor do you hear of Health and Safety legislation stopping restaurants serving rare meat or even steak tartare. Proper hygiene practices should be quite sufficient to prevent human infection here, keeping dog food separate from people food, cleaning any equipment thoroughly, and taking extra care with any humans that are very young, very old, or with otherwise compromised immune systems. Meat that comes from a reliable source and has been properly stored should be used, which is exactly what we do for ourselves as well. It will not stop your dog from bolting down the odd decomposing rabbit that it finds when out walking, which dogs seem to find more flavoursome than the prime-quality meat we give them, but then some of us have a taste for over-ripe cheese and well-hung game, which is close to the same principles.

ANTIBIOTICS

Another of the ways some people try to scare us away from natural feeding is to mention levels of antibiotics in carcases. Again, this is a matter of reliable sourcing. In the UK, lamb and beef are virtually organic, however raised, usually reared out of doors with expensive antibiotics given only to combat serious illness and with a strict withdrawal period before slaughter. Intensively-reared pigs and poultry are more at risk of a higher antibiotic intake, as is imported meat, and this should be borne in mind when choosing what to feed your dogs. What is also worth noting is that antibiotics and other chemicals are not always destroyed by mass processing.

FISH

There is no doubt that dogs love fish. It is tricky stuff to feed, though, for raw fish can be full of parasites, so ideally freeze it first for the requisite four weeks, or else cook it and take it off the bone. Do not risk feeding cooked fish bones as they can be every bit as sharp and troublesome as cooked meat bones. Tinned fish has soft bones and is good as an occasional treat, but some tinned fish has high levels of salt, so do not feed this too often. Fish canned in oil is good for the coat, and fish in tomato sauce provides some useful nutrients. When you cook fish for yourself, save the juices to put on the dog food and see how they enjoy your kindness.

VEGETABLES AND FRUIT

It is difficult for most animals to digest the cellulose that surrounds the nutrients in fruit and vegetables, and different species have different ways of accessing these. Some animals chew cud, others re-ingest their own faecal matter, we cook, and carnivores eat the semi-digested intestinal contents of their prey as well as the dung they find. Dogs will enjoy the muck of farmyard animals and wild ones, too, if we let them, though those loving licks are not quite so welcome afterwards. My own observations are that if my dogs are fed a meal that includes fruit and vegetables, they show no interest in other

Dog grazing on cleavers

83

animals' dung, but if they have had several meat and bone meals without added vegetables, they will graze freely of greenstuff and happily hoover up herbivore droppings. I live in the country and see a lot of dogs grazing with absolute desperation not just on grass but growing crops as well, because they are given dried food and are frantic for the missing nutrition they find in greens. Often, their owners try to stop them 'because it makes them sick' not realising that the dogs are self-medicating, and sick is exactly what they need to be. Dogs should be allowed to graze freely unless you suspect that the greenery has been sprayed; also if it is a farm crop that they favour, remember that it is somebody else's living, and be considerate.

If we are giving our dogs vegetables and fruit, we can make the nutrients much more available either by very light cooking, crushing in a mincer, or shredding in a liquidiser. You can even buy pre-shredded and dried vegetables for dogs from the same sources as the blocks of mince, and some manufacturers sell powdered greenstuff, which is very handy for those times when you have run out of the real thing. Any fruit in season is suitable for dogs except grapes and raisins, which have been shown to cause kidney problems in susceptible animals. Fruit should be given in sensible amounts, nothing to

Sharing blackberries

excess, and feeding a variety is important. Any vegetables can be used except for onions, leeks, garlic, or raw potatoes. Garlic has great medicinal use, but is better fed as a treatment when needed. Go easy on the root vegetables, because their starches are converted into sugars during digestion, but green leafy vegetables may be used in abundance. Like fruit, vegetables should be varied for best nutrition, and it should be noted that large quantities of raw brassicas (cabbage family) can affect thyroid function in susceptible dogs. Sprouts should not be fed whole as they can cause obstructions, and any hard plant material is in any case better ground up. Watercress and spinach are especially good for dogs, but we stress that the key to optimal nutrition is variety. Young nettles and nettle tips can be cooked for dogs and mixed in with their raw food, and apples and pears are very good for settling upset digestive systems. Dogs should be allowed to graze whatever herbs they choose when outside; mine are particularly fond of young wheat shoots, hogweed (not giant hogweed, which stings) and cleavers. Couch grass (otherwise known as dog grass) is a good emetic and diuretic sought by dogs that need to vomit up excess stomach juices, and sometimes worms will be brought up as well, alerting you to a job needing to be done. I had one dog

A good patch of couch grass

that would always seek out lungwort in order to empty her stomach of whatever was bothering her. Vomiting is not the problem to dogs that it is to us: they bring up whatever they need to, usually with two quick consecutive episodes, and then forget all about it, being ready to eat immediately afterwards unless they needed to be sick because they were ill. Couch grass can also go through the digestive system and be passed out more or less unchanged. On its way it seems to pick up excess mucus, and rids the bowel of that. It is useful stuff, and yet we humans too easily fixate on what looks uncomfortable to us instead of what is comfortable for the dog.

Some people have seen worms expelled following their dog's first raw-vegetable experience, and a huntsman once told me that if raw horseflesh is fed straight after slaughtering, it can have the same effect. Some followers of BARF say that you do not need to worm your dogs as often when fed on a rawfood diet, and while I would still use conventional wormers when appropriate, I have certainly seen far less need to since making the changeover. Please note that dogs can pick up worms from fleas as well as from outdoor sniffing around; they are a fact of canine life and their presence is not necessarily due to poor husbandry.

EGGS

There are foodstuffs you can give your dog which would only appear occasionally in a natural diet, but which are good for them in moderation. Eggs, for instance – a wild dog would only come across eggs at nesting time, and relatively few, so an occasional egg in your dog's diet will not be harmful. Egg-stealing dogs develop suspiciously shiny coats. A raw egg beaten and added to the meat and vegetable mix will often tempt a shy feeder, and one of the quickest ways I know of settling loose bowels is to feed scrambled eggs. However, it should be noted that loose bowels in a dog that is not otherwise ill are a cleansing process, and should be allowed to run its course before you feed anything to stop it. Nutritionally, there is an argument that eggs can inhibit the uptake of other nutrients, such as biotin, so keep these as an occasional treat. Raw eggs loosen the bowels just as cooked eggs have the opposite effect, and raw eggs can cause dreadful flatulence too. I learned this to my cost when a poultry farmer I worked for dropped half a bucket of eggs and fed the resulting mess to one of my dogs. That evening was spent suffering within a hideous cloud of sulphurous fart of which you just would not have believed such a dainty animal could have been capable.

DAIRY

Dairy produce is totally unnatural for dogs – and us – but has its uses. Few adult mammals have the necessary intestinal enzymes to digest milk properly – especially milk from a different mammal – and cows' milk can often cause diarrhoea. Milk really has no place in dog feeding, though countless people give it to puppies. Why? The best milk for puppies is in the bitch, and once the pups are weaned, she will top them up if she feels like it, and otherwise they are growing up and eating proper food. Cheese is one of the few processed foods that I find helpful in dog terms, and that is purely as a handy place to hide medication, and as an easily-carried titbit for training. Its strong smell and flavour makes it highly desirable to dogs, and small amounts will not do harm. Dogs find butter and cream delicious, but I find no nutritional reason for feeding either, and dogs with delicate stomachs may find them too rich. However, I possess an army of butter-stealing dogs, and one that hit the jackpot by ingesting the best part of a stilton cheese, so I have to be reasonable about these matters. Yoghurt is the one dairy product I will feed dogs on a regular basis, so long as it is plain live bio yoghurt where the 'friendly bacteria'

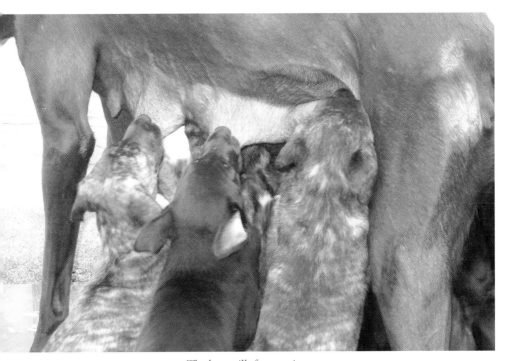

The best milk for puppies

are helpful to the gut flora, and the fermentation process causes a change in the milk constituents, making them already partly digested. Very good for settling minor tummy upsets, it is eagerly taken by most dogs.

Nuts and seeds

Nuts in season would form a very small part of a wild dog's intake, but they do love nuts, and a few as treats will be eagerly accepted by most dogs. Nuts contain all manner of useful nutrients, and are easy to store or carry. Never feed salted or coated nuts, only the natural nut kernel, and never feed nuts in the shell. Most seeds are acceptable to dogs as well, and a few, such as pumpkin seeds which are reputed to create a gut environment hostile to parasites, may be positively beneficial. Be aware of the risk of a greedy dog choking, and feed nuts carefully by hand with this in mind, rather than offering a pile of them in a bowl. Seeds can be mixed in with a meat and vegetable meal. Do not feed kernels of fruit stones, as these are harmful.

Oils

There are oils and oils. Pure cold-pressed vegetable oils are suitable to give occasionally, as are well-sourced (i.e. as contaminant-free as possible) fish oils, though you may not care for the fishy-breath aftermath of the latter. Heated and processed oils are not good to use, and if you prefer to keep away from genetically-modified food as much as you can, consider that most cheap oils contain maize and/or rape oil that is almost certain to be GM. Oils will loosen the bowels, so if you add oil to the dog's meal, make sure it can get outside as sometimes results are rather speedy. A small amount of oil in the food will put a shine on a dog's coat and improve a dry or scurfy skin. Elderly dogs with a tendency to constipation may also benefit from oil added to their meal (see also Chapter 4).

Titbits and leftovers

I am a great believer in 'a little of what you fancy does you good' and while I strive to feed my dogs in as natural a manner as possible, and would encourage anyone to do the same, I do not think the odd 'unnatural' treat should be out of bounds. Many people have a 'toast crust ritual' or a 'dregs of the cereal bowl moment' to share with their dogs, and it is a friendly, bonding time enjoyed by all. Similarly with leftovers from family meals, so long as these are plain and wholesome rather than lifting with artificial colourings, flavourings and preservatives. The closer food is to nature the better: butter is healthier than margarine (and I know dogs that won't touch the latter) and gravy made from meat juices is far better than gravy from a stock cube, which is mostly salt and colouring. So long as you are sensible with what you are giving your dogs, a small off-the-record treat here and there can be allowed.

CARBOHYDRATES

You will note that I have made no mention of carbohydrates. This is a food group that barely features in the diet of a wild dog. It may eat cereal from the stomach of a prey animal that has been feeding on crops, but ripe cereal is only available for a very short time each year, and not at all in uncultivated areas. It may dig up and eat root vegetables, or eat starchy fruit, but certainly not in large quantities. Processed ripe cereal and cooked starches are not good food for dogs, even though these are the chief constituents of many commercial dog foods. They are in there because cereal is cheap. Also cheap is soya, which features extensively in dog food, and is even more difficult to digest. Soya produces substances called saponins when eaten, which in susceptible dogs can present a bloat risk. While a dog can eat and benefit from fresh peas and beans, dried legumes are not at all good for them for the same reason. Most so-called 'natural' diets include some form of cereal, but dogs do not need cereal at all, process it poorly, and tend to convert starch to store it as fat. Dogs fed cereal-based foods present a quite different outline from those fed correctly, and seem to build up fat on ribs and abdomen. This may also be why some become diabetic, as a result of their bodies struggling with the sugars produced during the metabolism of the starches. Considering that commercial dog food started with Charles Spratt watching starving street dogs eating stale ship's biscuit, and from there having the idea of creating his range of dog biscuits, this may seem strange. Considering that many dogs over centuries were fed on bread, porridge and other starches, it might seem puzzling, too. But we are in a special position nowadays, for we can source and afford fresh meat for our dogs, and fresh vegetables all year round too. Time was, even in my childhood, that children were reared chiefly on bread, but it did not mean they were healthy, and it was just the same with the dogs. The difference is that the dogs of years ago could scavenge better food, and nowadays they cannot.

Properly-fed dogs live long and healthy lives, which the majority did not do in the days when they were mainly fed on bread. What about dog biscuits? These are very convenient to carry in a pocket and distribute as rewards, but I would say keep the biscuit feeding to a minimum, and do without it as much as you can. Ensure that any biscuit you do feed is free from colouring and additives, or even bake your own. However, as long as you have the oven on, why not bake some liver instead, until it is hard and dry, and store in the freezer? It makes much tastier treats and is better for your dog as well.

TIME

I can hear you say 'I don't have time for all that' but feeding rawfood is only as time-consuming as you want to make it. Certainly it is a lot quicker to dip a scoop into a sack of kibble, and you only need to stop at one place to buy that sack, but you might like to factor in time and money you will not be spending at the vet, because time and again, people feeding BARF find their dogs are far healthier. Freezers are the saving grace here: you can prepare all the food for a week or longer in one go, freeze it in meal-sized portions, and then all you have to do is remember to take out however many packets of food you need every day to thaw (naturally, please, not in the microwave, there being evidence that microwaved food can affect the immune system). You can whip up a quantity of vegetables in one go, or prepare them day by day to suit your own schedule, but vegetables start to deteriorate as soon as they are cut, so again, if they aren't going into the dog straight away, they go into the freezer instead. If you source the meat, bones and vegetables from shops that sell for human consumption – and you can often arrange some good deals with butchers and greengrocers – then you are probably going to those shops anyway. If you buy pet mince from the pet shop, then you are going to the same place from where you bought your kibble, but buying different food. It is possible to have large quantities delivered by some agencies, too. Wild meat can often be supplied by friends who hunt, shoot or fish, if you do not do those things yourself. It might cost you a cup of tea and a slice of cake, or a favour done when needed, but in the UK, only those licensed to do so may sell game. Feeding your dog the best food takes even less time than doing the same for your family, and many people, having seen the radical improvement in well-being shown by dogs on an appropriate diet, have amended their own eating habits to eschew processed food in favour of fresh. Thus we may shine with good health as well as virtue.

INTRODUCING THE NEW FOOD

Changing any diet is best done gradually, and in the case of rawfood, as much for the sake of the nervous human as the unsuspecting dog. There are dogs that will eat anything remotely organic (and in some cases, not even organic) without a blush, and dogs that react with horror to any change in their feeding regime. So far as personal experience goes, every dog to which I have offered a raw meaty bone or a chunk of raw meat has fallen on it with glee, and most will do the same with a bowl of meat and vegetables. If your dog acts as if it thinks you are trying to poison it, feed a main meal of the new food, and a little of the old food at a different time. Hunger is a great condiment, and feeding reduced quantities for a few days will encourage the dog to sample its change of victuals.

QUANTITIES

How much to give? This is easier than you think. Give a little more in volume than you did with the kibble, or in the case of meaty bones, start with a piece roughly the size of the dog's head. If the dog finishes the food and looks hungry, give the same amount again, but no more. If the dog leaves some of the food, give less next time. Within a few days, the dog's shape will begin to change and the coat will start to shine more than you ever thought it could. If the dog looks too lean, give more food, and if it begins to put on too much weight – very unusual with rawfood feeding but still possible with some breeds – give less. You have taken on the full responsibility for feeding your dog, guided by your eye and your experience of that dog. Awesome, isn't it?

BALANCE

A great fear among many of us revolves around the concept of 'balanced diet'. After all, those scientists involved in creating the processed dog food make a huge issue of the perfection of the nutritional balance of every piece of kibble. You are told not to add one bit of anything else because that would unbalance this flawless combination of nutrients, and you may have felt mortal guilt at sneaking the odd scrape of leftovers into the dog's bowl. Relax. Think of your own diet. There is no such thing as the perfect metabolism, and individual dogs – and people – make different use of their nutrients, some needing more, some needing less, of this or that. So long as the dog – or you, or any other animal – takes in all the essential nutrients over a week or so, what is eaten meal by meal does not have to be 'balanced'. The important thing is to give as varied a diet as possible, so that the opportunity is there to take in a wide variety of nutrients. What proportions of anything to feed? You will be guided by what you have available, and so long as your dog has some meat and vegetable meals and some meat and bone meals, with plenty of variety, that is all you need to do.

AGES

Dog food manufacturers supply different food for several stages of the dog's life. We can buy puppy, adult, working dog and 'senior' dog food, diet food, recovery-from-surgery food, stud dog and brood bitch food. How do we adapt rawfood? The answer is so simple – we do not. I wean my puppies straight onto rawfood, just as would happen in the wild, my brood bitches get the same but more of it, I increase the quantity for growing pups and hard-working dogs, and reduce it if a dog is laid-up with an injury and not getting

Weaning with raw food

Elderly dogs can benefit from supplements

much exercise. If dogs look lean, I give more, and if there is a suspicion of putting on too much weight, they get less meat and more bone and vegetable matter. Some dogs run up very light when working, and the best way to put healthy weight on them is by feeding fatty meat, such as breast of lamb, and if you can get green tripe with the fat still on, that is good too. Elderly dogs do not always make the most of their nutrients, and so a vitamin/mineral supplement made specifically for dogs will help them. Otherwise, generally dogs do not need supplements with a healthy BARF diet, and 'extra' vitamins and minerals can even be harmful if overdone (see Chapter 4).

STARVING

There was a great fashion until recently, which is still followed in some kennels, for not feeding dogs on one day a week. This was supposedly based on the idea that wild dogs would not eat every day. It was a very economical theory, as it saved fifty-two days of feeding over a year, but has no basis for health. True, sick dogs will lie-up and fast until they feel better, but there is no reason in our opinion to starve healthy dogs.

ROUTINE

Along with starving, old kennelmen swore by routine. In large kennels with plenty of staff, routine is the way to ensure that every job is completed and to the required standard, but the routine is for the people, not the dogs. It has always seemed strange to me that the same people who champion fasting the dog one day a week because in the wild it would not eat every day, also insist on a strict routine, which no wild dog could ever experience. Most of us have many demands on our time, and keeping to a routine is impossible unless we have staff. This is even more so for working dogs, whose days – and nights – vary depending on whether, when, where and how they are required to work. Dogs become accustomed to routine very quickly, have good clocks in their heads and some can begin to fret when the time approaches for a certain activity. My own dogs have always been well exercised and well fed, but not to any kind of routine because my lifestyle does not allow it. If routine works

Sleeping until needed

for you and your dogs, there is nothing wrong with it, but if you lead a more random lifestyle, do not feel that you are being a bad owner. Dogs are happy to eat or exercise at any time, and when they are not involved in either, they are equally happy to sleep. Whenever you are able to give them attention they will be ready to enjoy it, and they soon learn that there are times when they need to find their own occupation. The wise owner ensures that dogs have plenty to do that will not cause problems in the human environment, or else that the dogs have had their exercise and food, and are only too happy to doze when the owner is busy.

HOW OFTEN?

Again, the same people who make a case for starving dogs based on a hypothetical wild dog will tell you how often to feed your dog the rest of the time. Feeding intervals vary depending on the dog and the day. Very young puppies need to eat little and often, but once they are away from the bitch, they have to adjust to the human day as well, and of course that includes the human night, which means that supper can be a long time from breakfast the following day. Some puppies sleep through the night from the start, and others get bored and peckish at the sort of times you would rather be asleep. Some trainers can get very heavy about this and insist that the puppy 'learns' that it 'has to' sleep through the night. Puppyhood is such a short time, and a tiny pup that is hungry or needs to empty itself is not going to 'learn' anything except how to cry, and to soil its premises. Personally I prefer to interrupt my night for a few weeks, take the puppy out to get one end comfortable, and feed it to sustain the middle, after which it will want to play because it is a puppy. I do not join in this play because I am a human, and would like to get back to sleep, so I let the pup charge about for ten minutes or so and then settle it for the rest of the night by putting it back to bed and ignoring it. Daytime involves an early start to empty and feed the puppy, and usually pups under six months old will need three to four feeds a day. However, most pups are very good at deciding how often they need food, and you will often be able to cut down the number of feeds in a day long before the experts tell you that you 'should'. The pup is the expert here (I might make an exception for very greedy breeds) and if it does not want food so often, you do not have to offer it. Natural feeding puts you streets ahead in any case, because a pup is tired by the time it has wrestled a chunk of tripe or flesh into submission, or gnawed down a couple of raw chicken wings. Like human babies, pups have

Pup with raw chicken wing

hungry days and not-hungry days, and as long as the puppy is bright and lively and emptying itself normally, you do not need to worry about days when it wants less food. My latest one ate like a timber wolf every other day, only nibbling very small amounts on the days between, and many pups are similar in their eating habits.

By six months, pups are usually on two meals a day, and you have already forgotten the broken nights. Some people cut the feeds down to one a day at about nine months to a year, and others give a small 'breakfast' after the morning walk, or if a dog is to work that day, for the whole of a dog's life. Do whatever suits you and your dog best.

FEEDING FOR WORK

This does depend on the nature of the work in that a dog required to run hard should not do so on even a partly-full stomach, but a dog destined for a long day of shooting, picking-up or searching might be better for a very light snack. How light? A tablespoonful of mince and vegetables is quite sufficient for a springer spaniel-sized dog; adjust up or down according to the dimensions of the dog you have in mind. Similarly for the meal the night before, which should only be very small and given early for a coursing or hunting dog, while dogs in most other disciplines can have their usual rations at whatever time you like. Feed for the work the dog has done, not the work it is about to do, and you will not go far wrong. If the dog is working several days in succession, then it will be on light rations for the duration of the work. This will do the dog no harm, because once the working spell has finished, the dog can be fed extra rations, and more often if required, until it has made up its lost weight. I remember a trip to the northernmost tip of Scotland one winter, when I took a young, hard-going bitch. We went ferreting or bushing each day, and lamping every night, and it was really difficult to find enough time between these activities to feed her with sufficient time to digest her food. She was on small meals all week and ran up very light, but once we were home, she soon made her weight again. Dogs of this type are like falcons and have a weight at which they function best. This one was particularly weight-critical: as she became lighter, she became more and more fiery, crazy for her quarry and on a knife-edge of control. I am working her granddaughter now, a fey but much

Find your dog's best working weight

more amenable animal, whose best working weight is so light that I have had strangers comment on it. Learn the weight at which your dog does its best work while still remaining biddable, learn how your dog looks at this weight, and for all of its life you will be able to judge by eye whether it needs more food or less for the work it is getting.

FEEDING FOR ATHLETES

The dog that has to give an exceptionally athletic performance, generally in competition with others, has probably been on the receiving end of more inappropriate feeding than most. Generations of experts in their field (but not in nutrition) have given dogs all sorts of strange diets, including the sherry and blood mixture that once made up a large proportion of the pre-main (contest) diet of fighting cocks. Nowadays, many people base their dogs' competition diets on those of human athletes, which is not at all what the dog needs because its ways of using its nutrients are different from ours. I have come across so many people who believe in 'carbohydrate loading' the dog before sustained effort, because they are under the impression that the dog can create energy from starch the way that we can. In fact, cereal starch is a relative newcomer even in the human diet; a lot of us cannot metabolise it well, and it is one of the causes linked to type 2 diabetes in human middle age. The dog is designed to create energy from fat and protein, so rather than carbohydrate loading, the dog should be fat-loaded, and also receive red meat with the fat. If a dog is going to need to produce extra effort, do not feed large bones the day before or the day after the work, because these cost the dog more energy to eat and digest, and although a healthy dog will expel waste within twelve hours of eating that meal, bone waste can sometimes linger for another few hours while it gathers debris on its way through the gut. A meat and vegetable meal after the dog has expended extra effort will be good for its digestion, and then bones one or two days after the competition ends. No matter how many people tell you that they have always fed their dogs a large pasta meal, or that their Grandad was a highly successful greyhound trainer and fed brown bread before the big race, this is not the right way to get optimum performance from the dog, and it will have won despite the carbohydrates not because of them. Many people also give milk before sustained effort, and this is not good either. Mature animals seldom have the necessary gut enzymes for the processing of milk, and in any case your dog is not a growing calf. Milk generally loosens the bowels and can cause susceptible dogs to scour, which weakens their performance rather than strengthening it, in extreme cases even causing dehydration – definitely not wanted in a dog that is about to give its all. While you are bringing your dog to its highest fitness before competing, the normal rawfood diet will be all it needs. Dogs that are going to run hard will benefit from a series of small fat-rich meals the day before, the last one twelve hours or more before the start of the competition. Dogs are designed to hunt on a stomach that has been empty for hours, so there is no need to feel anxious that it might faint. Dogs that will be doing slower but more sustained work can have that tablespoonful of raw mince with or without a beaten egg before they start, and if the working day looks as if it is going to continue indefinitely, such as with Search and Rescue dogs, then the dog will appreciate a couple of mouthfuls of food after twelve hours or so – as will the handlers! It is worth remembering that a dog's sense of smell is much sharper when its stomach is empty, and a dog that has too much food in its stomach

Hard running

may vomit. For the duration of the dog's work, food should either be absent or given in very small quantities, preferably with an hour or so of rest so that the dog can start digesting it. Water, however, needs to be made available as often as possible, and if necessary to be given by syringe if the dog is reluctant to drink. However, the hard-running dog, such as the lamping lurcher or the coursing greyhound, has different requirements and is best worked fasting, with only a few laps of water and perhaps electrolyte until it has finished for the day or night. Working hounds can get very hot, no matter how cold the weather, and their day has a natural pattern of intervals, so their huntsman will endeavour to find them water at the end of each hunt, let them rest and roll and generally relax before they trot steadily to the next covert, draw slowly and diligently until they find their quarry or scent trail, and then run again. Good huntsmen also know when their hounds have done enough and take them home, no matter what the hour. Nowadays most packs have the luxury of motor transport: in the old days, hounds that had run exceptionally hard were often bedded down at a farm near where the hunt had finished, and taken home the following morning.

AFTER WORK

Once the dog has finished its work, it should not be given food or water until its breathing is back to normal and it seems relaxed and calm. Then a drink with or without electrolyte solution should be offered, but not too much. More fluid can be offered in half an hour, when the dog can drink its fill, and then after an hour, more fluid and a small meat meal when the dog arrives home, unless there is a long journey ahead, when the dog can have a few mouthfuls of food before leaving. Unless the dog has put in exceptional effort and is utterly exhausted, it can then have its main meal upon arriving home, followed by a good sleep. Very tired dogs are better having a small meal before their rest, and this is one occasion where a cooked meat and vegetable meal, served warm with plenty of liquid broth, is very welcome to a cold, tired dog. Then return to normal catering for the main meal, which should come after they have had several hours of sleep and been out for a potter about and an empty out, after which they should be left to rest again. Older dogs that might be past their prime but still enjoy a day's work will often try to do too much, and it is not always possible for the owner to stop this happening. Dogs too tired to eat need to be kept warm, either coated, in a heated kennel, or brought indoors, given plenty of fluid, and kept a stockman's eye on until they are back to normal, which may take a few days. Any dog that has apparently overdone it should not be worked again until it is completely rested and back to normal.

FEEDING FOR TEMPERATURE

Dogs are very efficient at using their body fat to keep warm. A dog that is otherwise healthy but does not hold its weight well will benefit from a coat or warmer surroundings as much as from more food. This is important for dogs being worked in winter conditions, for they will normally lose weight faster than they would in summer, and so would benefit from more fat in their food. Red meat tends to sustain weight better than white meat, and a nice fatty piece of beef, lamb or horsemeat is what is required if your dog needs a boost to its weight, while rabbit and veal are less likely to put weight on. Chicken, although white meat, is very fatty and so will be good for adding weight, whereas gamebirds are leaner with less fat unless they are corn-fed pheasants that have been raised for shooting.

GENDER FEEDING

Generally speaking, neutered dogs and bitches put on and hold their weight more easily than their entire counterparts, and feeding should allow for this. 'The eye of the master' is the key. It is better and far less stressful for the dog if the owner nips any weight gain in the bud than it is to let the poor beast get fat and then reduce its food to the point where it is hungry all the time. Entire bitches will gain weight over the abdomen at the time of their season and afterwards for the time they would have had pups and fed them. Nothing needs to be done about this as the weight is hormone-related, and will come off as soon as the false pregnancy is over and the phantom pups have been 'weaned'. Bitches coming into season will often show increased appetite, and bitches at the first week of conception sometimes go off their food and can even have spells of vomiting. Entire males can lose a lot of weight if working at stud, and some will fret off a whole lot more if there is an in-season bitch about, though others are not seriously bothered. Dogs accustomed to being used at stud are often less worried about bitches until exactly the right time for mating, and a few dogs can be badly affected by the presence of an unspayed bitch even if she is nowhere near her season.

PREGNANCY AND SUCKLING

For the first five or six weeks into the pregnancy, the bitch should not receive extra food, because this can result in big puppies and other birthing difficulties. It is far better to feed the bitch extra once the pups are born and she is suckling them. As the pregnancy goes into the sixth week, the bitch will start to change shape, filling out at the tuck-up, and now she can have increasing amounts of food (up to double by term) split into two meals. By the time she is into her eighth week, she will be getting short of internal space, and can be fed double her normal amount but split into four feeds daily. She will also need to empty herself more often, and ought to have the freedom to keep her quarters clean. Many bitches cannot last overnight by now, and so provision should be made for her to get outside when she has the need. It is not enough to put down newspaper or say it doesn't matter, because it does matter to the bitch. Most have the instinctive need to keep their sleeping area free from filth (there will always be the odd exception) and if she has to hold on to her waste, not only will she be distressed, but she will be holding toxins within a system that is already working at high capacity with processing waste from her unborn litter.

The birthing bitch should be allowed to eat the afterbirths of the puppies.

Bitch at full term

Some people stop this as it can make the bitch's bowels loose, which probably is precisely what it is designed to do, so that she can empty herself out more easily while bruised from the birthing. It is her instinct to eat the afterbirths, and she may well become distressed if not allowed to do so. Afterbirths are also reputed to be full of nutrients and hormones that the bitch needs at this time.

When suckling, a bitch can eat four times her normal rations. Give her more if she seems to need it. A good guide is the normal pre-pregnancy ration (N) times bitch plus pups divided by 2:

$$\frac{N \ \times \ (\text{bitch} + \text{number of pups})}{2}$$

but personally I would say feed ad-lib unless the bitch is exceptionally greedy.

WEANING

Here is a big secret: pups are self-weaning. I have never yet met an adult dog that was still on the milk bar. Yet we are told all sorts of methods, some quite bizarre, of inducing puppies to eat solid food. I have heard of scraped pulp off raw meat, rice pudding, goat milk, boiled mince, all sorts of cereal and of

Weaning

course commercial puppy food being essential for weaning pups. Some breeders even forcibly remove the pups at three weeks old, leaving the bitch at risk of mastitis, and the puppies stressed as well as unable to be taught appropriate social behaviour by their dam. It really does not have to be such a big process. Left to their own devices, many mothering bitches will regurgitate food for their weanlings, thus presenting it warm and with the digestive process already started. It is a queasy moment for a human witness, but just right for the puppies. Not every bitch does this, and what happens with mine is that I take the bitch a bowl of food one day and a litter of puppies piles into it. Maternal bitches will look on in motherly serenity, but greedy bitches can get quite agitated, and a minority will even attack the pups. If this is likely, then separate the bitch before you feed the puppies, making sure that she has not suckled them first. Then let her back in when they have all mumbled away at their food, and she can top them up with milk if they want. As the puppies get better at handling solid food, they will want less milk and the bitch will start to dry up naturally. When the bitch stops feeding is a very individual matter: I have had one that quit cold when the pups were

Feeding the suckling bitch

three weeks old and their teeth first started coming, and another that fed through to twelve weeks, and still offered a comforting suckle to the pup we kept until he was four months old and far too grown-up (in his eyes) for such baby behaviour. I use the same food for weanlings as I do for grown dogs, but I do supervise the puppy meals. How they love those chicken wings and lumps of raw meat. They shake the meat to kill it, *rrrrrr* at each other, back off their meat and pounce on it, and have great fun (remember being told not to play with your food?). Mince and vegetable mix gets hoovered up with glee, and I will sometimes add a beaten-up egg yolk or a glop of bio yoghurt. I admit to adding some honeycomb debris one year, when I was given a huge jar of it by a local beekeeper. I cannot construct a scenario where a wild dog would eat honeycomb, but I know that it is full of valuable minerals and trace elements, and the pups, which were hand-reared, did very well on it. Nor can I argue a natural-feeding case for plain bio yoghurt, but I can on nutritional grounds, so you can make allowances for me there! Make sure that any food carried off and buried by your baby wolves is found before it rots. I did have a pup that was really wild in her ways, despite having the same upbringing as

Bitch feeding six-week-old litter

105

the rest of the litter, and she would not eat out of any sort of dish at all. However, if you threw the food on the ground, she would stalk and pounce on it, shake and bite it until satisfied it was dead, and then carry it off to eat it in private. If there were other dogs about, she would take her food to eat on my lap. She grew into a normal dog eventually, and a very faithful one, but she was as wild as a hawk until nearly a year old, and we called her The Jackal.

GROWTH AND DEVELOPMENT

Ian Billinghurst in his book *Grow Your Pups With Bones* offers the interesting comment that pups should only grow to seventy-five percent of their potential. I am inclined to agree with this. Rapid growth such as that desired for farm livestock is not what is best for a dog, especially one that is needed for work. Slower growth minimises the chances of joint and bone problems, while ensuring that the body above the legs does not get too heavy for developing limbs to support. Slower growth leads to better bone density. Both of these mean that a pup with the potential for correct conformation is more likely to mature at the right shape, and as the osteopaths say: 'Structure governs function'. To a great extent, work dictates the shape and size of the working dog, which is why show dogs and working dogs supposedly of the same breed usually differ so vastly in size and conformation. It is a sad fact that once the 'work' is taken out of any breed, the dog loses correct shape and often health as well. What lunacy it is to breed only for genes, often recessive and harmful ones, for a particular size and structure arbitrarily set by a breed club for showing, with barely a nod at good health. Breeding at first was for function, but there is an optimum size for dogs, over or under which the body does not operate efficiently, and working dogs need to be of that correct size if they are to last at their job. Where there is a choice of breeds or types to suit a particular array of tasks, we need to take into account such important matters as the terrain that the dogs are worked over, and there will be localised differences to suit that. Fell foxhounds, for instance, that climb and scramble over rocks and really steep gradients are lighter and with longer toes than well-timbered cat-footed lowland foxhounds which have to pull their limbs out of heavy clay going all winter, and neither would function as well over the fast grassland country of the Shires as the hounds that are bred for it. Working beagles are so much smaller and lighter than the show version that dog rescues have been known to describe them as 'Jack Russell crosses'! Although many show-bred dogs retain the instinct to work, their physique has been changed

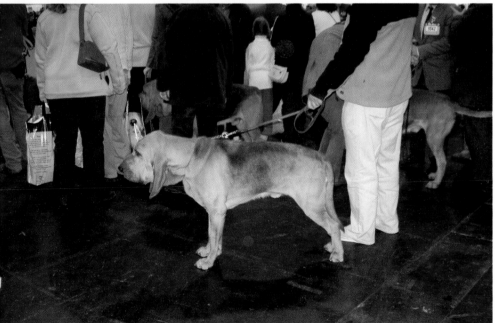

Show bloodhounds at Crufts

Show beagle with working beagle

to such an extent that they either could not work and remain sound, such as with the big heavy labradors and spaniels that you see, or could not work at all, as with the extraordinarily-shaped show version of the greyhound. Assuming that your pup has come from pure working stock, raw feeding should bring it on in the right form to mature at the right size and at the right age, but it may not be exactly to the breed standard. Many dual-purpose working breeds have the odd show dog in the pedigree, and so the potential exists for too much size and bone, but again, raw feeding will give the best chance for the dog to mature at the optimum size for working. Raw feeding means that the pup will grow on more slowly and be smaller at maturity than if fed a cereal-based high-protein diet, but we are raising working dogs not fatstock, and instead of being killed for the table while still immature, we would like our working dogs to remain fit and functional for years.

FOOD CONTAINERS

It might surprise you to know that what we put the food into has its importance as well. Bones and lumps of raw meat do not need to be put into anything, and I call each dog and give it its rations to carry off and eat in private. Mince and vegetable mix has to be fed in something, though, and the best containers are toughened glass or sealed earthenware. Stainless steel is convenient, lightweight, easy to store and keep clean, and is acceptable as a food container but not for water, to which we shall come shortly. Plastics should be avoided for bowls and storage bins as they can leach toxins into the food and can cause illness and allergies. They also carry their own smell, which many dogs find offensive. Indeed, many animals, including cats and horses, dislike eating out of food containers made from plastic for that reason.

WATER

And so to water, which is almost as important as food, but normally given very little thought. Water containers ideally should be toughened glass or sealed earthenware, not metal or plastic, or even a polythene bucket, for the same reasons as given above. Although stainless steel will be all right to use as a food dish, which only holds its contents for a short time, it is not the best

Clean water in earthenware dish

container for water because of the possibility of metal toxins leaching into the water. Tap water varies in quality from district to district, being very palatable in some areas and almost undrinkable in others due to the high concentration of so-called purifying chemicals. Therefore many dogs prefer to drink soft rainwater out of puddles, or fresh, well-oxygenated water out of streams. It can be very frustrating to the owner when dogs seem to prefer stagnant pond-water over the clean, clear supply made available by the owner, and of course some 'outdoor' water is not at all good for them. Puddles can contain chemicals from the run-off of sprayed fields, or oils from machinery, or even anti-freeze, which last will kill your dog shockingly quickly. Anti-freeze is sweet to the taste and very appealing to dogs. Standing water can contain toxins from dumped rubbish – humans are very good at polluting water supplies – or grow a poisonous variety of blueish algae. Water from a rain-butt may contain all sorts of extras, from chemicals picked up as the water runs off the roof to small life-forms, and of course the butt itself is liable to be made from something harmful such as plastic or aluminium.

The water you supply for your dog can be made more appealing either by being filtered to remove the worst of the chemicals, or by drawing it into a jug and allowing it to stand. If you want, you can purify the water by having two or three crystals in the jug, or even in the water bowl if you do not have the sort of dog that will try to eat them. I use rose quartz, clear quartz and amethyst, all inexpensive and easily found in New Age-type shops. You would be surprised at the dirt and calculus that these crystals attract from the water; they do a good job, are easily cleaned, and last for ever. If all this seems to be a lot of unnecessary trouble when you have always given your dogs water straight out of the tap and they have always drunk it, well of course you can continue doing that, but this is a book that shows the way to do the best for your dog's health. Try offering your dogs different water, and see how they will choose almost any option rather than straight out of the tap. Maybe you have really palatable mains water where you live, but that is not the case for every area. The tap water stinks of chlorine in my area, and I certainly would not drink it, unless there was nothing else available and I was desperate. Consider the increasing sales of mineral water and water filters. We in the UK also have the disquieting future prospect of mass medication, e.g. aluminium fluoride (an industrial waste product, the use of which is banned in some countries due to concerns both over cancer and intellectual impairment), being added to our water supplies by governmental decree, which would open the door to goodness knows what else if it ever happens.

Additives

Sometimes various substances can be added to water for the dog's benefit. Old kennelmen used to believe in rock sulphur in the water during the hot months, and our own dogs were given this when I was a child. It was supposed to cleanse internally and prevent 'hot spots' on the skin. It is also useful for dogs that eat their own or other dogs' excrement (coprophagia). There are several reasons for this behaviour, and sulphur will only work when the core reason is nutritional. Dogs on the rawfood diet seldom eat canine faeces, and when they do, it tends to be a psychological issue rather than a physical need, but you can never say 'never' where animals are concerned, and rock sulphur will often help stop this behaviour. If you use it, only in a glass or earthenware bowl, please, and you will have to scrub the sulphur now and then to stop it going green with algae. The instructions on the packet when you buy it recommend that you crumble a small amount in the bowl, but I think this is written by someone with a warped sense of humour or else the strength of a giant. Put the whole block in, and throw it away at the end of the hot weather.

Other helpful additives include colloidal silver as a general immune-system support, for it is believed to be antibacterial and antiviral. I put Bach remedy Crab Apple in the water as an internal cleanser if I have a dog that is showing skin sensitivity or having a stomach upset, and always use it for one that is on heat or has just given birth. These are gentle treatments, and will do no harm.

Out and about

A lot of working dog owners take the trouble to train their dogs to drink out of a baby's feeder bottle, which is light to carry and fits easily onto a belt or in a pocket. I always carry water in the car, and I expect you do as well, but sometimes we are a long way from the vehicle when the dog needs a drink. If you have your dog out and the day is warm, make sure that you have frequent stops for water and general cooling down, and learn where the cattle-troughs and streams are in the places you frequent. While carrying water and making use of available supplies, you will of course be using water from plastic and metal containers, but we have to live in the real world and do what is expedient from time to time. So long as you use fresh water in the container in the car and the bottle you carry, there is unlikely to be any major harm caused. Good care and maintenance is a lifetime project, and the odd straying from best practice is perfectly acceptable, indeed unavoidable sometimes. It is better to have a hot dog watered and cooled down than kept from water

Refreshment stop

Know where to find water

because the situation is not ideal, and the same applies with food. The occasional junk-food meal does them and us no harm if, most of the time, we have a healthy intake, and this goes for water too.

Away from home

Different water supplies can make a big difference to dogs, whose sense of smell is so much more sensitive than ours. Dogs travelling long distances for competitions, or going away to stud, will be appreciative of the owner carrying a supply of familiar water. I know a dog that was a hot favourite for a very prestigious three-day field trial refusing to drink the strange water, and his owner was up all night syringing fluids into him after the first day (incidentally, the dog won, and was none the worse). While some dogs will eat and drink anything, others can be extremely sensitive to changes of water, even more so than of food, and it is not unknown for a dog to get diarrhoea from this cause alone. Of course, this can work in a positive as well as negative manner, and my dogs loved the peaty, soft Scottish water every time I went up to the Highlands. It tasted pretty good in the whisky as well.

HALFWAY HOUSE

Life is unbearably stressful if we do not learn the art of compromise. It is very hard for those of us who have made the leap to raw feeding, knowing how we were once seduced by the convincing words of those who made their living out of selling canine junk food, to avoid being over-enthusiastic about recommending it. This can be irritating to others who have kept dogs for years, feeding commercial food or doing just what their grandparents did, and having no problems at all. Or perhaps there were problems but these were not traced back to the food. If your dogs do what you want and look pretty good, why change? It is entirely your decision. Few people who do make the change subsequently change back, because for the little more time and trouble involved – maybe an extra hour or two a week, and some forward planning – the improvement most see in their dogs is incredible. However, there will be those who are reluctant to commit to the rawfood diet in its entirety, and they ask if they can mix complete food with raw when they feel like it, or have an easy source of meat to use up. Yes of course this is possible, so long as the owner has a nodding acquaintance with nutrition, and feeds the raw part of the diet in its entirety, that is, with raw meat, raw bones and raw fruit and vegetables. However, the BARF and the commercial food should be fed at separate meals as there is risk of fermentation in the gut if they are fed together, because each is digested differently. Meat may be fed with mixer biscuit as a shortcut when expedient, but again it is far better for the dog if the meat meal is separate from the biscuit meal. Frankly, I believe the dog is better off having the occasional smaller meal of good ingredients, leaving out the commercial food entirely, and there is no need to worry about 'balance' at every meal as long as the dog is getting what it needs overall from the raw diet. Some people are really worried about feeding bones, or else have trouble sourcing them, but would like to feed raw otherwise. If that is the case, the diet is lacking not only in essential minerals, but in the critical ratios between these minerals which add up to them being properly absorbed. A reasonable halfway house in this case is to add a mineral supplement designed especially for dogs (see Chapter 4). The dog will not be getting as good a diet as if it were being fed in a totally biologically appropriate manner, but it will still be streets ahead of the dog that is fed wholly on processed food.

EXCEPTIONS

A very few dogs will not take to the rawfood diet because of metabolic disorders. If your dog has a health problem, then it is wise to liaise with a vet who is familiar with canine nutrition in relation to that disorder. Unfortunately, the only recognised qualification in dog nutrition in the UK at the time of writing is one given by a commercial pet food company, so you will need to seek out someone whose expertise extends beyond that. Otherwise you are likely to be recommended a commercial diet that reads more like a chemistry lesson than a recipe. It should be possible to create the basics of a good diet for a dog with digestive problems using fresh unadulterated food supported by probiotics and other carefully-chosen natural supplements.

HOMECOOKED FOOD

Ah, you cannot beat home cooking – not if your mother could cook like mine, anyway – and that is what you might like to do for your dog. A lot of people find dealing with raw meat is unpleasant, and would rather cook it. A lot of dogs enjoy cooked food. Would that be so bad? Again, a home-cooked diet is far better in our view than a totally commercial diet, and you can add cooked food to BARF. There is no doubt that raw food is healthier because a lot of fragile nutrients are destroyed by the cooking process, and a lot of human food contains additives that are healthy neither for you nor for your dog. So, if you are cooking from scratch with fresh ingredients, and you avoid giving cereals, cooked bones, salt and sugar, you can feed your dog this way, which is basically the rawfood diet, only cooked. If you cook vegetables al dente, so much the better. Again, what is missing are the nutrients in raw meaty bones, so you will still need to feed these, or else a mineral supplement, and the whole will not be so effortless nor as good as the rawfood diet. If you mostly feed raw but find it convenient to provide the occasional cooked meal, there is no harm in this at all. At appropriate times of year, my dogs wolf down game casserole with vegetables, and love it as a change from their raw diet. All cooked meat should be taken off the bone, though, and no cereals should be given. Dogs don't need bread to mop up their gravy.

WHY RAWFOOD?

Feeding raw can be a huge leap of faith, and many who hear about it naturally fear making that leap, especially if they consult their vet and he or she is one who a) sells commercial dog food as an essential part of the practice's profits, and b) has had little opportunity to study nutrition but has never let that hold them back from having an opinion about it. Plenty of people who should know better find the selling of commercial dog food is an important part of their income, and so the poor dog owner in search of the best way to feed his or her dogs will, instead of useful information, come across a bundle of self-interest from many vets, kennel owners and behaviourists. And of course, when in doubt it is sensible to stick with what we know – or think we know – or what 'experts' tell us we know. And you don't have to feed your dog in any way that does not suit you. I am simply promoting the rawfood diet as being the best for healthy dogs. You will only ever get out in terms of health and performance what you put in as food. Healthy dogs heal faster, have strong immune systems, can work to the peak of their inborn abilities and remain fit to do their job for longer. In terms of temperament, many a behavioural problem can be vastly reduced or resolved by changing to proper feeding. I have known dogs that were absolute head cases become calm and biddable once they were not reacting to the additives in commercial food. Physically, there is almost always a huge improvement in coat and skin, nails and pads, once the dogs are eating better food. We ask so much of our working dogs, and they ask little enough of us in return. Cynically, you could say that we invest a vast amount of time and money in buying and training a dog for work, and by feeding it properly, we get the maximum return on our investment. Experience shows that the dog, if injured, will be off work for a shorter time because it will heal so quickly, and if it comes into contact with dogs that are carrying infections, it will either not catch the illness at all, or will have such a strong immune system that it will throw off the infection with little to show for it. It is also far more likely to have a longer working life. For many of us, myself included, the dog is also a much-loved member of the family, and we want it to be happy and healthy for as long as possible. Feeding raw can achieve all this, which has to be the best reason for doing it.

4. ROCKET SCIENCE

SUPPLEMENTS FOR HEALTH

Nutraceutical Medicine

Nutraceutical medicine is the latest buzzword from the United States and is rapidly developing huge interest from those involved in the animal world over here. So what is it, and how does it apply to dogs and everyday UK veterinary practice, not to mention the everyday working dog owner?

The North American Veterinary Nutraceutical Council defines Nutraceutical products as 'substances produced in a purified or extracted form that are administered orally to provide or stimulate production of raw materials required for normal bodily functions'. This basically means dietary supplements, which have uses to help the body combat or prevent disease. My interest was sparked some years ago following my attendance at a medical conference where a paper showed that 42–43% of cases of asthma, eczema, and IBS (irritable bowel syndrome) in children responded positively to a 'Stone Age' diet (no wheat or other grains, no potatoes, refined sugars or processed foods). This is now more commonly known as the 'Palaeolithic' diet. I began looking closely at canine, feline and equine nutrition as a primary cause of disease seen in my patients.

'Let your food be your medicine' (Hippocrates); as ever there is nothing new under the sun. The advent of modern pharmacy has overshadowed the role of nutrients in enhancing repair mechanisms, the immune response and metabolic functions. More recently, as the limitations of modern drugs are realised, and as the veterinary profession loses more and more drug therapies to legislation, interest in nutraceuticals has increased.

The first thing one encounters when investigating this field is the vast array

A far from sedentary life

of advice given out in leaflets, articles and publications, often without any references supporting the claims. One only has to look on the Internet, searching 'minerals and supplements', to find nearly one million sites. This does nothing to help what I believe will become a valuable addition to the dog owner's therapeutic repertoire. The information is out there, but one has to search to find it, and all this marketing on the Internet would not have evolved if it did not have some validity. I began my search as a sceptic, but have now become a total convert to the principles.

Multivitamins and minerals

The first line of inquiry has to start with basic vitamins and minerals. We get enough via our food – or do we? Animals certainly fare better than humans in the number of these added to their basic diet if fed commercially prepared products, and this is one of the arguments used against natural feeding regimes. However, with all the nutrients in one form of food only, some vets feel that non-absorption of essential nutrients due to imbalances in the individual's bodily make-up can occur, but that this should not happen if the body gets a variety of foods over time. There are many differing views; however, the consistent theme is that the RDAs (standard recommended daily allowances) are simply not enough, because animals, and particularly those that work for us, such as dogs and horses, are far from the sedentary beings for which RDAs were calculated. There is plenty of research showing that optimum levels for each nutrient are far higher than the RDA. For example, reductions in overall mortality, and mortality from cancer and cardiovascular disease, have been reported in those who take supplements of vitamins C and E. A massive fifteen-year study on 13,500 people resulted in the establishment of Suggested Optimal Nutrient Allowances (SONAs) for vitamins. These levels are often ten times the RDA. People given the SONA-type supplements had fewer infections, a stronger immune system, and were generally healthier. A 75% reduction in birth defects, after SONA-type supplements were given to pregnant women, was shown in a study of 22,000 pregnant women. If these are the results being found in humans, we can broadly assume that these facts may well be true in animals as well. However, valid information is harder to come by. For example, a while ago megadoses of vitamin C were recommended for pregnant bitches, and puppies for two years after their birth, to prevent hip dysplasia, yet no studies have adequately documented the efficacy of this. Compound the RDA debate with theories about vitamin requirements being related to the metabolisable energy of the diet fed and we get even more complicated. So the assumption has to be, based on the human experience, that a well-formulated multivitamin/mineral supplement has to be a good idea to promote animal health. Certainly the public thinks so with the millions spent on supplements for themselves, for horses, and often on human supplements for their smaller animals where no other is available. This will become an increasingly important market with so many people opting for home-prepared diets, which may need appropriate supplementation.

BIO-AVAILABILITY

The next problem is the bio-availability of the product one selects. It is not much use taking the supplement in a form that the body cannot access. One of my favourite quotes from the marketing paraphernalia is about America's favourite multivitamin, which has allegedly blocked up Los Angeles sewerage plants as it goes through pretty well unabsorbed. Bio-availability is affected by a number of factors. Firstly, the balance of nutrients supplied in a product is important: many vitamins need major minerals in appropriate amounts to be absorbed, and similarly many of these major minerals need adequate levels of trace minerals for their absorption process to run smoothly – all are interconnected and, as such, over-supplementation with one nutrient can lead to iatrogenic (induced as a result of taking a supplement/medication) deficiencies of another. Secondly, the bio-availability of different nutrients is greater in one form than another. The current vogue developing in the human field is for oral sprays, where all the nutrients are in an aqueous solution and taken at frequent intervals throughout the day to avoid the 'peak and valley syndrome' of tablet medication. This presents some obvious practical difficulties with animals. There are many liquid preparations coming onto the market, but my own preference is for powdered colloidal multivitamin/mineral products, and for oil-based products to be made into stable powders by spraying the nutrients under high pressure onto micronised particles of silica mineral. The silica acts as a carrier and also stabiliser of the supplement. With appropriate flavouring, powders are highly palatable for pets and can be added to food easily and in a form that the animal is likely to take. Some manufacturers have added probiotics to their animal preparations of these powdered products, apparently to optimise gut flora activity and further increase absorption.

MULTI-MINERALS

The more people learn about nutrition, the more they appreciate the critical importance of minerals, and especially trace minerals, as the cornerstone of any nutritional supplementation programme. It was the use of multi-minerals in my practice which really revolutionised my way of working. I have found them useful in cancer and skin disease, but most especially I use them for musculoskeletal and arthritis cases. Many old dogs with arthritis (particularly spondylitis sufferers), do not seem to need pain control if supplemented with these types of products. This made me start questioning the neutering of pets, and wondering how much they suffer the effects of this induced 'menopause'. I have found unstable diabetics which improve on chromium and vanadium supplements, and the required insulin dose may even be reduced.

'Minerals are the forgotten dietary need. Often deficiencies are neglected whilst vitamins are taken in plenty. Yet most of the world's dog population is mineral deficient'. 'Lacking vitamins, the system can make some use of minerals, but lacking minerals, vitamins are useless'.

Few parts of the world exist where the human population (let alone the dogs), receives adequate minerals in the diet; this is primarily due to the inadequacies in the soil on which the food grows. 'Laboratory tests prove that the fruits, vegetables, grains, eggs and even the milk and meats of today are not what they were a few generations ago.' Much disease and premature death is said to be the result of these subclinical mineral deficiencies. People in areas which are not mineral deficient are said to suffer less heart disease, cancer, arthritis, strokes, and so on. Trace minerals have been shown to act as catalysts at a cellular level, regulating many cell functions including the bulk uptake of the major minerals in the diet that are needed in large quantities, as well as all the other ingredients in the diet, such as proteins, vitamins and carbohydrates. Other roles include the formation of bones and teeth, the regulation of body fluids and nerve function, working as partners for enzymes, and involvement in the formation of other body compounds such as iodine in the thyroid gland, chromium in sugar regulation, iron in blood cells, and so much more.

One of the most important factors in any supplement, along with the bio-availability of the product, is achieving a balance of the constituents compatible with the body's own self-regulatory mechanisms. Again there are no specific industry standards, although work is in progress on this. There is little point supplying individual minerals or incomplete sets of minerals as this will always lead to imbalance and occasionally deficiency states. For example, an excessive iron intake reduces the absorption of copper and zinc, which in turn can lead to secondary deficiencies. Balance is critical, the 'key' to health.

So is mineral deficiency being tackled in the world at large? One of the main reasons for deficiencies is said to be the changes in modern farming practices. Traditional farming moved onto fresh pastures once land was depleted, allowing longer-rooted perennial plants to extract deeper minerals to add to the topsoil. Alternatively organic manure was put back into the soil. Now modern methods add nitrogen, phosphorous and potassium to force plant growth, creating progressively deficient plants, and soil which is unable to regenerate for many years to come. This process is being reversed in countries such as Holland where the use of synthetic fertilisers is heavily restricted and organic systems, effectively soil probiotics, are being developed to bring the hardpan back into the soil. Recycling programmes producing composted waste will eventually benefit us all, but until this is universal (unlikely in the near future) it makes sense to add trace minerals to an animal's diet.

Essential Fatty Acids

Unsaturated fatty acids are increasingly becoming recognised as an important part of a dog's diet. They are needed for cell membranes and cell function throughout the body. Inadequate levels can have far-reaching consequences on cellular, tissue and organ function, thus contributing to many degenerative disorders. As well as this, fatty acids are necessary precursors for regulatory hormones, particularly the prostaglandins which play an important role in inflammation, blood clotting and viscosity, and arthritic pain, amongst others.

There has been increasing recognition of the potential of these fatty acids in the treatment of illness, especially dermatological disease, in the veterinary world. Initially this came with the launch of evening primrose oil supplements, and, more recently, borage oil. Fish oils have also been deemed important in promoting neutrophil (a type of white blood cell) activity. Not only is it important to have enough of these oils, but the balance has to be right as well. The body cannot make these 'essential' fatty acids for itself. Modern diets have shown a major shift towards high levels of omega 6, yet omega 3 is now recognised as an essential nutrient. An optimum ratio of 1:1 seems to be most often recommended for a supplement, yet many diets have as much as 25:1, omega 6: omega 3. Since omega 6 and omega 3 compete for enzyme pathways, this distorted balance can trigger multiple imbalances affecting neurological, immunological and hormonal balance, amongst others. In severe disease states it may be necessary to first increase the intake of omega 3 to redress the balance. One simple way for dogs is to grind one or two dessertspoons of fresh organic flaxseeds (linseeds) and add them to the dog's food just before serving (it must be freshly ground as the oils decay rapidly

122

after grinding the seed). Alternatively, flaxseed oil capsules can be used. This may be necessary for one or two months to correct imbalance, and thereafter a good supplement with a 1:1 ratio can be used.

It is not enough just to supplement essential fatty acids if they are to be useful in one of their major roles – as a source of precursors for synthesis of prostaglandins. It is necessary also to give various minerals and vitamins, such as zinc, magnesium, and vitamins B6 and C. This can be achieved by giving a good multivitamin/mineral supplement specifically designed for dogs. The list gives just some of the conditions for which essential fatty acid supplementation is said to be useful.

Omega 3 for:	Omega 6 for:
• Allergies	• Anaemia
• Arthritis	• Behaviour
• Cancer	• Cardiovascular system
• Cardiovascular system	• Fatigue
• Coordination	• Fertility
• Eyesight	• Glandular disturbances
• Immune system	• Hair loss
• Inflammation	• Immune system
• Liver problems	• Liver damage
• Mental decline	• Osteoarthritis
• Nerve problems	• Pyoderma
• Obesity	• Renal function
• Skin problems	• Skin problems
• Viral illness	• Viral illness
• Weakness	• Wounds

Antioxidants

The last few years have seen an explosion of information about the role of oxidative stress in causing, and the therapeutic role of antioxidants in preventing, any number of serious diseases.

Free-radical oxidisers are produced in the body and are used in enzymatic processes, hormone production, combating toxins, bacteria, and viruses and in waste elimination. They are essential to life. However, inappropriate free radical levels or free-radical attack can damage body systems by changing molecular structure, and this occurs when the body's own antioxidant enzymes are overwhelmed. To combat this, dietary antioxidants are said to be very useful. Excessive levels of free radicals are caused by toxins in food (herbicides, pesticides, antibiotics), pollution in the air (cigarette smoke, industrial smoke, etc.), UV (ultraviolet) light from the sun, illness, radiation, excessive exercise and many more – basically modern life.

Medical research is showing that this proliferating free radical problem is a significant factor in the escalation of degenerative and vascular diseases. At a cellular level, free radical damage tends to affect the unsaturated fats in cell membranes, preventing cells from importing nutrients efficiently, exporting waste, and resisting bacterial and viral attack. Cell DNA may also be affected, rendering the possibility of the chaotic growth of a tumour. On a larger scale, free radicals injure structural proteins, collagen and elastin with obvious results.

So what antioxidants are available? We have all heard of the role of vitamins E and C as antioxidants, and certainly they are useful, but there have been discoveries of so-called 'Super Antioxidants', the leaders in the field being oligomeric proanthocyanidins (OPCs) derived from grape seeds. OPCs are present at good levels in diets which contain plenty of sun-ripened fruit and vegetables. However, now that much more fruit is picked unripe for ease of transport and so does not have the chance to manufacture OPCs in the sun-ripening process, a supplement is almost always necessary for humans, and especially for dogs which rarely receive fresh unprocessed food at all. OPCs from grapeseed extract are said to be more than forty times as effective as Vitamin E. No self-respecting antioxidant preparation would now be worth its salt without good levels of OPCs.

Antioxidants are now used extensively in the US and France, and I have used them to help patients with cancer, allergies, diabetes, arthritis and many more diseases, especially finding them useful for assisting recovery after serious illness.

What conditions can Antioxidants help?

- Allergies
- Arthritis
- Asthma
- Blood vessel problems
- Cancer
- Cardiovascular problems
- Cataracts
- Diabetes
- Eczema
- Fatigue
- Fluid imbalance
- Gum disease
- Immune status
- Injuries
- Liver degeneration
- Mental ageing
- Muscular function
- Prostate problems
- Radiation sickness
- Strokes
- Toxic states
- Viral infections
- Wound healing

Chondroitin, Glucosamine and Type 2 Collagen

Of particular interest to working dog owners, these three products are now being used widely for the management of degenerative joint disease and tissue injuries, particularly now it has been recognised that anti-inflammatory drugs can suppress symptoms of arthritis but accelerate the progression of the disease. It is worth mentioning here that there is also the possibility of using shark cartilage supplements, but generally these have not been so popular due to environmental and ethical considerations. The development of poultry-sourced type 2 collagen supplements is arguably better therapeutically. It is probably best to consider these supplements individually.

GLUCOSAMINE

This naturally occurring substance, found in high concentrations in joint structures, is a rate-limiting step in glycosaminoglycan (GAG) synthesis and joint cartilage repair. Thus, when given as a supplement it is said to stimulate the manufacture of cartilage components and the incorporation of sulphur into cartilage, thereby producing the substances necessary for proper joint function and for stimulating joint repair (as far as this is possible). This addresses the cause rather than suppressing symptoms. Numerous studies have shown that glucosamine sulphate produces much better long-term results compared with a placebo in relieving the symptoms of osteoarthritis.

CHONDROITIN SULPHATE

This consists of long chain polymers that are the major GAGs found in cartilage. Oral administration of chondroitin as a supplement was found to have similar results to glucosamine. It is an effective and direct inhibitor of degradative enzyme activity, and long-term trials have shown supplementation to slow the progression of osteoarthritis, to improve joint mobility, and to reduce pain. Radiographic evidence of disease reversal has been seen. Chondroitin sulphate is often given in combination with glucosamine.

TYPE 2 COLLAGEN

This is a more recent player in this field, superseding shark cartilage on environmental grounds (it is derived from chicken carcases) and bio-availability (it is claimed to be significantly better absorbed). In people with rheumatoid arthritis there is selective destruction of type 2 collagen via an immunological response. Supplementation with type 2 collagen has been shown to affect the immune response, stopping the body attacking its own collagen type 2, thus causing a proliferation of T-suppressor cells (white blood cells that damp down the immune resonse) and ultimately decreasing the number of inflammatory cytokines that are partly responsible for the inflammatory reaction in arthritis. Whether this works in exactly the same way in animals, which rarely get rheumatoid arthritis, is not adequately established, but type 2 collagen seems to be beneficial in many cases. It is often given with glucosamine and chondroitin.

A note or two of caution. There is a thought that dogs can develop diabetes if given excessive amounts of glucosamine and chondroitin, and I have found that much more than 500 mg per 30 kg bodyweight doesn't really effect a better result so don't waste money giving your pet ever-increasing doses.

In Summary

The whole field of nutraceutical therapy is a rapidly evolving yet complex one, with a plethora of products coming onto the market, only a few of which I have been able to touch upon here. The best way forward for anyone wishing to utilise this type of therapy is to seek information from manufacturers of these products, to explore the vast array of information available on the Internet, and obviously to try them out.

ALTERNATIVE AND COMPLEMENTARY THERAPIES

Like the medical profession, the veterinary one has an exclusive monopoly on the prescribing and use of many drugs. This is quite correct as the side-effects and dangers of many of these if used incorrectly are numerous and serious. For the owner wishing to create a first aid kit for their dog there are still a number of useful options amongst complementary and alternative medicines (CAM for short), and the aim of this section is to give a few pointers to remedies that have been found useful in the field.

Remember it is illegal for anyone who is not a qualified veterinary surgeon to treat anyone else's animal without first obtaining veterinary referral, no matter how highly qualified they are in their particular discipline, with the exception of 'the rendering in an emergency of first aid for the purpose of saving life or relieving pain or suffering' (Veterinary Surgeons Act, 1966). You can, however, legally treat your own animal for minor ailments, provided you do not cause 'unnecessary suffering'. If you choose to use holistic therapies on your own animals, be aware that some of these therapies are strong medicines in their own right, and can cause harm if misapplied. It is always preferable to take the advice of a practitioner who is suitably qualified in the particular discipline that you are using if you are unsure. Equally, be aware that, as in every other area, some professionals are very much better than others. Word of mouth is a strong recommendation. Holistic practitioners are especially well placed to recommend others in related professions whose skills might be of use in a particular situation.

Treatments

Many treatments are non-invasive, and in the main they are safe to use in that if you do use the wrong treatment, or too much of it, you will do no harm. Most harm comes when someone does not seek professional help quickly enough when things are not going well. Some treatments work well with orthodox medicine (hence often being known as 'complementary') and some work so closely with the existing immune system that immune-suppressant medication, e.g. steroids, makes their use difficult or inappropriate. Some treatments are so straightforward that studying a few textbooks will be enough to give the pet owner adequate knowledge to use them, and some types require years of dedicated study. We have restricted the advice here to that relating to first aid, but don't let that put you off looking at these therapies in more depth as even the simpler disciplines are very rewarding for further learning. A particular therapy may draw your interest at once, or instead might repel you. This does not mean that this therapy is better or worse, but that you empathise more with one sort or another. If that is the case, then go with your feelings: we don't all like or work well within exactly the same framework.

Homeopathy

Homeopathy was the first holistic system of Western medicine to be developed, some 200 years ago. It is growing rapidly in popularity today as the failures of the drug culture in medicine are exposed, and homeopathy is often the system that offers the most realistic chance of cure when drugs fail. Homeopathy acknowledges that the body has a natural healing force: minor cuts and grazes heal on their own, and we quickly recover from mild coughs and colds. Science calls this healing force 'homeostasis' and homeopathy stimulates this.

Samuel Hahnemann, an eighteenth century German doctor and the inventor of homeopathy, called the body's self-healing principle the 'Vital

Force'. He saw it as an energetically active, living force, which is essential to life. His observations led him to discover that a non-lethal quantity of a toxic substance, or in fact anything that can affect the body, can stimulate healing where the symptoms of disease are similar to the effects of that poison. He created the saying 'Similia similibus curentur' – let likes be treated by likes. The idea that like cures like dates back to the fifth century, but had never before been used as the foundation of an entire medical therapy.

Hahnemann, throughout his lifetime, tested many substances on himself and his friends, and recorded the results in a volume he called the *Materia Medica*. This effectively is a book of symptoms, evolved from the original testing of a remedy, and amended by the detailed recording of cured symptoms and cases. This work has continued over some 200 years of patient and detailed observations by clinicians, and is expanding more rapidly now with the advent of computers and the collaboration of homeopaths worldwide, such that there are now literally many thousands of remedies available.

Part of the history of homeopathy led to the discovery of the concept of 'potentisation', and the fact that increasing dilutions of the original medicine that have been through this process have greater effect. This use of highly diluted medicines has led to misconceptions which are exploited by orthodox practitioners and the global drug industry. First, they state that the essence of homeopathy is the use of a tiny dose rather than the use of a 'similar'. Second, because science, as currently understood, says that there are no molecules left in the highly-diluted dose, they assume that the medicine could not possibly work. Third, because the treatment is specific to the individual, therapies cannot be tested like drugs, and the regulatory powers will only look at the drug system, homeopathy is denied research funds and opportunity as is it not 'accepted' by the corporate-controlled world. This suppression has been going on throughout the history of homeopathy. However, the results over 200 years speak for themselves, the public is not fooled, and to spend time working with a homeopathic practitioner is a huge voyage of discovery and wonder that no-one, in my experience, has ever been able to question.

The aim of a homeopath in selecting a treatment is to find the most similar remedy, or ideally the 'similimum'. A similar is the medical agent which produces symptoms closely resembling those of the sick animal when given to a healthy volunteer; if the symptoms match completely, it is the similimum. When a dog is treated, its physical, mental and emotional reactions to the world are analysed to identify the disease and its treatment. The totality of the animal and its condition is treated, and the more you know about your dog when it is healthy, the more you can help when it is ill. The smallest dose of the similimum that will stimulate the healing process is given. In acute cases, doses are repeated until benefits are seen. In chronic cases, each dose is left to have its full effect before it is repeated.

The second law of homeopathy is the removal of obstructions to a cure. This relates to the holistic idea that unless there are suitable nutrition and lifestyle changes, a permanent cure cannot result. This may seem so obvious, but is often ignored in our 'quick-fix' society.

Homeopathy and first aid
Whilst homoeopathic remedies are usually thought of as a means of treating chronic disease they can be invaluable in treating minor ailments, in assisting recovery after major illness or surgery, and in calming a dog whilst getting it to, or waiting for, the vet.

I have listed a few remedies here which can be readily obtained and kept in a first aid kit at home. Suggested potencies are also mentioned; however, if you cannot obtain the strength mentioned, the remedies sold in health shops and pharmacies will often achieve similar results with more frequent dosing. As a general guide, in acute conditions give a dose every quarter of an hour for four doses, then three times daily; in less urgent conditions give a dose three or four times daily. If there is no response in a few doses you probably have the wrong remedy, so think again. In all cases, where you are in doubt, or the injury does not respond to a few doses, consult your usual vet.

ACONITE 200C: Useful in all cases of **shock** or **fright**. The dog will be 'beside itself', desperate with fear. Aconite is also useful in all feverish states (day one only) and can often abort an infection. Dose quarter hourly until symptoms subside.

APIS MEL 6C: For swellings from **stings** and **allergic** reactions. The affected area is red, hot and sensitive to touch.

ARGENTUM NIT 30C: For **anxiety** from **worry/anticipation** of events. This type of fear builds up to the point where diarrhoea and even vomiting can occur.

ARNICA 6C AND LOTION/CREAM: The remedy for any **bruising**, and **stiffness after work**. In cases where **bleeding** occurs it aids clotting and recovery time. Hence it is also useful given pre- and post-operatively for a few days.

ARSENICUM ALBUM 30C: The commonest remedy for **diarrhoea** in the dog. Its indication is for diarrhoea after eating rotten food. However, it can also help in long-term colitis cases where dietary allergy is involved. Restlessness is a strong feature.

BELLADONNA 30C: Another **fearful** remedy, here dogs appear to have staring eyes, a burning skin and often a raging delirium with snapping and biting. Basically a more chronic version of Aconite for use in more chronic conditions than you would Aconite. Given early it may abort **inflammatory states** e.g. in eyes, ears or some other organ. Burning, redness, and raging anxiety are keynote symptoms.

BELLIS PERENNIS 30C: Useful for more chronic **deep bruising** and more appropriate in such cases. It markedly helps **deep muscle strains with stiffness**, and is useful for bitches badly bruised after whelping.

BRYONIA 30C: For all conditions made **worse for movement**: arthritis, rheumatism, mastitis, pneumonia, etc. In arthritis it is particularly useful if the wrist and hock joints are swollen and painful.

CALCAREA FLUOR 30C: A very useful remedy for **bony swellings, bone bruising and pain** (e.g. hips). It is thought that giving this weekly from six weeks of age helps the hip joints to form properly, and it certainly helps in young dogs with hip pain.

CALENDULA 200C (also available as a lotion and a cream): As a potency it is regarded as a cleanser of internal **infections**; as a tincture, or lotion, or as a cream (often combined with Hypericum) applied externally to clean wounds it rapidly promotes healing and hair growth.

CANTHARIS 6C: This remedy relieves the pain and discomfort of **insect bites** and **burns**. However, its main known use is in the treatment of **cystitis** where it can resolve the condition rapidly, often faster than an antibiotic.

CARBO VEG 30C: Known for its ability to restore extreme cases of **collapse**. Use for any condition with sluggishness, including poor circulation and poor digestion, difficulty in breathing, in fact any condition where the animal is cold and appears almost lifeless. It also has use alongside Nux vom for **indigestion**.

CHINA 30C: For complaints arising from **dehydration**. Loss of any body fluids from work without enough to drink, or vomiting, diarrhoea, etc. that lead to weakness and apathy call for this remedy as a first aid measure to pick up the patient whilst the cause is being tackled.

COLOCYNTHIS 30C: A remedy for pains in the abdomen, often described as a flatulent **colic**. Hence it is useful for puppy colic and for older dogs in severe pain with a gut infection or colitis.

ECHINACEA 30x: Known as the 'homoeopathic antibiotic' it is useful alongside antibiotics for all septicaemias and especially skin **infections**.

FERRUM PHOS 30C: Useful on the first day of **viral infections** especially of the chest. It can often stop them developing further.

GELSEMIUM 30C: Useful in **chest infections** where the dog becomes weak, trembly and may even have collapsed. Also another **shock** remedy, but here the patient lies quietly and is unable to move. Surprisingly, considering this, it can help dogs who have diarrhoea from excitement.

HEPAR SULPH 6C AND 30C: The remedy for **pus**. Give in 6c potency to encourage the ripening and bursting of abscesses, then 30c to heal discharging wounds, and to prevent re-infection.

HYPERICUM 200C AND LOTION/CREAM: This relieves the **pain** of open wounds, bites and penetrating injuries when applied to the affected area as a lotion four times daily, often combined with Calendula. As the 200c potency it relieves the nerve pain of crushing injuries.

LEDUM PAL 6C: Given to relieve the pain of **puncture wounds**, especially when the surrounding parts are bluish and cold. Useful also alongside conventional treatments to aid the healing of **corneal ulcers** and **conjunctivitis**.

NUX VOM 1M: The remedy for **vomiting**: affected dogs often can be irritable, snappish and hypersensitive to pain, noise, music and all stimuli. They are always chilly and seek the fire.

RHUS TOX 6C: Useful for all **joint and tendon** complaints where lameness improves after a few paces, but worsens after a long walk.

RUTA GRAV 1M: Useful in all cases of **ligament damage**, especially back injuries. Similar to Rhus tox, may be given when this fails.

STAPHYSAGRIA 200C: This remedy is used to help alleviate the **pain of cuts and lacerated wounds**. It is also useful for pain after surgery where the dog attacks the wound. This latter portrays one of its key indications, which is resentment towards the injury and help offered for it.

SULPHUR 6C: First aid for the **skin** condition, this helps almost all acute skin irritations where the coat takes on a coarse, shaggy unkempt look. Often the irritation is worse after a bath and all symptoms are worse from any heat and at night.

URTICA URENS 6C (also available as a lotion and a cream): Use the 6c tablets for **hives** and **itching** unresponsive to Sulphur, for bitches losing their milk and for urinary calculi. The lotion applied externally helps burns, insect bites and itching sores.

Lotions and creams, often called homeopathic, are nearly always made from the first extract of the herb, and so really fall under the category of herbal treatments. Common mixtures that are useful include: Hypericum and Calendula (often called Hypercal) for treatment of most wounds; Arnica, Calendula and Urtica (ACU) is commonly used for burns and grazes where the skin is not broken; Arnica, Calendula and Hypericum (ACH) can be used for eczemas and rashes. If purchasing lotions these usually need dilution as they are made in an alcohol base. Individual manufacturers will advise regarding dilutions.

Acupuncture and Acupressure

Acupuncture forms part of Traditional Chinese Medicine (TCM), which was first developed by the Chinese over 3000 years ago and is still practised today. This alone gives it the credibility it deserves, but additionally modern research is now beginning to create an understanding of how it works.

Acupuncture is based on a principle of the flow of energy, or Qi (pronounced chee), around the body through non-anatomical channels known as meridians. If the flow of Qi passing through any of the channels is disturbed, the health of the body will be impaired, which leads to disease.

Treatment is by the stimulation of precise anatomical points on the meridians to restore the healthy flow of Qi and thus facilitate the healing or pain-relieving abilities of the body. The knowledge of these points is based on results recorded over thousands of years.

The body's energy flow increases and decreases in each meridian in a fixed cycle each day, and as each meridian is linked to the organs of the body, distortions in those meridians can affect, or reflect, that organ's function. Correction of this is the basis for acupuncture being able to assist with many functional health problems.

However, acupuncture is probably best known for its ability to alleviate the pain of diseases such as hip dysplasia, spinal arthritis (spondylitis) and many other locomotor problems. Although not a cure, it is a very useful way to avoid the use of painkillers with their associated side effects, and should be considered for all early cases of arthritis.

An acupuncture treatment involves the insertion of fine surgical steel needles into a selection of acupuncture points appropriate to the problem to be treated. Not all dogs allow this, and so the use of high quality laser therapy is becoming more common, often with as good, if not better, effect. By law, only qualified vets are allowed to use acupuncture needles on animals. However, if you wish to provide back-up care for your dog, simple training from a qualified practitioner will allow you to perform finger pressure, or acupressure, at home in support of any conventional treatments your dog may be having.

Acupressure in first aid

There are a number of useful points to be aware of for emergency use, and these are detailed below. You need to know how to administer the pressure so here are some simple instructions first.

DIRECTIONS FOR USING ACUPRESSURE

To stimulate an acupoint properly, you must apply deep probing pressure. Therefore, only apply pressure as shown in the photos overleaf.

Practise on yourself first by exploring an area with a suitable pressure until an exact point announces itself to you with a sharp twinge. It starts as a jolt,

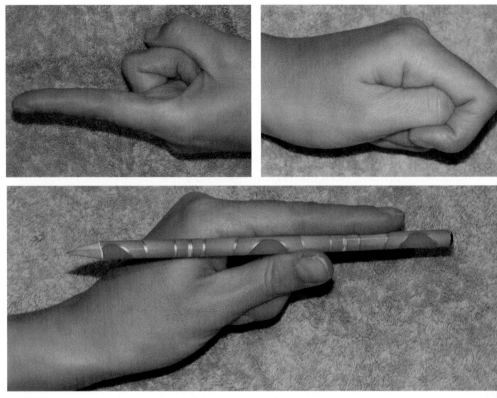

Different ways to apply acupressure

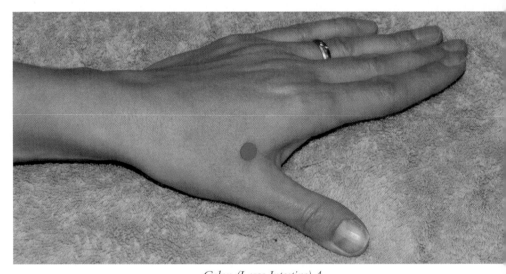

Colon (Large Intestine) 4

and after a moment becomes a numbing sensation, or a tingling radiating from the point. It can be quite a shock the first time. This will give you some idea of the effectiveness of the treatment, and how hard to press when needed. A good point to try on yourself is one known as Colon (Large Intestine) 4 which is in the web between your thumb and forefinger. It is a useful point for pain relief generally, and also for headaches. Note the difference in the way it feels and responds when you are well, and when you have a headache. When you decided to treat a point, apply pressure for fifteen to thirty seconds. Repeat using the same point on the other side of your body if not in the midline. Relief or effect should be fairly immediate. When you find a point that helps, use that point; if the relief is temporary, re-stimulate the point.

GOVERNOR VESSEL 26 : This point is very useful to know when a bitch is having a litter of puppies, and it has saved many a weak pup that is struggling to breathe. There is a wealth of research data on the use of this for resuscitation, respiratory arrest/failure, collapse from loss of body fluids (including blood), shock and strokes.

Governor Vessel 26

STOMACH 36: Use of this point is very useful to alleviate the pain and discomfort of bloat and intestinal problems generally whilst going to the vet for treatment. It is said to help the gastrointestinal tract to move and thus help expel some of the gas build up before a condition known as gastric torsion occurs. Once a torsion has occurred it will not be of use. The point is found by feeling the tibial crest, just below the knee. At the lower end of this crest move a centimetre or so to the outside of the leg, and in the belly of the muscle the point will be felt. It can be uncomfortable for the dog to have this massaged, but only for the first few seconds until relief starts to occur.

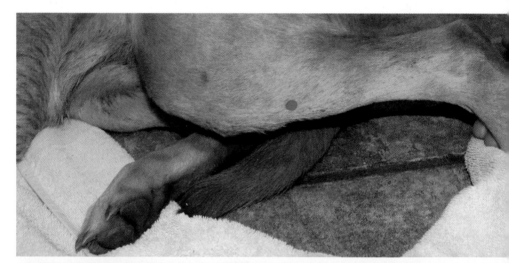

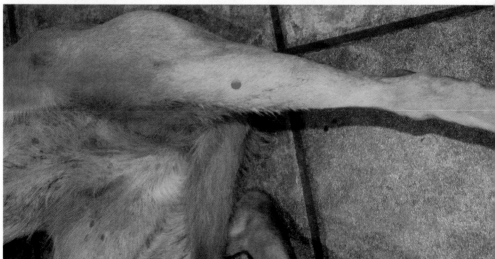

Stomach 36

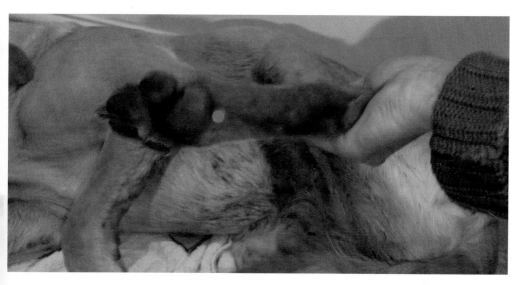

Kidney 1

KIDNEY 1: This point is used in combination with Governor Vessel 26 in desperate situations where the patient is in shock.

PERICARDIUM 6: This is the point for relief of nausea and vomiting, and also if gently massaged will help calm a bitch stressed by the birth process. It is useful for animals who are struggling to get over anaesthetics.

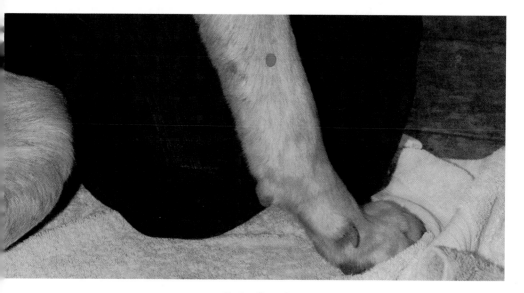

Pericardium 6

Further information on acupressure can be found in reference books and on the Internet, but a favourite book of mine is *Natural Healers: Acupressure Handbook* by Michael Blate (copies are obtainable from resellers such as Amazon.co.uk; it was published by Holt (Henry) & Co US (Dec 1977), ISBN: 0805001468). It is not difficult to transpose the points mentioned in this book to your dog by simply comparing anatomy.

Aromatherapy

Aromatherapy is the use of volatile aromatic plant oils to cause physiological and psychological changes in the patient. The molecules of these essential oils enter the body and the bloodstream by absorption either through the lining of the nose and lungs, or through the skin, thus imparting an effect on the body and mind. Due to their concentration, essential oils used for aromatherapy should always be handled with care and given the same respect as any other medicinal substance. Fragrant essential oils have been used medicinally in Egypt and the Middle East for thousands of years, although their use is not taught in medical or veterinary schools at the present time. Several parts of a plant may be used as a source of essential oil. Flowers, leaves, twigs, roots, seeds, bark and heartwood may all be used, depending on the plant. There are several methods of extracting the oils, the commonest being steam distillation and solvent extraction. However, the finest quality and therefore most expensive oils are obtained by carbon dioxide distillation. Cheaper synthetic oils are also produced for the mass market. Whichever type of essential oil you choose, always buy from a reputable supplier; regard cheap oils with suspicion, and seek organic oils for preference.

Dogs have a very highly developed sense of smell and use the secretions of their glands, and saliva, urine and faeces as a means of communication and to mark their territories. Because their sense of smell is so refined, most dogs will respond almost too well to aromatherapy, and oils should be used in much more dilute form than for humans. A one per cent dilution is often quite sufficient, though you may go up to two and a half per cent safely unless the patient is very young, very old or very ill. The rule of thumb is to note the volume of your carrier oil in millilitres, halve the figure, and add a corresponding amount of drops, e.g. 30 ml of carrier oil allows up to fifteen drops of aromatherapy oil to make a two and a half per cent dilution, which can then be scaled down for the one per cent. 'Less is more' is the rule for aromatherapy, so start with a few drops and never be tempted to exceed the recommended concentration. There are exceptions, such as lavender oil which may be used neat over small areas. Aromatherapy oils are usually diluted in massage oil for application, or alternatively in vegetable gel (obtainable from the better companies that sell aromatherapy products), which latter is often better for applying to furry areas. Remember, too, that a dog will always try to clean the oil off by licking and may ingest toxic amounts by doing so, so be careful to prevent this. If in doubt, rather than applying oils directly to the dog, use a diffuser, or add a few drops to a glass of hot water to allow the aroma to colour the environment of the patient, rather than applying the oil directly. The oils often work just as well this way.

Aromatherapy oils can be used to support any other therapy, although some feel that they can affect homeopathic remedies adversely as these can be destroyed by strong smells. Aromatherapy oils and homeopathic remedies should not be stored together.

Aromatherapy in first aid

The main use of aromatherapy in first aid is in harnessing its powerful but safe antibacterial and anti-inflammatory properties when dealing with wounds or abscesses. Bites, cuts, pulled nails and gashes can be rinsed out with a syringe full of water to which a few drops of either lavender or tea tree oil have been added. Tea tree is the more powerful of the two oils, although they are equally effective – you just use less tea tree than lavender. Both of these oils taste bad to dogs and will stop most of them from licking or picking at a bandage. Lavender is also useful when a dog has had contact with mange, such as from retrieving a mangy fox. Applied neat to the contact area, it is usually effective in preventing mange from developing. Lavender or tea tree dabbed directly onto a tick will kill it, and a few drops in water will make a good footbath for dogs that have picked up harvest mites. When using aromatherapy oils, we must understand that the smell of most of them is unpleasant to the dog. Although it is possible to buy parasite repellent which relies on aromatherapy oils, this is not, to my mind, justified for regular use on an animal with such a sensitive nose. In severe flea infestations, a one-off treatment combing gel with lavender or rosemary oil added through the coat will cause fleas to bale out in all directions, but it is not kind to the dog to do this often, and so it should be combined with a different and longer-term system of parasite control.

Flower remedies

The Bach flower remedies, prepared from the stalks, petals and leaves of plants, can be used to treat mental and emotional states in both humans and other animals, and are a wonderful facilitator to aid in correcting what we today describe as behavioural disorders. However, as with homeopathy, environmental obstacles to cure must be considered and resolved. Bach flower remedies were the brainchild of Dr Edward Bach. His experience as a homeopathic doctor had convinced him that physical disease was the body's reaction to a non-material cause. Changes in the body's fundamental vibrational energy resulted in a disturbance of mental state that could eventually lead to physical disease.

Dr Bach set out to seek a means of healing that used non-toxic materials rather than potentised poisons. He noted that his own moods could be strongly influenced by the plants he came into contact with, and so he theorised that these natural vibrations of certain plants could match the vibrations associated with certain mental states.

Bach discovered a range of thirty seven-plants, and rock water, which assisted his patients with mental and emotional problems. He also discovered that a combination of five remedies, in a preparation he called Rescue Remedy, could be used in emergency situations as a calming treatment for all types of panic, shock and hysteria. With its successes, Rescue Remedy probably converts more people to alternative medicine annually than anything else.

Stock solutions of single Bach flower remedies are now sold ready-prepared in health food shops and chemists. These remedies may be given alone or combined with up to five other essences at a time to make a medicine. To prepare a medicine, add two drops of each essence to 30 ml (two tablespoons) of spring water.

There are various written guides to the Bach flower remedies, but I prefer the original works of Dr Bach. Select the remedies according to the dog's mental state, using human emotions as a guide. The better you know your dog, the more you will deduce which remedies are needed. The simplest way to dose your dog is to add three to four drops of essence to its drinking water, or you can give them directly into the mouth.

Since the work of Dr Bach, other series of flower essences have been developed, such as Californian, Alaskan and Australian Bush Flower Remedies. These have been developed with modern life in mind, and offer treatments for such factors as the ill effects of pollution and stress. These remedies are prepared and used in the same way as the Bach Flowers, and can also be used successfully on dogs.

First aid and the Bach flower remedies

In first aid treatment, helping the patient cope with stress factors is known to improve not only recovery times, but in some cases the actual chance of recovery. The most widely known of all the Bach remedies is Rescue Remedy, a combination of five of the Bach flowers. Rescue Remedy is known as the emergency first aid remedy, but it is also useful for chronic stress and anxiety, often working so quickly that you can see the patient become calmer.

Like all complementary therapies used in first aid, Rescue Remedy is not a panacea or a replacement for orthodox medical care. However, many doctors, vets, homoeopaths, other physicians and health care professionals throughout the world carry Rescue Remedy with them.

Bach classified the following seven major emotional and psychological states:

- Fear
- Uncertainty
- Insufficient interest in present circumstances
- Loneliness
- Oversensitivity to influences and ideas
- Despondency or despair
- Overcare for the welfare of others

Not all of these relate to an emergency, but for completeness we have included them all with their connected remedies. Shock can result in a variety of responses, not always immediately recognised. Loss of interest is as likely in some patients as blind panic is in others. Inability to make decisions (uncertainty) can also be a symptom. So look at your dog objectively, compare how it is behaving with its normal behaviour. How is it different? Is the change real or imagined? Treat on the basis of how you feel the animal has changed, and remember your first hunch is usually the right one as only you can know your dog that well.

You can do no harm with Bach flower remedies: they work when given correctly, but if not then they have no effect. Kits are available with the full range of remedies, and they are well worth having to hand.

The following is a brief summary of all the thirty-eight Bach flower remedies and their uses. These are listed within their appropriate categories.

This list is not intended as a definitive explanation of all the Bach remedies; for more information we would recommend reading one of the many books available that have been written about these for use on animals.

FEAR

Rock Rose *(Helianthemum nummularium)* for extreme terror, panic, hysteria, fright, and nightmares.

Mimulus *(Mimulus guttatus)* for known fears and oversensitivity; for example, fear of vets, thunder and lightning, darkness, being alone, of other people and dogs, etc. Also for timidity and shyness. A less well-known use is to take the edge off dogs obsessed with bitches.

Cherry Plum *(Prunus cerasifera)* for fear of losing mental and physical control; uncontrollable rages and impulses, causing harm to itself or others. Useful for puppies who lose their tempers!

Aspen *(Populus tremula)* for vague fears and anxieties of unknown origin, a sense of foreboding, apprehension, or impending disaster. Useful therefore for dogs who get anxious when separated from their owner.

Red Chestnut *(Aesculus carnea)* for anticipatory anxiety that something unfortunate may happen. Useful for the dog that gets diarrhoea from going to a shoot, or that has problems with training and wants to run off, and for dogs that don't go well in the show ring or trial yet are fine at home unless told off.

UNCERTAINTY

Cerato *(Ceratostigma willmottianum)* for those dogs who cannot make decisions. They are constantly looking to other dogs to take the lead and are often misguided.

Scleranthus *(Scleranthus annuus)* for those who are indecisive, being unable to decide between two choices, first one seeming right then the other. They may also be subject to energy or mood swings.

Gentian *(Gentianella amarella)* for those easily discouraged, in whom even small delays may cause hesitation, despondency and self-doubt.

Gorse *(Ulex europaeus)* for feelings of despair, hopelessness, and futility (hard to ascertain in dogs).

Hornbeam *(Carpinus betulus)* for tiredness and a tendency towards procrastination.

Wild Oat *(Bromus ramosus)* for those unhappy in their work, or with kennel mates, or who don't seem happy wherever they are.

Clematis *(Clematis vitalba)* for those who tend toward escapism, living more in the future than in the present (the dog that knows it all!); for lack of concentration, daydreaming, lack of interest in present circumstances, and spaciness.

Honeysuckle *(Lonicera caprifolium)* for those dwelling too much in the past, reminiscing about the 'good old days'; nostalgia, and homesickness (hard to see a use for this remedy in dogs).

Wild Rose *(Rosa canina)* for those who are apathetic and have resigned themselves to their circumstances, making little effort to do anything.

Olive *(Olea europaea)* for total mental and physical exhaustion and weariness; for sapped vitality from a long illness or overtraining.

White Chestnut *(Aesculus hippocastanum)* for persistent, unwanted thoughts, mental arguments, or preoccupation with some worry or episode. Basically the scatty spaniel with its mind not on the job.

Mustard *(Sinapis arvensis)* for deep gloom that comes on for no apparent reason, bringing sudden melancholy and heavy sadness. This can be useful during and around the season in some bitches.

Chestnut Bud *(Aesculus hippocastanum)* for those who fail to learn from experience, continually repeating the same patterns and mistakes.

LONELINESS

Water Violet *(Hottonia palustris)* for those whose preference is to be alone; seemingly aloof, proud, reserved, self-reliant, sometimes 'superior' in attitude. Capable and reliable they will not get 'personally' involved with other dogs. Ideal for saluki types.

Impatiens *(Impatiens glandulifera)* for those quick in thought and action but often impatient, especially with those who are slower than they; for those who show irritability through lack of patience. A good terrier remedy.

Heather *(Calluna vulgaris)* for those talkative persons who constantly seek the companionship of anyone who will listen to their troubles (kennel barkers).

OVERSENSITIVITY TO INFLUENCES AND IDEAS

Agrimony *(Agrimonia eupatoria)* for those not wishing to burden others with their troubles, covering up their suffering with a cheerful facade; they often seek escape from pain and worry through the use of medications or alcohol (another one hard to see in dogs).

Centaury *(Centaurium umbellatum)* for those who have difficulty in saying no, often becoming subservient in their desire to serve others; anxious to please. This can be the pup getting too forward in training and then collapsing in on herself.

Walnut *(Juglans regia)* for stabilising emotions during periods of transition, for breaking past links and adjusting to new beginnings, such as new homes, trainers, owners, companions etc. It is also good for bitches pining when the pups have left. Probably the most widely used remedy for dogs after Rescue Remedy.

Holly *(Ilex aquifolium)* for negative feelings such as envy, jealousy, suspicion, revenge, and hatred.

Despondency or despair

Larch *(Larix decidua)* for those who, despite being capable, lack self-confidence. Anticipating failure, they often do not make a real effort to succeed.

Pine *(Pinus sylvestris)* for those not satisfied with their own efforts, who are self-reproachful and suffer much from guilt and the faults they attach to themselves, feeling they should or could have done better. Typical situations include the dog who is never sure it was right to retrieve that bird, and so will hang onto it despite getting into trouble for doing so.

Elm *(Ulmus procera)* for those who over extend themselves and become overwhelmed and burdened by their responsibilities. Again a good remedy for forward pups who get too far ahead of themselves then lose it.

Sweet Chestnut *(Castanea sativa)* for those who feel they have reached the limits of their endurance.

Star of Bethlehem *(Ornithogalum umbellatum)* for mental and emotional stress during and following such traumatic experiences as grief, loss and accidents.

Willow *(Salix vitellina)* for those who have suffered from some misfortune or circumstance they feel was unjust or unfair. As a result, they become resentful and bitter toward others. One example of use would be for the dog attacked by another that now holds a grudge against the rest of 'Dogdom'.

Oak *(Quercus robur)* for those who despite illness and adversity never give up. They are brave and determined to overcome all obstacles in order to reach their intended goal.

Crab Apple *(Malus pumila)* for feelings of shame, uncleanliness, or fear of contamination; for poor self-image, particularly as it relates to parts of or growths on the body (hard to see in dogs). Will assist in detoxification and the cleansing of wounds, both internal and external.

Overcare for the welfare of others

Chicory *(Cichorium intybus)* for those who are overfull of care and possessive of those close to them; they can be demanding and self-pitying, with a need for others to conform to their ideals.

Vervain *(Verbena officinalis)* for those who have strong opinions, always teaching and philosophising. They are easily incensed and can be overenthusiastic, argumentative, and overbearing towards their kennelmates.

Vine *(Vitis vinifera)* for those who are strong-willed leaders in their own right. However, when carried to extremes, they can become autocratic, dictatorial, ruthless, and dominating. For the 'alpha' dog that takes things a step too far in asserting his position.

Beech *(Fagus sylvatica)* for those who, while desiring perfection, easily find fault with people and things. Critical and intolerant at times, they may fail to see the good within others, overreacting to small annoyances or other people's idiosyncrasies.

Rock Water *(Aqua petra)* for those who are strict and rigid with themselves in their daily living. They are hard masters to themselves, struggling towards some ideal or to set an example for others. This would include strict adherence to a lifestyle or to religious, personal, or social disciplines (hard to see in dogs but obvious in some trainers, and dare we say it, judges!).

The more you look for it, the more you see the subtleties of canine behaviour. Understanding gives both the human and canine partners in a team a more meaningful and successful relationship and so even if you never need to use them, reading about these remedies can be really useful.

Herbs

The use of plants to heal - Herbalism - is probably the oldest form of healing still in use today. Herbal medicines play an essential part in both Traditional Chinese Medicine (TCM) and in the Indian Ayurvedic system. Today some eighty per cent or the world's population still rely on herbal medicine for the treatment of disease, and even in 'developed' nations, many drugs derive originally from herbs. Interestingly, few active agents have only one effect: they also tend to have other unwanted actions or side effects. Herbalists believe that the balance of active ingredients in herbal medicines works together to counteract harmful side-effects, and it is the purification into ever-stronger drugs which makes those side-effects become more of a problem. As we understand more of this medicinal system, this idea reveals itself to be more and more accurate, and hence there is a modern resurgence of interest in this field. With this interest has come problems, as we have been indoctrinated in the idea that bigger is better, and high doses of some herbs can be toxic. Just enough to heal is needed, and so consulting a qualified practitioner is always a good idea for anything other than first aid.

Finding healing herbs

The fact that dogs and other animals actively seek out and eat plants that are known to have medicinal properties as and when they need them also supports the view that herbalism should have an established and widespread place in orthodox veterinary medicine today.

Herbal medicines can be administered in many ways. The traditional method is in the form of herbal infusions or teas, which are made from fresh or dried herbs. Good-tasting herbs can be fed directly to the dog if mixed with its food (you and your dog may disagree over which herbs taste good). Commercial herbal extracts in the form of tinctures are also available, and these can be given directly into the mouth, if your dog will tolerate it. Herbal capsules and tablets are available from some suppliers and herbs can also be used to make poultices and compresses. Details of some of these are listed in the A–Z section (see Chapter 5). You will not generally have herbs to hand, and they take time to make into remedies, so we have not taken ideas beyond first aid here.

Herbalism is best used to support conventional care. If ever the dog's condition appears to deteriorate at all, stop the treatment and consult your vet.

Physiotherapy

In a similar way to massage, physiotherapy aims to restore the strength and full range of movement of an injured area by manipulation or by a series of controlled exercises. It can help to control pain, speed up healing, and preserve the function of injured tissue. It is of especial use after surgery, but can be used alongside all other therapies as well. Veterinary physiotherapy is slowly becoming more widely used in general veterinary practise, although its benefits have been recognised for years in the horse and greyhound racing industries.

Owners can use simple massage, ice packs with care, and gentle warmth as first aid at home. Local dog swimming pools are also of great help in arthritic and post-surgical cases and your vet will have a list of recommended ones. However, the more specialist physiotherapy techniques and equipment can inflict further injury if misapplied, and only a qualified physiotherapist should ever use these.

Qualified physiotherapists are registered and legally recognised and will only work following referral from your vet. Always ask your vet if there are any therapies he or she can refer you to, and about other techniques that can help your pet.

5. HEALTH AND SAFETY AT WORK
FIELD FIRST AID

Working dogs are, by the very nature of what they do and where they do it, at increased risk of accidents, as well as exposure to some illnesses. Should your dog be unlucky enough to be badly injured, become seriously unwell, or even be poisoned, then your first port of call should always be the vet. However, it is useful to have some idea of first aid measures, as well as simple home remedies, to enable you to treat minor problems either before a vet is seen, or when the problem occurs out of surgery hours and is not serious enough to necessitate a call-out. Vets never mind being contacted at any time if you are worried, but they have lives to lead too, and their support should never be abused. It is also vital to know your dog's normal parameters, for example gum colour, resting/normal heart rate, respiratory rate and so on, enabling you to assess changes, but more on this shortly.

Typical field hazard

When selecting a veterinary practice to register with, many owners will simply opt for the nearest clinic, without exploring the facilities offered or the vets' particular interests. Today's vets are not only becoming more technology orientated, but individuals are becoming specialised in different fields, so that there is now plenty of choice for the service you require. Whilst the old system of building a dog's lifetime relationship with your vet is an excellent basis for healthcare, this can be difficult in some areas as modern practise is changing and the vets themselves may not be there forever. The specialisation issue may well mean you need two or more practices to get the complete service you require, as no one person can be an expert in everything. Some vets have a particular interest in certain breeds, whether because they themselves own them, or just because they see a lot of them. For instance, some will be more

At increased risk of injury

sympathetic to breeds that are docked* than others, and this is an important consideration as it can be so difficult needing working pups docked when no vet in the area will perform this essential service. Is there open-mindedness in the practice should you wish to consult a vet practicing homeopathy and/or acupuncture, which are very important for the treatment of chronic or recurring cases? What is the arrangement the practice has with other specialists for the services they cannot provide? Good vets will never mind a client seeking a referral or second opinion as they will be confident in their own abilities, and will happily direct you to a reputable practitioner; in fact they will often suggest it. In today's ever-advancing medical world there is no place for a clinician who believes he/she can do it all when there is so much specialist help out there in times of trouble. The service you want will be down to your own preferences, but it is well worth looking into what is available.

Some general points to remember are:

1. Learn what is normal for your dog through a routine of checking it over regularly.

2. Keep your vet's telephone number easily to hand.

3. Always phone before dashing to the surgery to ensure that he or she is ready for you. The vet may also be able to give some life-saving advice before you set out.

4. Learn to restrain your dog so that it understands the concept before a problem occurs, and ensure you and any helpers do not get bitten.

5. Never offer treats to calm a dog as an anaesthetic, and therefore an empty stomach, may be needed.

6. Rescue Remedy and Arnica are worth carrying everywhere to aid treatment of shock (owner and dog!) and bruising.

7. Remember dogs are used to us communicating with them, so talking to them in a calm voice can be reassuring, even if they cannot understand the words.

8. Make and keep handy a basic first aid kit for your dog, which is much better than wishing you had done this after the event.

* Docking is illegal in some countries, and only certain breeds may now be docked in England and Wales, though some may be legally docked in England that may not be in Wales. You are probably aware that docking is totally illegal in Scotland, legal in Eire and I'm not sure what is happening in Northern Ireland!

ESSENTIAL REGULAR CHECKS

Dogs who are used to being examined are much easier to treat when something goes wrong. Owners who, similarly, are used to examining their dogs will have a good idea of what is normal for them, and be better able to assess the situation in a crisis. This not only helps first aid, but is immensely useful to the attending vet, speeding assessment and treatment planning.

What to do?

I believe it is a good idea to check your dog over from head to tail at least a couple of times a week, getting used to what is normal for it, and enabling early spotting of problems. In many cases it will need a trained vet to interpret the change, but a problem treated early is much more likely to have successful outcome, so this is very important as an exercise.

First look at gum colour and teeth simply by lifting the dog's upper lip at the side and round the front, and gently pulling down the lower lip. This will expose the teeth and gums, and there can be quite a variation in appearance between individuals and breeds. Gums that have become pale can indicate more chronic problems such as anaemia, but also occur when the dog is in pain or shock. Dark, almost red-brown gums, or a grey appearance, are both indicators of ill-health, whilst yellowing can indicate liver problems. A bluish tint to the gums indicates a lack of oxygen suggesting heart or breathing difficulties, infections can give the gums a bright brick-red colour, and small haemorrhages can indicate a clotting problem. So this one simple act can give an immense amount of information upon which prompt action can be taken.

Continuing with the head, it is useful to see inside the ear canals (as far as one can without poking anything down), looking for normal/abnormal wax and discharges. Become familiar with the normal smell of your dog's ears, as infections or mite infestations are often easier to detect by a change in smell. Run your hand over the skull and jaw to feel the normal structure and any lumps or bumps that might occur. Look at the eyes for brightness and clarity of the corneas (the glassy part of the eye). When the dog is used to being examined you can gently press down below the lower eyelid to look at the colour of the conjunctiva (the whiter parts of the eye) to check all is in order there.

Carrying on from the head, work down the spine and around the abdomen, feeling for areas of increased heat, or even cold, which can be a marker of injury and pain. Check the tail and below it, around the anus and vulva/testicles for normal appearance and presence of any swellings. Then run your hands down each leg, stopping at the joints to massage the muscles gently, and look for swellings, heat and/or cold, and any pain response. Feet should be looked at closely after a working day as cuts can quickly get infected, and seed burrs and matted hair should be removed from between the pads to stop excoriation of the skin. Always look on the top side between the toes as well as underneath. It is surprising how often this is forgotten as it is easy to turn the foot over and look underneath, but to check the tops of the feet you have to get down to the dog's own level.

It is well worth getting to know the normal pulse and heart rate for your own dog. The easiest way to feel the pulse is to feel into the dog's groin with your middle finger, and roughly in the middle of the inner thigh, just below the abdominal wall, is a groove in which lie the larger blood vessels of the leg. Gentle pressure will allow you to feel the pulse, and the rate can be recorded by comparing with a watch that has a second hand. If you find this difficult, start the same process with the dog lying on its side, lift one leg gently and feel for the groove.

The pulse rate is useful as an increased rate at rest can often be an early indicator of illness, whilst the quality (weak, thready, hard, bounding etc.) can be a pointer to what is happening. As an alternative to feeling the pulse, you can find the dog's heart rate by feeling between the ribs approximately one third of the way up the chest wall, in line with, and just behind, the left elbow. A normal resting rate for a dog is eighty to 120 beats per minute, but this will be affected by fitness, age and how calm the dog is when examined.

Another very useful indicator of health is the dog's breathing. The rate of this varies quite a lot at rest, and normals are given as eight to thirty-two breaths per minute, which tells you that you need to know what is normal for your dog in different situations. What is perhaps more easily noted is any difficulty in breathing. Normally there should be only minimal effort, with the most movement being that of the chest wall. Unless the dog is panting to lose heat, the mouth is closed, and breathing occurs through the nose. When there are problems, the rate of breathing will increase, the movement of the chest wall will become exaggerated, panting may become uncontrollable, and in severe situations the abdomen will be used as well. Dogs in this state are often restless, possibly even standing with the front legs wide apart and the head and neck stretched down and forwards. Obviously this will be a situation necessitating veterinary care.

For the really keen, you might wish to get your dog used to having its temperature taken using either a glass thermometer, or preferably a plastic digital thermometer (they are less breakable). Normal body temperature for a dog is between 38 and 39 degrees centigrade (100.4 and 102.2 degrees Fahrenheit) depending on what it has been doing just prior to taking the temperature. To take the dog's temperature first apply a little lubricant (KY gel or similar) to the tip of the thermometer, insert it about an inch into the rectum, and angle it to one side so the tip is against the wall of the rectum. This latter is important as you want to measure the temperature of the patient, not its poo! Leave the thermometer in for approximately one minute (or until the alarm sounds if digital), clean and read.

Remember, the main reason for all these checks is so you can spot a problem early, which improves the chance of a successful outcome to any treatment. It also gets the dog used to being handled, which makes applying any treatment easier, and helps the human/animal bonding that makes for an enjoyable and easy relationship.

Get into the habit of checking your dog after working and before you feed, as you do not want to discover an injury and then find treatment has to be delayed due to a full stomach preventing an anaesthetic.

RESTRAINT AND NURSING

It may seem that your dog is so loving that you cannot envisage ever having to restrain it, but a dog that has been bitten, is injured or is even just ill can change in temperament due to the pain. Some simple rules that are easy to remember and practise are worth knowing: a dog that is used to being held still by your holding a bit of the neck's scruff will not be frightened if a tighter grip is needed for restraint. With a larger dog, it is best to take hold of both sides of the neck. Always face the dog away from you so it cannot bite at your arms and face. A simple muzzle can be created from a strip of bandage, a tie, stocking, or a lead, and tied over the muzzle, crossed back underneath and passed back around the head to be tied. Legs are an issue as a scrabbling dog is hard to hold, so wrap a dog in pain in a blanket or coat.

Nursing care

When nursing a dog, the rules to remember are that a good nurse doesn't fuss: he or she does what is needed, then allows the patient to rest. Again simple rules apply:

1. Many homes are draughty at ground level so make sure the patient is not sleeping in a draught.

2. Wrapping hot water bottles well, inside a towel which in turn is inside a pillow case avoids burns from exposed bottles. If you find stone hot water bottles in junk shops, buy them, for they are just the job, giving out heat more slowly, holding warmth for longer, and being unchewable. You will probably need a new rubber seal for the stopper, but these can be cut from any piece of rubber that is the right width. I wish someone would start making these again, because they are by far the best to use.

3. Clean fresh water should be to hand, and offered to the patient at intervals.

4. Noise and bright lights upset patients.

5. Bedding should be clean and replaced immediately if soiled. Specialist fleece products are excellent for this, as they wash easily and dry quickly; a thick layer of newspaper underneath picks up surplus moisture and is easily changed. Straw and shavings are not recommended as they can stick to and contaminate wounds.

6. If not moving, patients should be encouraged to turn over every few hours to help prevent further problems.

7. Clean eyes and nose with salt water if discharges build up.

8. Keep an eye on any changes in body temperature using a thermometer.

9. Follow any veterinary instructions to the letter.

10. Lastly, if in doubt ask for professional help.

A BASIC FIRST AID KIT

It is sensible when working a dog to consider carrying a first aid kit in the car so that it is easily to hand when needed. Few shoots seem to do this and I have on occasion had to spend a lot more time than was needed dealing with the life-saving aspect of a case before attempting repair, when much of the problem could have been prevented by a little foresight on the owner's part. Many of the better first aid kits designed for human use can be a good place

First aid kit

to start when putting together a kit for your dog. Often they are combined by owners for both purposes. Portability is a key part of design, as there is little use having the best kit at home instead of in the car when it is needed.

Basic Items

At least two **strong soft rolled bandages**. Cohesive ones are more practical (see section on bandaging), and are a quick and easy final-covering bandage readily obtainable from most pet shops, chemists and saddleries.

Two crepe knit bandages for fixing dressings or to make an improvised muzzle.

Adhesive rolled plaster (you cannot fix ordinary plasters to hair so you need a type to wrap around the dressing and stick to the hair – see section on bandaging techniques).

Curved blunt-ended scissors, blunt-ended as you don't want to add to the injury in a stressed and not necessarily still animal.

Cotton wool for padding over injuries and absorbing blood and other discharges. Used under bandages it prevents too much pressure building up in one area. Cotton gamgee pads obtainable from equestrian outlets are ideal as they avoid the fibres sticking to wounds.

Lint pads for covering small wounds and preventing bandages sticking.

A large (20 ml plus) syringe can be very useful to flush water or saline into wounds when cleaning, or very carefully into the eyes if they have become contaminated. Alternatively spray cans of saline are available from chemists and are useful as a source of sterile wash solution.

Water/saline and water bowl. Saline can be purchased from pharmacies, or easily made by dissolving 1½ teaspoons of table salt in a pint of boiled water. Plastic 35 mm film cases are ideal for carrying salt.

Tweezers for ticks and thorns.

A thermometer.

Washing soda crystals. These are crystals of sodium carbonate and used to induce vomiting if a dog is poisoned – see poisoning section.

Hypercal cream, a mix of calendula and hypericum to aid healing of wounds and reduce pain.

Bach Rescue Remedy to treat shock and to calm the patient and owner (four drops each).

Arnica tablets for the pain of bruising. They are also said to help stop bleeding.

A blanket to wrap the dog in if needed, or to use as a stretcher.

Disinfectant such as Betadine solution, or diluted tea tree or lavender oil, and a **hand cleanser** for yourself. Disposable gloves can be useful to cover dirty hands, or to prevent contamination the other way as well.

A torch (accidents always seem to happen as the light is fading). Check often for battery life, and watch out for people borrowing and forgetting to return it.

Wire cutters for the dog caught on barbed wire.

A tea towel, useful as a thick absorbent pad, used to apply pressure to an area when there is a lot of bleeding. Doubles as a clean area to lay items on when in the field.

Kitchen paper. The toughest kind, excellent when you run out of pads and towels.

An appropriate **container** to keep this all in.

A list of contents so anything used can be quickly replaced.

Your vet's telephone number.

A mobile phone carried with you when working your dog is now almost an essential item, even if you only use it to make calls out, as veterinary advice is more immediately available, you can call for help, and you can put the vet on alert if you are rushing a patient in that needs immediate attention.

If your dog is on essential medication, for example because he or she suffers allergic reactions, then the appropriate medications should also be included. Painkillers, such as paracetamol, should not be given without veterinary advice as human medications can harm dogs, and vice versa. They can also interact with drugs the vet may need to give, compromising recovery.

Also of use are proprietary first aid kits of homeopathic remedies, sold now by many pharmacies. Whilst mostly packaged for humans, the indications are the same for dogs and thus these can be useful to keep to hand to help with many of the treatments outlined below. Please note that homeopathic remedies should be kept separately from strong-smelling substances such as disinfectant or aromatherapy oils.

Complementary and alternative therapies we covered in more depth in Chapter 4.

HOW TO RECOGNISE AN EMERGENCY

Owners who are used to checking over their dog will be ahead of the game here, and will spot changes in their dog earlier than otherwise might occur. Whilst trying not to point out the blindingly obvious, such as the dent in the car and the patient lying by the side of the road, this next section aims to give you some ideas of when you need to seek professional help.

Allergic Reactions

These range from itchy nettle rash to large swellings and collapse. There are various ideas for treating minor reactions later, in the A–Z section, but severe cases that cause collapse, or even vomiting and diarrhoea, will necessitate professional help. Any swelling of the head, or reaction which causes breathing difficulties, is an emergency.

Behaviour

Dogs are in some ways like young children in that they cannot talk directly to us about their problem, so you need to look at any change in behaviour and try and understand it in dog terms. Although dogs are pack animals and so by nature tend to hide their illnesses, those that have a good relationship with their owners will often try to attract our attention when they feel unwell. With strangers most animals will attempt to hide any pain or illness as a preservation strategy. So you also need to look at any behaviour from the perspective of your relationship with the dog as well.

Bleeding

Technically known as haemorrhage, any bleeding that is spurting, doesn't stop with applied pressure, or carries on despite best efforts is a medical emergency and must be seen by the vet. Often forgotten is that injuries can cause internal bleeding too, and this is not always obvious to an outside observer. When in Poland recently I encountered a terrier looking terribly sorry for herself after a tussle with a large wild sow. Closer examination revealed a hot soft swelling underneath the lower neck that was clearly filled with blood. Arnica (see section on first aid, and the A–Z) helped this case enormously and, but for her

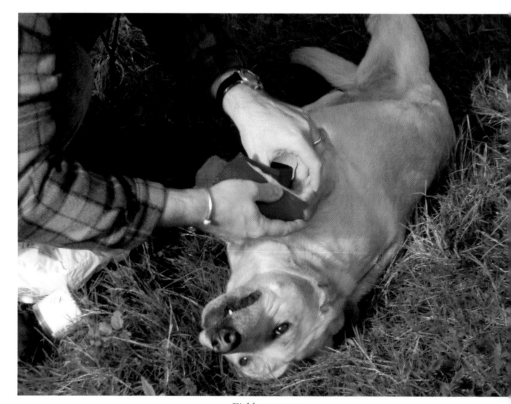

Field emergency

owner pulling her out of work, she would have preferred to have been back in the fray the next day. Bleeding can also occur into the abdomen and/or the chest, with the first sign being seen coughing blood, vomiting bloody fluid or even blood in the stool.

Bloating

Any situation where the belly of a dog becomes distended quickly is an emergency and help should be sought.

Breathing difficulties

The causes of this are many, including trauma and bleeding as mentioned already. If the reason is not obvious always seek professional help. Dogs get very distressed by these problems, and it affects their thermoregulatory ability as they use panting to control temperature. In the unfortunate event of your dog developing breathing difficulties, remember to keep it calm, and also out of direct heat, fanning if possible, whilst you seek help.

Diarrhoea and Vomiting

Dogs are pretty good at vomiting, often at the most inconsiderate times, and this is a leftover from days of scavenging, when the vomiting and re-eating of food helped deal with decaying and bacterially loaded meat. Unless there are other signs of distress, or the vomiting is severe and recurrent, then this alone is unlikely to constitute an emergency. If the dog cannot hold down water, this is a clue that matters may be more severe than first thought. If diarrhoea, a fever, bloating of the abdomen or signs of pain (especially if touched) accompany the vomiting, then this is not usual and attention will be needed. Bleeding into the stomach and upper intestine may cause vomiting, and unless fresh, the blood may come up looking like coffee grounds, calling for urgent medical attention. Similarly black or bloody stools appearing from the other end also indicate the need for veterinary help. Dogs' stools can vary quite a lot naturally, and like us they don't necessarily produce a perfect stool every time. Unless there is a lot of straining and indication of pain with behaviour changes do not panic at the first soft stool. It may be that they snaffled something tasty on a walk, or you gave them something that for some reason did not totally agree. Matters usually resolve quickly but if loose stools become persistent, mucous covered or bloody, and don't respond to simple steps you can take at home, then seek help.

Eye and Ear Injuries

Any eye problem is a potential emergency, and these can be indicated by swelling, running clear discharge, pawing at the eye, redness, cloudiness of the glassy cornea, a bluish tint or any blood.

Ear problems in the field, aside from lacerations, are commonly due to material such as grass seeds getting lodged down the ear canal. This can be acutely painful and the dog will stop whatever it is doing, paw at the ears and shake its head uncontrollably. Some dogs do not show dramatic symptoms, but instead carry the affected ear differently, or the head on one side with the painful ear lowest. Because of the damage to the eardrum that can be caused, this is always an emergency. Foreign objects can cause the inner ear to swell, making the vet's job much more difficult, so help should be sought without delay.

Fits, Faints and Collapse

The causes of any of these are multiple, and often impossible to assess in the field. Some are transient and only last a very short time, but they often indicate more serious matters developing and so even if recovery is quick, do get your dog checked out.

Hyperthermia, Fever and Hypothermia

Despite everyone's best efforts to raise awareness of the problem, dogs do still get left in hot cars, and collapse with heat stroke (also known as hyperthermia). Similar situations can occur in the field when working on a really hot day, as dogs have in the main only panting and use of the environment (lying in a nice cool puddle, for example) as their methods of cooling body temperature. Black and dark coloured dogs whose coats absorb more heat, and heavy-coated dogs, are worse affected so you should consider this possibility when your dog slows or refuses to work. A body temperature of over 40°C (104 Fahrenheit) is an emergency and requires intervention (see heat stroke in the A–Z section). The opposite state of hypothermia (too cold – see A–Z) can occur in dogs over-exposed to cold or wet weather, and affected dogs will also stop working, become weak and even collapse. Dogs are quite good at raising their body temperature, but we do ask a lot of them. Wildfowling dogs in particular can suffer this after retrieves from icy cold water and it is important to have blankets, or even a metallic 'space' blanket in your car (these are available very inexpensively from outdoor expedition kit retailers) if you ask

Cooling down

Bitter cold wildfowling – hypothermia risk

Wildfowling

your dog to work in cold conditions. A body temperature below 37°C (98.6°F) is hypothermic and demands attention. Worth knowing is that unexpected occurrence of hypothermia without obvious cause can indicate the presence of other illness and merit veterinary attention.

Poisoning

Poisoning symptoms vary so much, and some guidance is given in the A–Z section. If you find a chewed up packet of a poison, or any evidence that your dog may have come into contact with some, take that information, and some of the poison, to the vet. Many poisons are colour-coded and so actually seeing a sample is very useful to the clinician.

Remember, if in doubt in any situation, no-one can be an expert in everything, and it is always better to seek help from those who know what to do rather than risk the patient.

Is that poisonous?

BANDAGING

Bandages, and practising using them, are well worth the effort involved and have saved many a working dog from life- or career-threatening injury in the field.

Attempting to bandage an injured dog can be likened to trying to bandage a moving cone with both shape and gravity colluding with the patient to cause the whole thing to fall off, thus frustrating the poor owner who has to try and put the whole thing together, often in a crisis. The only consolation perhaps is that vets are often not much good at it either, and it is only the vet nurses, who spend hours practising, who save the day and get the things to stay on.

We have included here some simple guidelines and examples which will enable the owner to use bandaging successfully in first aid.

Why bandage?

The reasons are multiple, and mostly obvious at the time. In summary the main reasons include:

1. To hold dressings, poultices and compresses in place.

2. To help control bleeding and swelling.

3. To prevent further wound contamination.

4. To prevent licking, scratching and self-mutilation.

5. To support fractures in order to aid pain relief, and to prevent them becoming more complicated.

6. To support injury repair in areas where immobilisation is needed, for example a wound over a joint.

7. In extreme situations, such as the use of tourniquets to prevent fatal blood loss.

Bandages must serve the purpose for which they are intended, and if incorrectly applied can make matters worse, so there are some rules that are worth considering:

1. Wash your hands before commencing, and be as clean as possible in the process.

2. Gather all the required materials together before starting, as the canine patient will invariably get up if you have to leave it to retrieve an item, and your good work will be dragged along the ground.

3. The bandage must be applied firmly and comfortably, while ensuring that it is not too tight and the circulation is not impaired.

4. When bandaging limbs, start from the foot end to prevent pocketing of blood.

5. Unroll small amounts of bandage at a time as this enables easier and more even application of pressure.

Bandage material and types

Conforming

These bandages have some degree of elasticity, and will spring back to shape when stretched. Care must be taken with these as they can easily be applied too tightly, but are useful when some pressure is needed. They are best applied over good padding as this reduces the risk of over-tightening, and they hold padding in place very well.

Non-conforming

These are usually made of cotton and have no ability to expand. They are difficult to apply as they do not wrap around body contours as conforming types of bandage do, and so they are not commonly used today.

Cohesive

A conforming bandage covered with a thin layer of latex which enables it to cling to itself, but not to animal skin or hair. These are extremely popular and sold in most animal supply outlets. They are easy to apply, comfortable, and also have the advantage of being easy to remove, which is a major blessing if dealing with an animal in pain.

6. Apply rolled bandages with a half to a third overlapping in spiral fashion.

7. If supporting a fracture, you must include the joints above and below the injury.

8. If the bandage needs to be held onto the limb or tail, you can tape over the hair using an elastoplast finish to the process to hold it on. Do not use an increase in tension as you will affect the circulation. If possible you can split a bandage to enable tying a reef knot part way up, again not too tight.

9. Choose the right bandages for the problem being addressed.

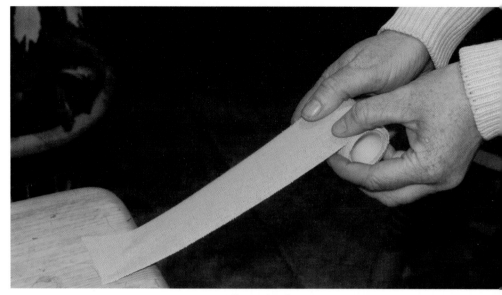

Adhesive bandage

Adhesive

Elastoplast-type bandages, these have a layer of adhesive, and are commonly used by professionals to hold on awkwardly positioned or longer-term bandages. Thinner strips can be used to bind into hair to hold bandages onto areas where they can easily slip off, for example tails.

Stockingette

In the case of dogs, these are usually used by professionals to hold dressings in place.

Tapes

More usually used to bind in hair to hold bandages on in places where they can easily slip off, for example tail bandages and those on lower limbs.

Padding

The classic padding is cotton wool, which can now be obtained in many forms. My preference for a first aid kit is the sheets of cotton wool in a roll, which can easily be applied around a leg, or torn into strips/pads/balls as needed and appropriate. The structure of these also gives consistency of padding and pressure when applying a bandage around an awkward area, and ensures areas are not left uncovered.

Dressings

When covering a wound with a bandage, it is important to put a gauze or similar dressing over the wound to prevent the bandage material sticking to the injury. Trying to remove a dressing where the blood has soaked into the bandage, hardened and then become fixed to the patient adds unnecessary stress to vet and patient. Most chemists will sell a range of dressings, and a selection of sizes can be handy, but if space is limited, get larger sizes which can be cut down as required.

Bandaging in the field

Detailed below are examples of bandaging methods that suit some common situations in the working dog environment. Not every situation can be covered, but in these descriptions we have tried to address the basic principles. Owners will no doubt have to adapt to circumstances as needed.

Always remember, a dog in pain can bite, even your own dog, and it is worth applying a muzzle as detailed at the beginning of the first aid section. If possible have an assistant to hold the dog, so that you can concentrate on the bandaging.

Foot and lower limb bandaging

A common site of injury and bandaging need in working dogs, split pads are highly vascular, and seem to bleed disproportionately to anything else. When bandaging the foot, you should first pad out the toes as shown, which ensures the toes will not rub together causing swelling and moisture build-up, possibly leading to nasty lesions. The next move is to apply some padding, commonly

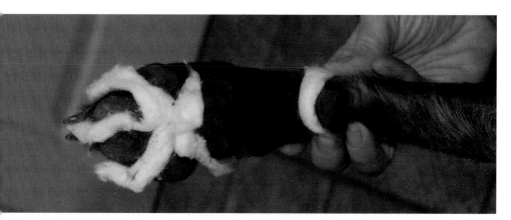

Bandaging foot injury

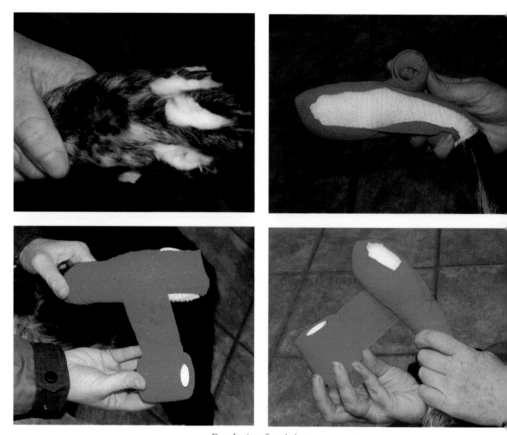

Bandaging foot injury

sheets of cotton wool, around the limb. If using cotton wool bandage, first roll the material longitudinally down the limb, back up the other side, and then change direction and roll the material diagonally around the limb, allowing one half to one third overlap of the material. Next take a conforming bandage and apply similarly to the bandage roll, starting at the toe end of the dressing. Often a layer of cohesive bandage is then applied in a similar manner over the top as a protective layer, preventing soiling of the more absorbent materials underneath, and some tape can then be fixed to the top of the bandage, including some hairs for security if required.

Head and ears

Commonly a spaniel problem, torn ears can affect any breed that needs to work in thorn cover or around barbed wire, and like pads they can bleed seemingly out of proportion to the injury when isolated. Bandaging can be

168

Simple ear bandaging

useful whilst getting to the vet, especially if you don't want your car interior looking like Dante's Inferno. This will hold the ears close to the dog's head and minimise blood being flicked everywhere every time it shakes its head.

Correct bandaging is useful in any ear problem, including infections, which benefit from ventilation of the ear canal (again a typical spaniel problem). Dogs' ears generally will fold easily onto the top of the head, and this is best done by grasping gently the end of the pinna (ear flap) and folding it over in one movement. One or both ears can be folded as needed. Place some padding, or a dressing, both under and on top of the folded ear(s) and use a figure of eight pattern to the bandage (as shown) using a conforming or cohesive bandage. These types of bandages are well tolerated and not too bulky, and being elastic they do not impede movement of the jaw. It is important to ensure that the bandage is not too tight around the neck as this can cause problems with breathing, and you must also be sure the bandage will not slip for similar reasons.

Bandaging tails

Tail injuries are common in breeds such as the labrador, and will unfortunately become more so in the spaniel breeds as docking of tails becomes less common. The tail is a particularly awkward thing to apply a bandage to that will stay on – the line of the hairs, the tapering effect as you get the end, enthusiastic wagging, and the ease of teeth access all contribute to frustrating the situation. It has become common to use a plastic tube (vets use old syringe cases, and I have seen a plastic hair curler used, which has the advantage of letting plenty of air to the wound) to cover the end of the tail, which is the most commonly injured area, and also any dressing. It is a particularly useful technique for the stubby, shorter tail.

When using the tube method, ensure the end is open to allow ventilation of the injury, dress the wound as appropriate, and attach the tube with some adhesive tape, including some tail hair in each turn of the tape to ensure the tube stays in place. It is common then to use a cohesive bandage over the top as protection from contamination, and to protect the owner's legs and possessions from an enthusiastically wagging plastic-reinforced tail. If you thought a labrador's tail could be hard, try it with the addition of armour plating and beware the mugs of coffee at dog height that get in the way.

Another method of tail bandaging is to use a spiral binding. Here, having dressed the wound appropriately, use a conforming (or cohesive) bandage rolled lengthways along the tail as shown and then from the tip spiral the bandage towards the top of the tail allowing overlap of half the material, including some tail hair in each turn as you approach the top of the tail. With dedicated waggers it is worth using some adhesive tape for the last few turns, making sure the whole bandage is not too tight, affecting circulation.

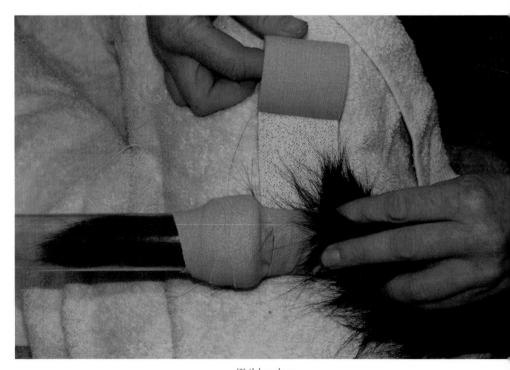

Tail bandage

Chest and abdomen bandaging

In the UK, barbed wire tears are probably the most common cause for which these bandages will be needed, but wounds from sharp sticks are perhaps more common than is thought, and as wild boar grow in population, we may expect tusk injuries to be added to the list, as they are in other countries.

Abdomen bandages are difficult to keep in place, so the principle is to apply the bandage, once a dressing is placed on the wound, as shown, allowing a large amount of bandage overlap (at least half, and ideally two thirds) such that the whole thing has its own inbuilt structural integrity and won't ruck up. Wide bandages are better, and you must not apply them too tightly or you will interfere with the dog's ability to breathe. A good alternative is stockingette if you have it, pulled over the body and the dressing, with holes cut for the limbs to keep it in place. In an emergency, the sleeve off a pullover or a small T-shirt will hold a field dressing in place while you travel to the vet; how you obtain either of these is a matter for your powers of persuasion.

A chest bandage is a very useful technique to know as injuries here are quite common. After applying a dressing to the wound, the principle is a

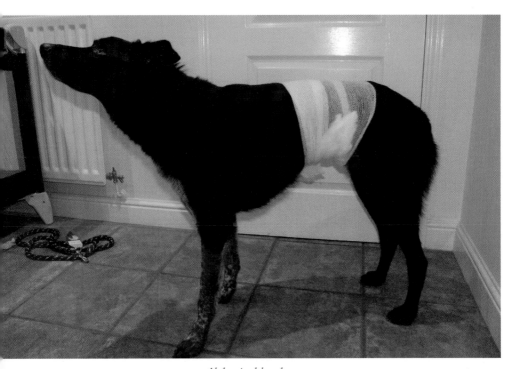

Abdominal bandage

figure of eight bandage, starting at the top of the shoulder. From here take a wide conforming bandage down to the front of the chest, then through the forelegs, up under the opposite armpit, up over the shoulder, down to the other armpit, forward under the legs, and back to the starting point (have you got that?). Then take a turn around the chest and repeat the process. Keep going until an adequate area is covered. A cohesive covering can be applied over the top similarly if required. Do remember again not to apply this too tightly as it can affect breathing.

Immobilising or Robert-Jones bandage

As mentioned before, if your dog has a fractured leg, you have to immobilise the limb such that the joints either side are included. A Robert-Jones bandage is often the ideal way to do this. However, this is a difficult bandage to apply correctly, and should really be done by a professional as incorrectly applied it can do more harm than good. It may be better to call out the vet to the site rather than move a dog with a severely injured leg as any movement of the fragmented bone could cause further damage, compromising recovery and future working potential. Few dogs in extreme pain will lie still enough to bandage anyway without sedation. If in a corner, and you have to do something to salvage the situation, it is always better to have some idea what to do, and do your best, so for completeness the process of a Robert-Jones bandage is as follows.

Having dressed any wounds as appropriate, pad out the toes and cut two lengths of adhesive tape and apply as shown, overlapping at the toes (these are known as stirrups). Wrap cotton wool spirally four to five times around the dog's leg, as firmly as possible. A 500g roll is sufficient for a labrador-sized leg. Compress the padding with a layer of spiralling conforming bandage, using a half-layer overlap and starting at the toe end. This compresses and supports the limb. Completely cover the cotton wool layer, but leave the middle two toe nails exposed below to allow the dog to balance and to facilitate checking the limb's circulation. If firm enough, when flicked the dressing will make a resonant sound likened to a ripe melon being tapped. Take the free ends of the stirrups and fold them back, securing them to the cotton wool bound layer. This secures the bandage and prevents it sliding down the limb. Lastly apply a cohesive layer to the full length of the bandage, further securing the stirrups in the process. The finished result will be a thick bandage like a form of soft cast, three or more times the width of the dog's leg. Finally transport the patient to the vet for professional attention.

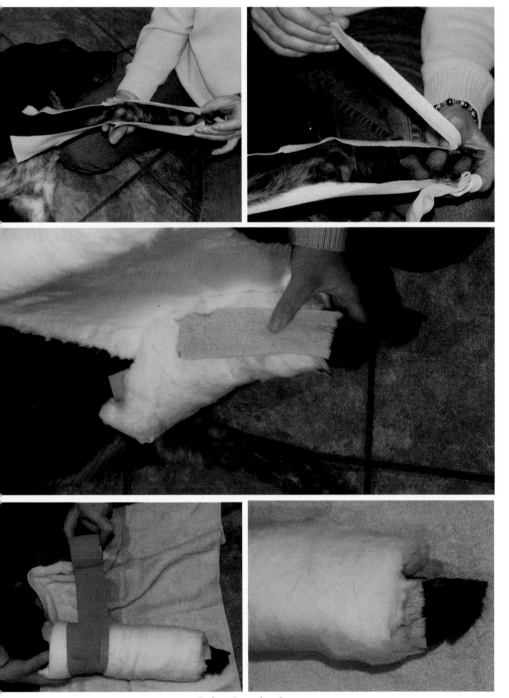

Robert-Jones bandage

Protecting the bandage

Aftercare

Once bandaged by the vet the dog will still need to go outside several times daily to empty itself, and if the injury allows some degree of exercise, the dog will enjoy a little fresh air and a sniff around. The bandage itself will need to be protected from getting wet and dirty while the dog is outside, even if it is only pottering about for a few minutes, trying to find exactly the right spot to anoint (how many hours of my life have I spent waiting for an injured dog to perform?). Orphan socks can be pressed into use in dry weather, and are especially helpful with limb and head injuries. Very small paws can be protected with a condom, but larger feet and limbs might need a carrier bag taped over the bandage, or better still, most vets keep old drip fluid bags for this very purpose which are hardwearing and reusable. Parcel tape is another cheap and easy solution for fixing the covering temporarily. As wounds need to breathe, any waterproof coverings must be removed as soon as the dog is back indoors.

Similarly, plaster casts need to be protected from wet and dirt. A dog with a broken leg still has three good ones itching to be exercised, and so long as your vet is in agreement, a short, controlled on-lead hop about for a few minutes is refreshing for the dog. Do not, however, give in to temptation and let the dog off the lead, because they can still motor along faster on three legs than a human can on two. Changing a cast is nuisance enough for all concerned without your having to think of an explanation of what the dog was doing in the stream in the first place.

When not to bandage

Many injuries, however, are better not bandaged at all, but left for the air to get to them, and superficial wounds are often better left unstitched as well. There are many places on a dog where there is just not enough skin to bring together for stitching, and if these places are stitched, they can pull and irritate to the extent that the dog will worry at them constantly. If a wound is not in contact with the ground, then it may often be left to heal by itself, so long as you keep an eye on it. Doing 'nothing' like this does not mean that nothing is being done; by letting Nature take its course you are still keeping the area under care. It is fascinating how injuries heal. Let's take a simplified look.

The classic barbed-wire wound, a three-cornered rip with a flap of skin hanging loose and the flesh punctured underneath, is so common in the working dog. First of all, unless excessive let it bleed: the blood is pushing

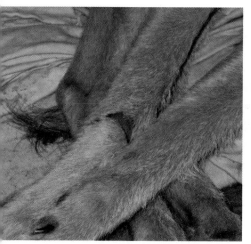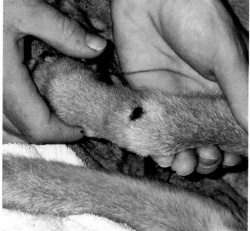

Wound left to heal unstitched, unbandaged and no antibiotics, but under veterinary supervision

debris from the wound. Then the blood will start to congeal, first around the edges of the wound and then in the middle. You might like to rinse the wound out gently with some salt water in a syringe, or just let the dog lick it if it can reach. This is sufficient cleaning unless the wound has collected a lot of dirt within it, in which case you will need veterinary help. Long-haired dogs will benefit from having the hair clipped close around the edges of the wound, so that hair does not trail into it. I use honey a lot on wounds: it can be messy but it is an accepted natural antiseptic and healer. Assuming such an injury is then left open, it will start to granulate at the edges, while the loose flap of skin will die back. The surface of the wound will accumulate a straw-coloured sticky fluid. The wound will heal according to holistic principles 'from within to without' and so its diameter will hardly seem to alter for days, or might even increase slightly as your dog licks away the dead skin, but what is actually happening is that the flesh is healing upwards to skin level. Once the flesh has reached the top, the granulation will start to cover the surface from the edges inwards to form a scab, and the dog may well niggle at the scab and remove it a few times. Let it, unless it is one of those dogs that over-grooms and chews into the flesh. You, however, must resist all temptation to pick at the scab with your monkey-human fingers, no, not even if you have disinfected your hands first. A lot of trouble is caused by human picking. Eventually, the scab will stop itching and the dog will lose interest in it (no you may not pick it now) the skin will be growing under the scab, and when it is complete, the scab will start to lift on the new-grown tissue (leave that scab alone), and you will see the new scar underneath. Length of time varies with depth of wound, but two weeks from injury to completion is about average.

Puncture wounds are also better left open to avoid sealing in infection. They should at first be thoroughly rinsed out with salt water to which a drop or two of tea tree oil or similar antibacterial can be added. Do not over-use your chosen disinfectant: if the first clean is thorough, you may not need to repeat the process. The risk with punctures is for the top to scab over before the inner healing has been completed, which can trap bacteria into a nice warm friendly environment for infection. Normally the dog will lick off the scab as it forms, preventing this, and a few minutes' application of a pad of dressing with honey on it will loosen a scab that has formed prematurely. Any heat around the site of a puncture wound means that it needs attention in the shape of more cleaning and perhaps antibiotic treatment. If you are in any doubt over whether a wound may be left or should be bandaged, then go with the advice of your vet.

First Aid and Simple Treatments for Common Ailments A–Z

In this section a variety of common problems seen in working dogs are flagged up, and a range of possible treatment choices that are readily available are detailed. When considering treatment for a minor illness that seems not serious enough for the vet rather than first aid, remember the following simple rules.

1. It is better only to try the seemingly most appropriate treatments one at a time to avoid confusion over what is actually happening, although using both an external application and an oral tablet is fine.

2. Watch closely for responses as often minor problems such as vomiting will clear quickly with well chosen homeopathic remedies, and the vet may not be needed at all.

3. Do not overdose. This is very important.

4. Lastly, if in doubt, remember it is often better to do nothing yourself if you are unsure, rather than make things worse. When there is doubt seek professional advice.

For all homeopathic remedies, the treatments mentioned are easily available tablets, given by mouth unless specified, and most will be found in suitable first aid kits. It is also possible to obtain homeopathic remedies in tincture form, in a spray or dropper bottle. Ideally, tablets should not be touched by fingers, and are given most easily by crushing between the backs of two sterilised teaspoons and then tipping the powder into the mouth. Some dogs, including two of my own, will eat the tablets straight off the spoon. Tinctures are either dripped onto the dog's nose or sprayed into its mouth. Bach flower remedies may be obtained from health stores or homeopathic pharmacies, and are liquid, given by mouth unless specified. Herbs and aromatherapy treatments are administered in a variety of ways and these are mentioned in each section as applicable.

Abscess

An abscess is a collection of pus resulting from the body attempting to wall off an infection. At first an abscess will appear as a hot swelling with a reddened area of skin over it. With time, it will mature by the skin covering weakening until it bursts, often discharging an amazing amount of pus everywhere, or so it seems. Sometimes an abscess does not burst, but cleanses internally, leaving an area of thickened skin that gradually disperses, often over a long period of time.

Action in the field

The causes can be many; often blackthorn spikes or splinters are the culprits and so these should be removed, if possible, as soon as they are noticed. Once beneath the skin they are next to impossible to dislodge and an abscess is the body's way of doing this.

Simple home treatments

An abscess should be gently poulticed (see Wounds) or bathed in warm salt water (made using sea salt, or alternatively Epsom salts, at a rate of four teaspoons to a pint of water) until the abscess bursts and drains. The area can then be washed out with warm water, to which a little hydrogen peroxide has been added – this will make it bubble and foam – but note, do not use hydrogen peroxide around the eyes or ears, and if made up to anything more than an extremely dilute solution it can sting (a one in fifty dilution would be the strongest I would suggest, and it is effective at greater dilutions).

Herbs

Poultices of comfrey, marshmallow root, plantain and chickweed can be made up by grinding the herbs, either together or separately depending on what is available, and strapping this as a compress to the abscess to draw the infection.

Homeopathy

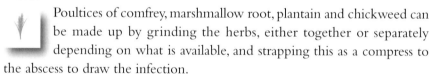

Apis mel 6c is an especially good remedy in dogs for relief of the pain caused by the early red and hot swelling. Dose hourly for four doses, then as needed. Some early abscesses will be aborted by this treatment and no further remedy will be needed.

Hepar sulph 6c can be given three times daily if the area is very painful to touch and the infection needs to be encouraged to discharge. It can be given with Apis.

Hepar sulph 30c is useful once the pus has discharged in assisting with clearing up the infection: it is given three times daily.

Silica 6c helps clear up wounds where they have burst, but the pus fails to come away properly, often given with the Hepar sulph 30c.

Staphysagria 30c hourly for four doses can help with the pain of thorn and stick injuries, and can settle a dog that is reluctant to allow examination.

Aromatherapy

Chamomile and lavender oils can be used externally to draw infection by adding to any poultice.

A single topical application of diluted tea tree oil is often sufficient to remedy a minor abscess.

Bach flower remedies

Rescue Remedy for the pet that is very distressed is calming and aids settling.

Crab Apple will support the cleansing of the abscess and expulsion of any foreign material.

When to call the vet

An abscess should mature within 24 hours and burst, healing rapidly afterwards. If this doesn't happen, or if the dog appears unwell at all (possibly indicative of infection spreading), then your vet should be consulted and antibiotics may be needed.

Abscesses that recur can indicate an underlying problem, and if the abscess is near the anus there may be a problem with the anal glands. In each of these instances a vet should be consulted.

Accidents

Despite all precautions possible, accidents can still happen.

Action in the field

Most accidents will be minor and a learning experience, but if more severe and you don't know what to do the first rule is to do nothing except keep the dog still and warm whilst waiting for help, giving Rescue Remedy and Arnica 30c in alternation every fifteen minutes. If you have to move the dog, then improvise a stretcher with blankets, boards etc. If there is a lot of bleeding try to stop it (see Bleeding and bandaging) and if the dog is hysterical then apply a muzzle (see Restraint).

Herbs

Chamomile, skullcap and oats can all be used to make a calming tea that can be offered to dogs every few hours. They will often drink this enthusiastically as dogs, like many animals other than humans, have not lost the ability to know which herbs are good for them, and when they are needed.

Homeopathy

Aconite 30c is a must for all shock cases. Give two doses ten minutes apart then move on to give Arnica.

Arnica 30c. This remedy in whatever strength you have it is so useful for reducing pain and bruising, and it is also said to prevent minor haemorrhages. Dose every fifteen minutes for four doses then hourly for four hours. Certainly horse riders swear by it for falls, and many sportsmen now take it routinely for competition. More people are converted to homeopathy each year by this remedy than any other. Arnica is also available as a cream for bruising, but this must not be put on open wounds as it can affect healing.

Carbo veg 30c, known as the homeopathic 'Corpse Reviver' should be given to collapsed cases every twenty minutes for three doses.

Aromatherapy

Eucalyptus, lavender and tea tree oils are all useful remedies, diluted and applied externally to bruises for pain relief and healing, but do not apply to areas where the skin is broken. Use singly: do not combine.

Peppermint oil is said to aid recovery from shock and to calm nerve pain. Hold the open bottle under the patient's nose.

Birch oil, dropped into a little hot water in a glass, and placed in the room helps ease dogs in pain.

Bach flower remedies

Rescue Remedy: like Arnica, this is a must for any first aid situation, given neat as a few drops per dose to alleviate shock and at the same intervals as the Arnica. Again, this combination of five flower remedies converts many people to holistic therapy each year, as it is so successful and reliable a treatment.

Sweet Chestnut will help calm an inconsolable patient. Dose twice in ten minutes.

Rock Rose will calm terrified patients. Dose twice in ten minutes.

When to consult your vet

 It is always worth getting a professional opinion after any accident, and in more severe cases the need to get to the vet will be obvious.

Allergic reactions and Stings

Contact with chemical irritants, insects and plants that sting, or more unusual things such as toads, can set off reactions in dogs. Toad poison can cause mild fit-like episodes, foaming at the mouth and drooling, but most irritants will just result in rashes or mild swellings that can often be quite painful. If affecting the face the whole head can swell up, more typically with wasp and bee stings.

Action in the field

 Wash off any irritant as soon as possible, including gently flushing the eyes if contaminated.

Calamine lotion is found in many households and if available this can bring relief.

Witch hazel diluted at one in fifty is a great reliever of minor external irritations. It can even be made up in a small spray container and sprayed onto rashes and sores to give immediate short-term relief.

Many people carry Piriton tablets now, and they can be used in dogs quite safely. I suggest a dose of one tablet per labrador sized patient, scaling up and down according to bodyweight. The patient may get a little sleepy but this usually passes quite quickly.

Simple home treatments

 For wasp or hornet stings, alkalis (such as vinegar) diluted in water and applied to the sting will relieve the pain. Similarly for bee stings use bicarbonate of soda, but you have to watch that you don't get bitten at first when applying it.

Vitamin E and fish oils have an anti-inflammatory effect on dogs with a tendency to allergies, and can be given to dogs in similar doses to humans, but scaled down to their bodyweight.

Herbs

 Chamomile and yarrow as a tea will help sooth an allergic reaction, given up to four times daily. Echinacea and elderflower are also good herbs for calming the over-response of the immune system and are both often readily available.

When the eyes are sore some chamomile and eyebright as a diluted infusion can be a very useful relieving eyewash, applied as often as needed.

Homeopathy

Apis mel 6c can be given hourly for relief of any skin rash, and is especially good for swellings around the eyes and ears, a must for bee and wasp stings.

Caladium 30c is good for mosquito bites, given two or three times daily as needed.

Ledum pal 6c is good for puncture wounds, including dog bites, horsefly bites and wasp stings. Dose as often as needed for relief.

Urtica urens 6c is good for hives (nettle rash) given hourly for four doses.

Ledum, Pyrethrum and Rumex can all be bought as lotions and combined with Hypericum and Calendula to make up an anti-sting lotion, which is then applied by diluting and holding on with a damp cloth.

For severe reactions to stings a lotion made from Arnica, Calendula and Urtica (ACU lotion) can be applied to soothe and reduce inflammation. Best applied by putting a few drops onto a cold flannel and holding on to the area, allowing your hand's heat to warm the wound over a few minutes.

Aromatherapy

Chamomile and lavender, mixed into a massage oil, can be rubbed into the areas of affected skin for relief. If skin is broken, a few drops of lavender oil on a pad of kitchen paper may be applied for a few minutes. Other than lavender, and diluted tea tree for initial cleansing, aromatherapy oils should not be used on broken skin.

Bach flower remedies

Rescue Remedy cream can be applied to any skin reaction, and is especially useful if the skin has broken and many of the other options are not possible.

A combination of Agrimony, Beech, Cherry Plum, Crab Apple and Walnut can be given as a few drops by mouth, or diluted in a spray bottle and squirted onto the affected area a few times daily.

When to consult your vet

The vast majority of acute allergic reactions will pass in an hour or two, but if the face or throat area is affected, or the problem persists, then you must consult your vet before more serious problems occur.

Some dogs will tend to suffer allergic responses quite often, in a similar way to humans, and for these it is a good idea to consult a holistic vet for a longer term solution.

Anal Glands

The cause of many a trip to the vet's, these little, marble-sized glands that sit either side of the anus are an evolutionary remnant gland that dogs have not yet learned to delete for our convenience from their genetic make-up, though the scent we find so revolting is an important communication method for our dogs. Modern processed diets can result in a stool that is not firm enough to massage these glands clean as the dog defecates, and the situation is often made worse by the shapes that people have bred into dogs in the pursuit of different breed types. If not emptied properly, the glands fill up with a thick, foul-smelling liquid that can become infected. Early warning signs of problems are when the dog rubs its bottom along the floor or new carpet in an attempt to express the glands, and follows this with licking around the anus. It is wise then to get them checked before matters get worse.

Simple home treatments

 If they become a persistent problem ask your vet to show you how to empty these glands yourself. Whilst quite a foul smelling task, routine emptying can prevent problems recurring. Look at the diet also, and consider changing to a Bones and Raw Food (BARF) diet to achieve a better stool. If infection occurs, loads of live plain yoghurt added to the diet will help colour the stool so that a dose of 'friendly' bacteria will reach the gland as each stool is passed, and this should always be given after any antibiotics are prescribed in any case (see Antibiotics, below). A warm compress made from a mix of Epsom salts and water soaked into a flannel and held onto the dog's bottom for ten minutes twice a day gives great relief, often causing the glands to express naturally.

Herbs

 Dandelion root, goldenseal and yarrow made into a tea and either offered to the patient, or added to the food twice a day can help with irritation and pain, as well as improving circulation in the area.

Homeopathy

Apis mel 6c is good for relief of pain when the area around the anus is red and swollen, given hourly for four hours.

Hepar sulph 6c is useful to encourage blocked glands to discharge, give three times daily.

Merc cor 30c will help healing when the pus from the glands is bloody, black and thin in constitution: dose three times daily.

Natrum mur 30c helps the distressed dog that is producing a green, often almost fluorescent, discharge, dose three times daily.

Silica 6c daily for a few weeks will often help a dog that has suffered recurrent problems, and where the openings of the glands have now become scarred and closed.

When to consult your vet

In any case where the patient is distressed the local vet, and in all recurrent cases a holistic vet, should be consulted to work out a solution. When visiting the vet, always ask to see the discharge from the glands as the colour and consistency can be a guide to remedies needed.

Antibiotics

These may seem an odd addition to a first aid section, but I include these here to make a few points that can stop the development of long-term problems from their use. Firstly, if your vet has prescribed antibiotics you must use them at the advised dose and for the time specified. This is important to prevent resistant bacteria building up and causing problems further down the line. Secondly, dogs have quite short intestines, and they need 'friendly' bacteria to aid the digestive process. Most antibiotics will kill off these 'friends' as the drugs are not discriminatory, and so you will need to put some back *after* the medication has finished to restore a healthy gut, and also to prevent any 'nasty' bacteria establishing. Many a chronic diarrhoea and bowel problem has been the result of neglecting these simple rules, and it is much harder to correct the problem months or even years later when long-term changes have occurred in the intestines.

For puncture wounds and other deep injuries where infection may be trapped, your vet will often prescribe more than one antibiotic, and one of these may be for anaerobic bacteria. These are bacteria that do not need oxygen to survive, and they can set up quite nasty abscesses. If courses of

184

antibiotics do not run out concurrently this may be for that reason, but check if you are worried.

Anxiety and Shock

Anxiety is defined as a state of uneasiness or apprehension accompanied by tension that may or may not have an obvious cause. Often a result of us owners failing to recognise the 'wolf' in our companions, neglected anxiety states are a major cause of long term health problems through stress effects on the immune system. Behavioural problems as a result of inappropriate adopting of avoidance techniques, such as wrecking furniture or unearthing houseplants, are typical signs indicating this problem. If spotted early and treated with medicines described below, as well as by changing our lifestyles and attitudes to allow normal canine behaviour, a lot of expense and grief can be avoided.

Action in the field

First take the dog away from the stressful situation and give it time to calm down. It is often useful to return to a known safe area such as your car. Remedies to calm the dog, both homeopathic and Bach flowers (see below) can be given, and then reintroduce it gradually to the situation, though if necessary, you should abandon the day to prevent a more permanent or difficult fear ingraining itself in the dog's psyche.

Simple home treatments

The DAPs (Dog Appeasement Pheromones) that have been mentioned in a preceding chapter can be bought from your vet to calm a stressed dog on a longer term basis for treatment of some issues, but the most important thing is to sit down and think out the problem, and set about changing your and your dogs' lives to get around whatever it may be.

Herbs

Catnip, chamomile, hops, passiflora, skullcap, and valerian are all herbs that have been used with success to calm stressed dogs. Often these can be obtained from herbal suppliers in various mixes, and easily given as a tablet, or added to the food. Of especial use I find is an Indian herbal formula of astragalus, ocimum, phyllanthus and withania marketed by specialist importers Global Herbs Ltd (see Useful Addresses).

185

St John's wort (hypericum) is often used for depression and anxiety in humans, and there is some indication it can be used for the chronically anxious case in dogs too.

Homeopathy

Aconite 30c is the remedy for an acute shock.

Argentum nitricum 30c is a remedy par excellence for the dog that gets diarrhoea with anxiety or excitement, such as when going shooting. Diarrhoea before work can reduce endurance due to the dehydrating effect so it is important to resolve this. Often these patients have other issues as well, such as fear of the dark, fear of approach and so on.

Gelsemium 30c for the 'frightened rabbit' syndrome, where a stress creates paralysis and inability to move. I have used this successfully for dogs that have stopped retrieving after a shock, such as that occurring when trying to retrieve a bird stuck on an electric fence.

Ignatia 30c for anxiety related to separation, grief and loss, as well as change in environment. Timidity and hysteria characterise this remedy.

Natrum mur 30c for the dog that has developed odd behaviour traits from the stress. We all remember the polar bears in zoos that pace up and down all day as a response to stress. These can be Natrum mur cases. Dogs may also have odd obsessions such as watching birds in the sky, snapping at flies, and a tendency to hide in dark places. These dogs do not take to kennelling alone, and are better kept with companions.

Proteus 30c is a very useful remedy for the recently rescued dog that has intermittent stool problems, often a poor skin, and a history of recent separation from its owner. It is also useful for dogs who don't settle after being bought in from professional trainers, where diarrhoea is a concurrent feature of the problem.

Sulphur 30c is for dogs who have developed a fear of approach after a trauma.

For all of the above dose twice, an hour apart, repeating as needed.

Aromatherapy

Basil, lavender, and rose oils: adding two or three drops of each, or all, to a cup of recently boiled water will create a gentle aroma perfusing the room to calm a stressed pet.

Neroli and frankincense oils can be used in a similar way for pets who suffer separation anxiety problems on a longer term basis.

Bach flower remedies

 There are almost too many of these useful here to describe in depth, and I would recommend anyone with a dog that has developed behavioural problems to read one of the many books on these for guidance. Many such problems can be resolved with these so long as changes are made to remove the cause as well. A selection includes:

Agrimony for fear of being left alone (often given with Mimulus). Useful especially for dogs who don't settle when left in the car.

Mimulus for fear and apprehension relating to known events.

Oat for the odd behaviours such as pacing and rocking.

Red Chestnut, for fear and anxiety about others, such as other dogs and the human family.

Rock Rose for extreme anxiety and panic.

White Chestnut, for the persistent thoughts that go round and round in the head. Hard to see in dogs but many anxiety states, often early in training programmes, will be helped by this, so dogs must dwell on things.

Other

 Reiki can be particularly helpful for anxiety cases.

When to consult your vet

 Basically when none of the above has worked, and you have been unable to determine the problem, it is time to call in the professionals. Your vet will have a list of local behaviour therapists or homeopaths, and be able to recommend one, or more often now your vet may also have an interest in this field.

Arthritis

We tend to think of arthritis as a longer-term issue of age, but some modern dog breeds can develop problems as growing puppies, and injuries can happen at any time. Any joint inflammation is technically an 'arthritis', and early effective treatment can prevent damage to the delicate cartilages in a joint and thus also reduce the chances of developing age-related arthritis.

Action in the field

All joint inflammations must be regarded as potentially serious, and work for the day should be abandoned to avoid longer-term problems from damage to the sensitive tissues.

Simple home treatments

For most joint problems there are supplements available from health shops that can be of great help in longer-term cases. Glucosamine, combined with chondroitin sulphate, can be easily obtained and given to great effect. A simple guide is to take a 500 mg tablet as a daily dose for a 35 kg labrador and scale up and down accordingly (see Chapter 4).

Another useful tip is to massage the acupuncture point that is known as the 'Aspirin point'. This is BL60, and is to be found on the top of the ankle joint on the outer side.

Massaging for sixty seconds a side twice a day can bring great relief.

Cider vinegar, honey and corn oil (must be GM free), mixed together in equal portions and given at a rate of one teaspoon twice daily in the food is a good and easily available remedy that helps many mild cases.

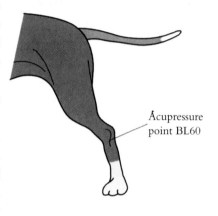

Acupressure point BL60

Acupressure 'Aspirin point' BL60

Herbs

My favourite herbs here are two Indian, or Ayurvedic, remedies, boswellia and turmeric. The former is the number one arthritis treatment in India, and is said to outsell more conventional painkillers. Mixed together they are a powerful formulation, but if you have nothing else, you will often have turmeric as a herb in the kitchen, and you can add a little powder, typically a quarter teaspoon for a labrador, to your dog's food (but don't panic if the stool goes orange for a while).

Homeopathy

Rhus tox, Ruta grav and Arnica in 30c are the main remedies for joint pain and injury, and they are often combined and given together, up to three times daily.

Calc phos 30c should be given daily to all puppies with growing problems to promote healthy bone and cartilage formation and is especially useful for large breeds with a rapid early growth rate.

Aromatherapy

 Chamomile, eucalyptus, juniper and lavender are all said to provide relief, added to massage oil or gel and worked around a sore joint above and below.

When to consult your vet

 In all cases it is especially important to consult a holistic vet as the causes and potential treatments for best outcome must be found as soon as possible. Treatment with painkillers (often called anti-inflammatory drugs) just masks a problem and is not a solution in the majority of cases. Young dogs especially need assessment as they may develop a condition known as OCD (osteochondrosis dessicans) that is potentially serious if left. It is worth noting, however, that breeders whose dogs used to suffer this problem but then changed to a BARF diet for their puppies have reported the problem disappearing – convinced yet?

Bandaging

Most dogs have a desire to lick their wounds, and will try and chew off bandages and dressings unless they sensibly realise it is hopeless. Unfortunately some dogs will get so distressed by bandages they will actually cause further injuries by tearing frantically at dressings so care is needed to ensure this cannot happen. Vets will therefore often bandage right around the limb or body, even if it is only a small area that needs dressing. A good bandage will be firm and wide, but not so tight that it cuts off the circulation, and will be typically covered in Elastoplast to protect it from biting. Plastic collars to prevent chewing may be needed as well for persistent offenders. Very sensitive dogs can become frantic when wearing the 'Elizabethan' type collar. Depending where the wound is, a very wide collar that covers the whole of the neck, preventing it bending, may be less upsetting for them and many vets will offer this option.

Simple rules to remember at home are: cover the wound with lint, or similar dressing, to ensure the bandage doesn't stick to the skin, then apply a thin layer of rolled gauze bandage. A layer of cotton wool is placed around that and a further layer of bandage applied around this before an Elastoplast or Vet-wrap outer is applied. The resulting dressing should be firm, but not so tight that it acts like a tourniquet and cuts off the blood supply (with obvious devastating consequences if not spotted in time). If in doubt over what to do, always ask for advice regarding bandages (see also Bandaging, above).

Barbed Wire — See also Bleeding, Wounds and Bandaging sections

Barbed wire injuries are very common, and cause a characteristic three-cornered rip in the skin, with the barb often going in deeper. Dogs caught up in barbed wire, whether victim of the loose rolls concealed in a ditch or from having miscalculated when jumping a fence, can panic and struggle, making the problem worse. When dealing with this, the first action must always be to get something in the dog's mouth that isn't you, because you will cause the dog even more pain while detaching it, and you will be very close to the biting end. It is not easy to get a makeshift muzzle on a screaming dog, so a strong thick stick that will not break placed crossways in the mouth may be used, or else a rolled-up article of clothing. In the hunting field, one of the uses of a traditional hunting whip is to place it horizontally in the jaws of a hound before attempting to free it, though I know of a huntsman who sustained a horrific bite to his face because he neglected to do this when rushing to the aid of a favourite and normally gentle hound. A coat over the dog's head is another option, but be careful as this can slip off just when matters are getting close and personal. You can tie a sweater on by the sleeves going between the jaws, which is better.

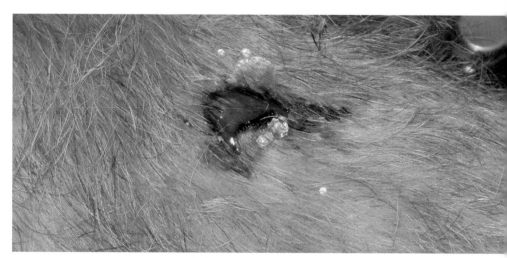

Barbed wire injury treated with honey

Ideally, you will then need someone to take the dog's weight while you unpick it from the fence, or even cut it free, but in practise this sort of horrible situation often occurs when you are on your own. If using wire-cutters on a fence, remember that the wire will spring back if previously under tension. Rather than cutting the barbs free, cut the fence between the barbs if you can, even if this leaves the barbs in the dog. These can be removed later under less stressful conditions. If the dog has been caught by a leg in between the two strands of barbed wire that top a stock-fence, remember that the leg can be injured at any point from taking the whole weight of the dog while it struggles. The best way to release the dog caught like this is to take the weight and release the tension by lifting the dog as close to the fence as possible. If you work your dog in barbed-wire country, consider carrying wire-cutters at all times, or else teach it to go through rather than over. This can still catch it on a barb now and then, but the injury is comparatively trivial. Smaller barbed-wire tears are best left unstitched but cleaned very thoroughly. The wounds heal well, and the spare flap of skin will shrink away as the new hide grows across.

Bites

Despite the best socialisation classes and early puppy training, some dogs seem to be prone to getting into scraps, even if it is not always their fault. Working dogs inevitably come into contact with quarry that can bite. Rats, foxes, mink, squirrels etc. all have sharp teeth and the resulting bite wounds can be very

Biting quarry

Working terrier's badges of honour

painful, often for some time after the initial bite as the swelling develops. However bites are generally best left open and bathed rather than covered up. Covering can seal infection in and lead to an abscess forming, or worse, septicaemia.

Action in the field

 Often minor bites do not prevent the dog working the rest of the day, and terriers in particular will often seem mortally offended if they cannot display their war wounds as a badge of honour. Be aware that adrenaline will keep the dog in action beyond when it should be so, and if it seems sorry for itself once the excitement has died down it should be retired for the day and attention given to the problem. Obviously if the dog is bleeding a lot to start with then follow the rules for bleeding (see Bleeding), and also follow the rules for wound care (see Wounds). When checking a bite from an animal with large canine teeth, such as a dog or fox, always find all four puncture wounds, as there will be two that are less obvious but often deeper. Similarly with the chisel bite from a rodent, which can mean a large slice in two places on the injured party.

Fox bite injury

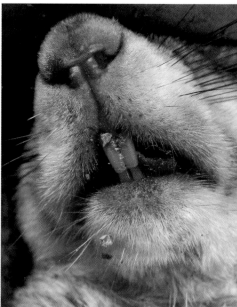
Rodent teeth give chisel bite

Simple home treatments

Clean the bite with witch hazel diluted one in forty. This is a level at which it will not sting and upset the patient, yet is strong enough to be mildly disinfectant. If you do not have witch hazel to hand, then salt water at a rate of two teaspoons to a pint of water is a good fall-back position.

Herbs

Marshmallow made as a tea, to which is added some Arnica tincture, can be soaked into a flannel and applied as a warm compress to relieve bruising and swelling once the wound has been cleaned.

Calendula (marigold) can also be made as an infusion and dabbed on at regular intervals to cleanse and promote healing.

Homeopathy

Arnica 30c should be given to all patients to relieve the pain and swelling of the bruise. Alternatively Rhus tox, Ruta and Arnica 30c combined can be used. Dose hourly for four doses then as needed.

Ledum pal 6c is a major remedy for dog bites, which tend to become swollen and inflamed. Dose hourly for four hours, and thereafter three times daily.

Vipera 30c can be given along with Ledum for snakebites.

Mezereum 200c seems especially useful for relieving the pain and infection from fox bites and bites on the face. Give twice daily for a few days.

Aromatherapy

Tea tree or lavender oil can be diluted and applied around the wound for pain relief, and also syringed directly into a deep puncture wound as an antibacterial.

Bach flower remedies

Rescue Remedy drops and cream can be used, the former to calm the patient, the latter to put on the wound to cleanse and promote healing.

When to consult your vet

Many bites do not need more than cleaning and the care as described above, but those near the eye, ear, belly or anal area should always be checked by a vet for other complications. Any case where pus starts to form may need antibiotics (one never knows how clean the teeth of the biter were), and any case where the patient becomes quiet and withdrawn should be checked over, including the temperature taken to see if infection might have spread. Snakebite cases should always have veterinary attention, and as soon as possible after the event, with a description of the snake if possible.

Bleeding

Action in the field

Rule 1 – Don't Panic. A little blood goes a long way, and if a dog is wet it can seem that there is a vast amount of blood everywhere. If there was that much you probably couldn't do much about things anyway, which is generally not the case.

In a panic situation it is hard to know where best to bandage so the best rule is to first restrain the dog so it cannot hurt you (including muzzling). Then apply firm pressure to the wound area using a tea towel from your first aid kit, or a handkerchief, torn shirt or even a pack of tissues. Once this is achieved either use bandages or torn cloth to bind the area firmly (see Bandaging), then wrap the patient in a blanket and get it to the vet.

Laceration injury

Bandaging leg wounds is straightforward as you can simply wrap around a leg. Tails are more difficult as you often have to wrap the whole tail, and even then it can be hard to keep a dressing on. Body injuries are best wrapped in a criss-cross fashion around the whole body. Eye injuries are hard to bandage correctly and it is probably best just to hold a pad against the eye whilst on the way to the vet. Ears can be bandaged by folding up over the head and bandaging around the whole head, again easier in a criss-cross pattern. A quick and effective bandage for a torn ear, which will save your car from a lot of blood, is to cut the toe off a sock and pull the rest of it over the dog's head like a balaclava. Tough luck if you only have your vastly expensive wool shooting socks to hand – consider pleading with the beaters, or even buying a sock off one of them. Noses and bums are impossible to bandage so here the rules of restraint and warmth apply (i.e. wrapping in a blanket) whilst getting to the vet.

We're beginning to see here the importance of that blanket and tea towel in the first aid kit. Combining as a stretcher, restraining method and warmth provider they are so useful to carry in the car.

Remedies to carry always are Arnica and Rescue Remedy, and both should be given to all cases that are bleeding, often both every fifteen minutes, whilst heading to the vet.

Bruising

Injury to the body can result in bleeding into tissues or underneath the skin. This accumulation of blood initially causes redness and swelling, before causing the more typical purplish appearance of a bruise as the bleeding settles and the blood gradually breaks down. Deep bruises may not be obvious from a surface examination, but typically will cause discomfort, and later on stiffness on movement. Some bite wounds, such as from a horse, crush rather than puncture, and bruising can then be extensive. You will usually know when your dog has sustained an injury likely to bruise, unless it has been working out of sight. Bruises that appear for no reason can indicate other illness and merit a check by your vet.

Action in the field

Stop work for the day if the bruising is severe, as to carry on exercising will only cause more bleeding. Ice packs applied quickly can help slow the bleeding and relieve pain, but care should be taken in their use as you have to remember your dog cannot tell you when the area

Bruising injury

is too cold, and pain relief can encourage working on an injury, which is never advisable.

Herbs

Arnica lotion or cream is probably the best known topical remedy for bruises and its results can be spectacular. Many people are converted to holistic therapies by seeing the rapid results of this on their own injuries. Arnica is also used in homeopathic form taken internally as a tablet.

Comfrey, marigold and St John's wort can all be made into an infusion and applied as a compress to a bruised area four times a day or more. Comfrey promotes healing, marigold does too, and St John's wort relieves the pain.

Homeopathy

Aconite 30c has a long history of use to alleviate shock and bleeding, and is useful for the dog that is wide-eyed and panicked by the injury. It should be used immediately after the injury, and typically dosed every fifteen minutes for four doses.

Arnica 30c should be given to all patients to relieve the pain and swelling of the bruise; alternatively Rhus tox, Ruta and Arnica 30c combined can be used. Dose hourly for four doses, then as needed.

Bellis perennis 30c can be used to alleviate the pain of deep tissue bruising, and is especially useful for back injuries. Dose hourly for four doses, then as needed.

Hypericum 200c is the remedy for injuries, including bruising, to nerves and so has uses for alleviating spinal injuries, crushed toes and facial injuries, and is especially known for relief of pain from injuries to the pelvis and base of the tail.

Natrum sulph 30c is used for dogs who have suffered a head injury, often after Arnica has been used and there are still some residual effects. Dose twice daily as needed.

Ruta grav M can help relieve the pain of bruising to bone, given twice daily for a few days.

Staphysagria 200c is worth thinking about as a remedy for the patient who tries to attack the pain. Dosed twice a few hours apart it can be of real help.

Aromatherapy

Lavender oil, dropped onto a wet flannel and held against the bruise, can give a lot of relief.

Bach flower remedies

Rescue Remedy applied as a cream onto the bruise is almost as good as Arnica cream, and taken internally as drops can be used to calm the patient.

When to consult your vet

In any case where the symptoms persist for more than 48 hours, when the dog shows signs of increasing pain, or if the dog becomes listless and slow to respond to commands.

Burns and Scalds

The most common burns affecting dogs involve the pads through walking on hot ash, or else on the back and head as a result of spilling hot water or food as they get under your feet at the wrong time. Aside from the initial pain, symptoms may take some time (even days) to show, as fur can be not only protective, but also hides problems from view. Treatment of severe burns is really a matter for the vet, but minor burns can be treated safely at home.

Burns can also result from chemicals contacting the skin, and here it is vital that the vet is informed of the type of chemical as a guide to treatment, especially as it may also be a poison (see Poisoning).

Action in the field

Most burns will happen after work, but all cases respond best to immediate attention so focus on the dog and leave the work for later. Dog hair holds hot water against the skin, so it is important in scalding to soak the area in cold water first and keep the area clean afterwards (do not let the dog roll around in mud).

Herbs

Aloe vera is an excellent remedy for all burns, and every vet practice and home should grow a plant. If you have a plant, break off a leaf and squeeze out the gel-like liquid onto the burn. If you only have it as a commercial ointment or liquid, that will suffice, and you can literally plaster the area with it if you have enough.

Comfrey, marigold and St John's wort can all be made as an infusion and the burn bathed four times a day or more. Comfrey promotes healing, marigold does too and St John's wort relieves the pain.

Urtica urens (nettles) can be made also as an infusion and washed onto the wound for pain relief.

Homeopathy

Cantharis 6c, dosed three times daily, will help relieve the pain where there is blistering.

Causticum 30c twice a day is said to help severe burns heal quickly.

Kali bich 30c twice daily should be given later to help with the skin itching that occurs as a burn heals.

Urtica urens 6c three times daily can be used for mild burns to relieve the pain and aid healing.

A lotion of Arnica, Calendula and Urtica can be applied as soon as possible to the area burnt to soothe and promote healing, and as an ointment is excellent at promoting healing if the wounds blister.

Aromatherapy

Lavender oil is excellent for burns, its properties first being documented following a laboratory accident. Applied diluted, it will soothe and prevent infections: it is also said to promote tissue repair. The fragrance calms the patient and helps to avoid panic. Neat lavender oil can be applied directly onto burns and scalds, and every kitchen should keep some nearby.

Bach flower remedies

Rescue Remedy can be again applied as a cream onto the burn, as well as using drops given orally to calm the patient.

When to consult your vet

In any case where the eye is affected, and in anything other than very mild cases.

Choking and Collapse

Working dogs are exposed to situations that can cause choking, and if severe, they can collapse and stop breathing. Causes can include running onto sticks, broken bones from the quarry species getting lodged in the throat or across the roof of the mouth between the teeth, tennis balls thrown as dummies (much better to use the shaped versions now available for training), the list goes on. Symptoms of something wrong in the airway can include pawing at the mouth, gagging, drooling and in severe cases bluish gums and collapse.

Action in the field

For the patient distressed but conscious, seek help in holding the dog as you obviously cannot muzzle it to prevent panic biting of yourself and the volunteer help. This is the sort of situation where your training the dog to be examined will pay dividends as it will be more confident in allowing you to open its mouth even when distressed. Once open, secure the mouth if you can to stop it closing on your hand. Using a pair of forceps, tweezers or even a pair of pliers, attempt to dislodge anything obvious with the exception of sticks that have gone down the back of the throat or under the tongue as these need professional attention to avoid further problems with bits left behind. If you cannot remove or deal with the problem, get to the vet without delay.

For the unconscious patient a good rule to remember is the ABC: Airway, Breathing and then Circulation as the order of events to consider.

Extend the head and gently pull the tongue forward to open the airway, check the mouth and throat (your torch is now useful) for anything causing an obstruction and remove it. If there is a lot of saliva, position the dog with its head lower than its chest to encourage the flow outwards.

Next check the breathing. If this has stopped you will need to breathe for your dog, and the technique for this is to close the dog's mouth and cover the dog's nose with your mouth. Breathe in to the dog's nose for a couple of seconds until you can just see you are inflating the chest, and then allow it to deflate before repeating the process. The breath rate to aim for is said to be thirty breaths per minute but this is probably impractical. Every so often stop for a bit to see if the patient has started breathing for itself.

You should also now be checking for a pulse or heartbeat by feeling the

CPR Large dog

femoral pulse or chest wall. If the dog has a heartbeat just continue breathing for it until it starts to breathe on its own again, checking the pulse from time to time as well as that the gums are pink and well oxygenated. If there is no heartbeat you will have to try CPR. CPR is Cardiopulmonary Resuscitation. It is much easier with two people and should be kept up until either you reach the vet, or the patient has obviously passed away. You will effectively be both breathing for the dog and keeping the circulation going with chest compressions. These latter vary in method according to the size of the dog and two pictures of the possibilities are shown here.

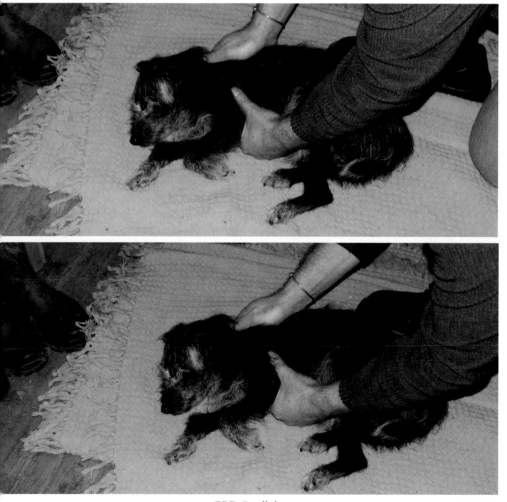

CPR Small dog

If you are alone, then you should aim to breathe for the dog at a rate of thirty breaths per minute, applying chest compressions at a rate of about eighty per minute. Aim for two breaths per fifteen compressions, bearing in mind you cannot do both at once and have to alternate between them. If there is help, then give one breath every three to five compressions. Reading this you will be wondering how these figures add up, but take heart from the fact that your compressions also move air in and out of the lungs, and so compressions take priority over breaths.

In any dog that has no heartbeat then your chances of success, it has to be said, are minimal but it is worth trying. If you have not been able to resuscitate the dog after fifteen minutes then it is probably best stopping your efforts as there will be other damage occurring due to the lack of oxygenation.

Homeopathy

 In acute situations giving first aid remedies frequently and together can be well worth trying. Although it breaks all the rules of classical homeopathy to do so, it has helped me get patients through crises many times.

Aconite 30c should be given for any shock, and to calm fears, including that of the head being approached.

Arnica 30c has uses in shock as well as for tissue damage and is said to help the heart.

Carbo veg 200c is well worth trying on any collapsed case.

Ferrum phos 30c is said to be a reviver if the collapse is following a fever, and also from loss of blood or any body fluids.

Aromatherapy

 Frankincense and rose oils as well as lavender may be used as 'background scents' to aid restorative rest once the situation has stabilised. All three may be used together if available, but should not be applied directly to the patient; instead put some on a tissue and allow the scent to circulate the patient's immediate area.

Bach flower remedies

 As always, Rescue Remedy is the first port of call, and this can be given every five minutes. I have used this many times during operations in elderly and sick cases where the patient has been struggling, and their situation has then stabilised. I also used to use it routinely on recovery from anaesthetics but we had to stop giving it to young bitches after spays as they became too bouncy! Dose every five minutes at first, then hourly on recovery to try to prevent relapse.

Rock Rose can be used to calm panic on recovery.

Acupressure

 Governor Vessel 26 has been researched and used extensively as the point for resuscitation and to stimulate breathing (see Chapter 4).

When to consult your vet

 Always after any incident of this kind to ensure there are no long term or other associated problems that merit investigation and treatment.

Claws

Just like your nails, claws can be broken and torn. Amazingly, if this happens during a day's work, the first thing noticed may be the blood all over the car on the way home. The pain tends to come later when the adrenaline rush has worn off. However, the majority of nail injuries are immediately painful, with the dog unable to put the paw down, or limping badly.

Action in the field

 If the affected nail is broken and loose you can grip the broken bit firmly and tug it off sharply, but beware, the pain can cause the mildest dog to bite so if in doubt, ask the experts. Cracked or firmly held fragments may need an anaesthetic to remove. There is an awful lot of nail unseen inside the skin of the toe, so do not attempt to pull if the nail is broken right up by the cuticle. In all cases where there is bleeding, apply firm pressure with a pad for a few minutes until bleeding stops. Remember prevention is better than cure, and well-trimmed nails are less likely to tear than overgrown ones. Puppies should be accustomed to having their nails clipped from the start, and where dew-claws are present, these must be kept trimmed as short as possible. If the dew-claw digit sustains damage so that it sticks out at an angle, it may be appropriate to tape it close to the dog's wrist until it can be examined by a vet.

Simple home treatments

 Some people swear by applying honey to the cut to slow bleeding, and certainly honey has antiseptic and antibacterial properties. It is however, pretty sticky if you have to clean the area afterwards, so do not use this if your next stop is the vet.

Healthy nails can be encouraged by adding omega 3 fatty acids such as fish or flaxseed oils to the diet. I especially like halibut oil, and the knock-on benefits of this can be seen in energised and gleaming dogs. It is a sad fact that there can never be enough omega 3 when compared with omega 6 in processed foods, and this can be a cause of poor nails in some dogs.

Herbs

Calendula and St John's wort tincture can be used as a rinse on nail injuries. This reduces swelling and helps to prevent infection. If removal of the nail is needed, washing with this before and after is said to reduce bleeding.

Homeopathy

Staphysagria 30c given twice on the day of injury helps reduce pain and also phobia about the foot being touched after an injury.

Phosphorous 30c given hourly for four hours to cases where the blood is oozing persistently will often stop the flow.

A lotion made up from Arnica, Calendula and Urtica is excellent for soaking the foot in to heal any injuries to feet and claws.

When to consult your vet

When the torn nail needs to be removed, or if lameness persists for more than 24 hours.

Collapse – see Choking

Concussion – See Bruising

Cuts and Scrapes – See Wounds

Cysts – See Abscess section as the treatment is more or less the same

Dehydration and Heat Exhaustion

Dehydration in dogs can be a serious matter. Whether caused by illness, exposure to heat, or a simple lack of fluid intake, dehydration must be

Panting causes loss of body fluids

addressed immediately. If left untreated, it can cause health problems, and in extreme circumstances, death. It is very easy for a dog to become dehydrated; easier than many owners realise. Fortunately it is also easy to prevent dehydration in dogs and it is very important to do so.

Dehydration is an excessive loss of bodily fluids. It most often involves the loss of water and minerals such as sodium, chloride, and potassium, collectively called electrolytes. It can be caused by illness (especially if the dog has a fever) such as diarrhoea or vomiting, exposure to or working in extreme heat, and a number of other factors. A dog's natural act of panting causes a loss of fluids and can result in dehydration if these are not replaced. Remember that dogs lack sweat glands to keep them cool and they pant in an effort to regulate their body temperature. A panting dog is a hot dog.

Dogs may also be seen to thermoregulate behaviourally as a response to dehydration. Dehydrated dogs make few movements of the head and limbs, generally lying with the head resting on the forelegs. They will certainly be reluctant to work.

Heat exhaustion is a form of dehydration in the dog, as a well-hydrated dog can tolerate high temperatures and physical demands when working. A heat-exhausted dog will show disorientation and loss of responsiveness to command, as well as the progression to collapse that dehydration causes.

Symptoms of dehydration:

1. The skin loses elasticity as it loses moisture. This can be somewhat misleading because younger and fatter dogs will have more elasticity than older, thinner dogs. It is important to have an idea of what your dog's skin looks and feels like on a normal basis. Pinch a little skin between your thumb and forefinger on your dog's back. When you release it, it should pop back into place immediately. (You can try this on the back of your own hand as an example.) As the tissue under the skin loses moisture, the skin moves back more slowly. In extreme cases, the skin doesn't pop back at all.

2. The eyes appear sunken and lack moisture.

3. The mouth appears dry, as do the gums and nose.

4. Delayed capillary refill time: pull up your dog's lip and look at its gums. Place your index finger firmly against the gums so that they appear white. Remove your finger and see how quickly the blood returns to the gums (they will become pink in that area again). This is called capillary refill time. If you do this when everything is normal, you will have a basis with which to compare. The gums of a normal dog refill immediately; the gums of a dehydrated dog could take three seconds or so to return to their pink state.

Action in the field

Lots of water is the best way to replace fluids, but a severely dehydrated dog should not be allowed to take in large amounts at once. This will result in vomiting and a further loss of fluids. Instead let the dog drink small amounts over a period of time. Some dogs will accept liquid syringed into their mouths, and will take more that way. Electrolytes can be replaced with a hydrating solution, and there are many commercial products for this on the market, any of which are worth considering keeping in your first aid kit. However, when these are not immediately available, a dessertspoonful of honey, with a pinch of salt dissolved in a pint of water, is a useful second best.

See also Choking section for homeopathic remedies which help with fluid loss and collapsing.

When to consult your vet

Any dog that seems dehydrated or refuses to drink should be seen by a vet to determine appropriate treatment and whether the dehydration is a symptom of some other ailment.

Diarrhoea

It has been said that diarrhoea always has character! Observing the colour, development and progression of a diarrhoea problem is a vital aid to diagnosis in more severe cases. However, dogs are fairly prone to mild diarrhoea and they do not need to be rushed to the vet at the first sign of anything other than a perfect stool. Diarrhoea can vary from a soft, cow-pat like stool, to watery mucous, the latter obviously being the more serious. Causes can be many: viruses, bad food (that lovely rotten rabbit crunched enthusiastically on a walk), contaminated drinking water, even just excitement at going out for the day.

The first rule of diarrhoea is to not feed any infection, so starve the patient for twenty-four hours. Often this alone will solve the problem. Following the period of starvation a small amount of bland non-irritant food for a couple of days is a good idea, and in this circumstance, starches may be fed. Scrambled egg with rice or mashed potato is a good standby, before introducing normal food again. Chicken and rice used to be the recommended bland diet but many dogs now are becoming sensitive to chicken, possibly as a result of the chemicals used in the poultry industry, so I advise to steer clear unless you have a good organic source of this meat.

Simple home treatments

Kaolin oral liquids from the chemist are a good way to help most diarrhoea. These contain a clay which absorbs the diarrhoea-causing bacteria and poisons in the gut, as well as having well-known ingredients such as charcoal and bismuth. Doses generally are a teaspoon per 10 kg bodyweight hourly for four hours. If you don't have this then arrowroot powder, oatmeal porridge, tapioca or semolina are useful alternatives.

If the diarrhoea is very watery, rehydration of your dog can be aided by offering a mix of one pint water to one dessertspoonful of honey and a large pinch of salt. Water is carried better across the gut wall in the presence of glucose, and the salt, similar to many of the sports drinks one sees sold today, assists the glucose.

Once over the 24-hour starve, it is useful to add some dietary fibre in the form of freshly crushed flaxseed, at a rate of half a teaspoon per 10 kg bodyweight to each meal. Dogs that are reluctant to drink much may be tempted by that good old-fashioned panacea chicken broth, made from real chicken of course, with a little salt and honey added.

Herbs

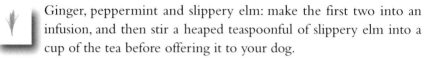

Ginger, peppermint and slippery elm: make the first two into an infusion, and then stir a heaped teaspoonful of slippery elm into a cup of the tea before offering it to your dog.

Chamomile tea is a good alternative to calm the gut, and is probably preferable for puppies.

Homeopathy

Aloes 30c is indicated for spluttery, jelly-like diarrhoea. Dose three times daily.

Arsenicum alb 30c is probably the major diarrhoea remedy in the dog. Its indication is for watery burning diarrhoea, often caused by eating bad food, and it will calm the restless and anxious patient. Dose hourly for four doses.

Colocynthis 30c may be given hourly for the dog that is hunched up with pain.

Merc sol 30c can be given for foul-smelling, watery and bloody stools with constant urging and straining. Dose three times daily.

Podophyllum 30c is for painless watery stools that gush from the rectum, and there will be the characteristic rumbling of the intestines. Dose three times daily.

Sulphur 30c is indicated for the bright yellow to orange diarrhoea that greets you at breakfast, with that foul, rotting odour. Dose three times daily.

Aromatherapy

Peppermint is an anti-spasmodic oil, and can be diluted in a little massage oil (or vegetable oil if nothing else is to hand) and massaged into the ear tips. Dogs get a lot of stomach pain with diarrhoea and the response to this can be quite remarkable at times.

When to consult your vet

Vets generally are taught to let most diarrhoea run its course, to starve and treat as we have discussed. However, if the diarrhoea persists for more than 24 hours, blood is seen in the stool, or if the patient appears obviously lethargic and unwell, then advice should be sought. It is worth noting that older dogs may become weak in their back legs, even to the point of collapse, and puppies can dehydrate quickly with diarrhoea and so need veterinary care earlier. Diarrhoea with vomiting is also serious in the dog, and needs attention.

Drowning

Not a common problem, but wildfowling dogs that get into trouble in rough water are at risk, and I have had to treat a spaniel that dived for a bird in a ditch and came up under bramble debris such that she couldn't get her head above water. She was only saved an untimely end by the Gun ignoring risk to himself and jumping up to his waist in the freezing water, pushing through the brambles and hauling her out. Dogs that fall through ice and then get trapped underneath will need urgent treatment for hypothermia as well.

Action in the field

 Suspend the dog by its hind legs to encourage the water to drain from the lungs.

Press your palms either side of the chest and push firmly to expel water from the lungs.

Close the dog's mouth and blow hard into the nose to clear it and to open the lungs.

Once recovering, keep the dog's head down relative to the chest for a while to aid any further water left in the lungs to drain.

If the dog is not breathing, or if there is no heartbeat, follow the instructions on resuscitation.

Homeopathy

Aconite 30c for shock, can be given every few minutes to calm the patient and help reduce collapse from shock.

Sulphur 30c can be given after Aconite for the more chronic symptoms of shock. Cases that will be helped by this will show signs of disorientation and the gums will be bright red.

When to consult your vet

Any dog that has taken brackish water into the lungs will need antibiotic cover for the probable pneumonia that will result, and this is best given immediately rather than waiting for symptoms to develop.

Ears

Man has bred many different types of ear into dog breeds, and not all have a lot of logic in their design. Folded over ears are warmer and can be more prone to infection that is at the same time hidden from view, while some breeds have narrow ear canals that hold wax and get infected. Others have ears hairy on the inside, resulting in the same problems. It is a good idea to check your dog's ears regularly, ensuring they are clean and not inflamed in any way.

Most ear problems only affect the outer part of the ear and can be simply treated at home. Remember never to poke anything into the ear, such as cotton-buds, as you cannot see what you are doing and may cause more harm than good.

Action in the field

 During dry weather, and in all dogs with spaniel-type ears, check the ears for plant seeds and remove any before they have a chance to fall down the ear canal. Visible seeds can be removed with tweezers.

If they are distressed, to sooth the dog temporarily you can fill the ear canal with olive oil to try and float up any seeds.

For cuts which bleed enthusiastically, pressure with the tea towel, and in severe cases bandaging (see relevant sections), is a good idea, and some use honey applied to the wound to both clean it and stem bleeding.

Simple home treatments

 If there is mild inflammation then some warm almond or olive oil poured into the ear, followed by gentle massage of the 'ice-cream cone' of the ear canal that can be felt below the outer ear, will float most problems to the surface.

For dirty waxy ears a dilute solution of white vinegar, one teaspoon to half a pint of water, is a useful cleaning aid and can be syringed into the ear canal, which is then massaged and wiped clean. This will also clear many mild yeast (musty smelling) infections.

Herbs

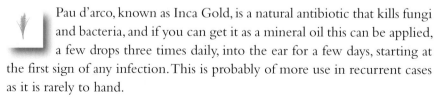 Pau d'arco, known as Inca Gold, is a natural antibiotic that kills fungi and bacteria, and if you can get it as a mineral oil this can be applied, a few drops three times daily, into the ear for a few days, starting at the first sign of any infection. This is probably of more use in recurrent cases as it is rarely to hand.

Homeopathy

 Belladonna 30c given hourly for four doses will relieve an acutely hot, red ear.

Ferrum phos 30c is very useful to give after the Belladonna if there is no discharge and the redness has not completely gone. Dose three times daily.

Hepar sulph 6c for any pus or creamy discharge from the ear. Dose three times daily.

Merc cor 30c for ears that produce a black, thick waxy discharge with a dark redness to the visible ear canal. Dose twice a day.

Pulsatilla 30c for thick yellow discharges. Surprisingly often the ear canal will not even appear inflamed in these cases. Dose twice a day.

Silica 6c for yellow or greenish discharges. These cases will often have swelling around the ear. Dose three times daily.

Aromatherapy

Lavender oil, dropped onto a warm wet flannel and held against the ear, can give a lot of relief.

Bach flower remedies

 Mimulus can help calm the patient that will not allow you to look at the ear.

Rescue Remedy is useful on arrival at the vet if ears have been a recurrent problem and the patient dislikes having them examined.

Other

'Thornit' is gentle and very effective (see Useful Addresses). Many breeders and trainers swear by it as a treatment for long-term problems, for alleviating acute problems and treating ear mites.

When to consult your vet

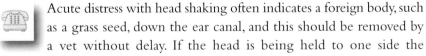 Acute distress with head shaking often indicates a foreign body, such as a grass seed, down the ear canal, and this should be removed by a vet without delay. If the head is being held to one side the infection is deeper and may be affecting the middle part of the ear – seek professional help soon and put nothing yourself down the ear until it has been checked. Dogs can also suffer a problem known as a haematoma, where a blood vessel is broken in the earflap, which swells with blood. This needs

Electric fencing hazard

212

to be drained to prevent the ear scrunching up like a cauliflower with scar tissue at a later date.

Electric Fences

Common on many shoots – all too frequently a dog can get a nasty shock while working, and with young dogs, this can confuse them and possibly put them off for life. I have found the homeopathic remedy Staphysagria 200c, which resolves issues around resentment of injury and invasion of personal space, given before training a few times goes a long way in helping the dogs get over this. It also works too for the human companion that didn't check for the electric fence the other side of the hedge beside which he had answered the call of nature! Gelsemium 30c is useful for the "frightened rabbit" syndrome, where a stress creates paralysis and inability to move.

Electric Shock

Puppies are notorious for chewing electric wires, and quite nasty burns can result. IF you find an electrocuted dog, the first rule is to STOP and THINK as you could end up in trouble as well if not careful. Many animals urinate when shocked, and if you tread in that urine, which is a good electrical conductor, you could get a shock too. Find and switch off the electrical source first before doing anything at all. Once you are absolutely sure this has been done, separate the patient from the wire and then, if they are not breathing, apply artificial respiration (mouth to nose, gently holding the muzzle closed) and massage the chest vigorously in between breaths, while someone phones the vet.

Herbs

The main problem with electric shock survivors is organ failure some time afterwards. Herbal treatments should be directed towards supporting the liver and de-toxifying the body. Burdock, centaury, dandelion, nettle and cleavers can be obtained as tincture, or combined and made into a tea. Give a dessertspoon of the mix three or four times daily.

Homeopathy

Natrum sulph 6c twice daily for ten days can be given to support the liver.

Bach flower remedies

Rescue Remedy should be given immediately, and hourly for at least six hours.

When to consult your vet

Always!

Exhaustion – see Dehydration

Eye Injuries

Dogs need to search under bushes and brambles for their quarry, and eyes can occasionally get scratched and infected; fragments of dirt, grass and bark may also get trapped under the lids. Again difficulties have been created for some dogs by selective breeding for odd head shapes, where the relationship of lids, eyeballs and sockets is not as evolution determined, and so the eyes can become more exposed to injury. This is particularly seen in short-nosed

Working conditions for getting sore eyes

breeds. Problems show first as watery discharges and a squint, and may progress to soreness and pus-like discharges if more severe.

Action in the field

 Mild problems often respond to simple bathing of the eye in salt water (one teaspoon added to a pint of boiled water and allowed to cool before applying) or the liberal application of Optrex drops. If dirt or some other foreign body is trapped, use bathing liberally to flush the problem out. Attention should be immediate when the problem is spotted to prevent more serious injury.

Do not attempt to remove objects such as thorns that have penetrated the eyeball. This is a job for the vet.

Simple home treatments

Cold tea, made with fresh leaves and stewed for just a minute, then allowed to cool, is a good old-fashioned cleansing lotion for eyes. A mistake many people make is to use teabags, but these are held together with glue that can be an irritant and so should not be used.

... and the result

Herbs

Euphrasia, the everyday name of which is 'eyebright', can be purchased as a sterile tincture, and a few drops added to an eyebath then applied to the eye. It is very soothing and antiseptic, as well as having antioxidant properties which help healing.

Homeopathy

Argentum nit 30c should be given if any infection starts to appear, and especially if there is any cloudiness of the cornea (the glassy part of the eye). Dose three times daily.

Arnica 30c given following any injury helps prevent bruising and haemorrhage. Dose hourly for four doses.

Ledum pal 30c is given for 'poking' injuries such as a stick into the eye. Dose twice a day.

Symphytum 30c should be given three times daily to any case where the eyeball is injured to relieve pain and encourage healing.

When to consult your vet

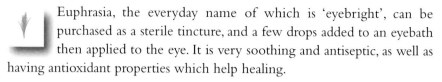

If problems persist for more than 24 hours, or immediately if there is any cloudiness or obvious scratch affecting the glassy part of the eye – the cornea – and if the discharges turn coloured, indicating infection.

Falls – See Bruising, Fractures and Bandaging sections as needed

Female System

Bitches can suffer from a number of problems relating to their cycle. The first are excessive symptoms of false pregnancy, and this is thought to indicate an increased likelihood of developing the second major problem, which is pyometra, after subsequent seasons. Pyometra is a type of womb infection and it can occur at any stage within the nine-week period after the season, but typically sooner rather than later. The bitch will start drinking excessively, may produce a discharge of pus from the vulva, and as the problem progresses will start vomiting. This condition is a medical emergency and the only solution is an emergency hysterectomy. However, the majority of bitches will not develop these problems, and prevention of these problems is not, to my mind, reason enough for spaying a bitch in the middle of her life unless indications are that they are happening.

Herbs

Raspberry leaf tablets from the middle of the season until three to four weeks afterwards are thought to cleanse the uterus and make pyometra less likely. They should not be used if the bitch is pregnant as raspberry leaf tea is an abortifacient.

Homeopathy

Pulsatilla 30c is useful to relieve the symptoms of false pregnancy, especially the behavioural changes. Usually given twice a day until symptoms subside.

Prolactin 30c is the main remedy used for bitches that produce milk at this time. Give three times daily for five days.

Aromatherapy

German chamomile or rose oils help ease female reproductive problems, and can be applied in diluted form massaged gently into the abdomen, or used in diffusion, or else by putting a few drops on the bitch's bedding. If she refuses the treatment, then do not persist because if the oils are needed, the dog will often seek them out.

Bach flower remedies

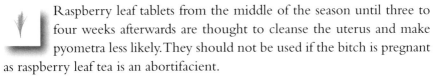

Mimulus is a very useful remedy for the male dogs in the house (or next door). When the bitch is in season the males will sometimes do anything to get to her, or pine and stop eating if they cannot. At its worst they will howl constantly, with the associated neighbourly complaints flooding in. Mimulus is excellent at reducing all these symptoms, dosed three times daily, but note that it produces a reduction in the behaviour only, and should the couple get together it will not stop them mating. I've even known one client so impressed with Mimulus that she added it to her husband's mineral water!

When to consult your vet

This section is included more because one needs to know the normal aspects, rather than any treatments. The best thing one can do if problems occur is seek professional help, and all problems are best treated sooner rather than later.

Fish Hooks

We tend to take our companions with us wherever we go in the field, even if it is just for a stroll if they are not required to work that day. When with us fishing, or investigating places where others have been fishing, dogs can suffer two types of injury.

Firstly, they can get hooked in the lip, mouth or body. This is obviously very painful so unless it would prevent access to the hook, muzzle the dog first before attending to the problem. To remove the hook push the barb all the way through, cut it with wire cutters (or similar) and remove the pieces.

The second common situation is the dog eating a baited hook and line. This can be especially serious if the line has a swivel and weight attached as this can cause the intestines to bunch up and even perforate. Surgery may be needed to resolve the problem. If just a hook and line is swallowed, it is unlikely you can pull it out, so do not try to do so or you may set the hook. Instead, cut off the line as short as practical and feed bread to try and dislodge the hook and carry it through the intestines. Often it will go through but watch out for signs of problems beginning.

Homeopathy

Staphysagria 200c is said to relieve the pain and trauma of tearing wounds similar to those created by fish hooks.

When to consult your vet

Keep an eye on rectal temperature and whether any vomiting or other sign of illness occurs. If in doubt seek help quickly as peritonitis can set in if the intestines are punctured. Occasionally surgery will be needed to remove the offending hook and/or line.

Fits, Faints and Collapse

The causes of any of these are multiple, and often impossible to assess in the field.

Action in the field

In all cases keep the dog quiet, ideally in a darkened place, and be aware that in the immediate recovery period dogs can panic to the point of lashing out with their teeth, and they can even sometimes run away blindly, so pop a lead on. If the dog is sick whilst unconscious, or if breathing stops, then refer to the section on choking and collapse. On the dog's recovery from a fit or collapsing episode, offer some sugary food, as the brain will have been depleted of glucose by its frenetic activity in a fit, and in other cases collapse can be simply due to a drop in blood sugar whilst working hard. Usually someone on a shoot has some biscuits or sweets. Chocolate, whilst poisonous in large amounts, is probably better than doing nothing, bearing in mind that most chocolate bars have very little actual chocolate and a lot of sugar in them, but avoid dark or catering chocolate, or blocks of solid chocolate. If working on a hot day, check the dog's temperature to make sure the cause is not heatstroke, and if so treat accordingly (see Heat Stroke/Hyperthermia).

Check the pulse and note its rate and character as information for the vet.

Homeopathy

Aconite 30c given every few minutes for four or five doses will help if the patient is choking and panicking.

Carbo veg 30 or 200c is of use if the dog has lost consciousness, and seems cold to touch.

Plumbum 30c seems to help cases that have instability of the head, eyes and/or limbs after a fit.

When to consult your vet

Some collapsing episodes are transient and only last a very short time, but these often indicate more serious matters developing and so even if recovery is quick, do always get your dog checked out afterwards.

Foreign Bodies

For eyes and ears this has already been covered, so what we are discussing here is the swallowed or chewed item. Puppies especially are devils for swallowing bits of plastic toys, bits of rubber balls and all manner of other objects. Occasionally this can persist into adulthood, and some dogs, spaniels especially it seems, will chew and swallow items such as stones, clothing and so on. Therefore if you have a pup in the chewing phase, or an adult with a chewing history, be alert to signs of trouble. The first sign is usually vomiting, especially vomiting back anything eaten or drunk. Then, as the problem persists, tenderness around the abdomen can occur, and the patient becomes quiet and withdrawn. Thinking around the subject may reveal a missing sock, underwear, plastic toy or similar, and it is as well to consult a vet as soon as practical. These cases can present a diagnostic challenge, especially if the item swallowed will not show on an X-Ray. Often the dog will need surgery to remove the offending item so the guidance below is really preparatory for this.

Action in the field

In the field, dogs can chew sticks and bones, or worse can run onto sticks which penetrate the throat, eyes, chest and so on. Anything stuck in the mouth can be removed with forceps, or even a pair of pliers, taking care not to get yourself bitten in the process. Sticks that have penetrated deeply are best removed by the vet as any small fragments left behind can set up severe abscessing. For chest penetration see Gunshot wounds.

Homeopathy

Arnica 30c should be given before going to the vet, to ease the bruising of any possible surgery, and for the relief of pain. Continue the treatment three times daily post-operatively at home.

Carbo veg 30c; dose every fifteen minutes whilst on the way to the vet, for any animal that has collapsed, has blue mucous membranes, and/or is cold to touch.

Colocynthis 30c can be given hourly for the relief of gut cramps, and dogs that need this will be restless and walk around with a hunched back, and often also a bloated abdomen.

Aromatherapy

Lavender oil massaged into the ear tips can bring great pain relief.

Bach flower remedies

Use Rescue Remedy if the patient is collapsed. Dose every fifteen minutes for four doses.

When to consult your vet

Always if you believe your dog has swallowed an item.

Fractures

Broken bones are usually pretty obvious to almost any observer, and they necessitate a trip to the vet to define the problem and how it may be resolved, often surgically. However, dogs can be surprisingly good at coping with a limb fracture, and the only outward sign may be an intermittent lameness, or holding a leg up. With a prop on each corner they can get around quite well on three legs. Obviously pain on examination will be revealed, often with a detectable 'click' or grating as the broken ends of bone rub together. Limb fractures are not necessarily a life-threatening emergency, apart from relief of pain, so many surgeons will prefer to wait for swelling to subside before operating, but attention will always be needed to stabilise the problem and prevent complications. Spinal fractures will usually result in paralysis, or in some cases paralysis of some parts with rigidity of others. Pelvic fractures may just present as reluctance to walk on one or both hind legs, while broken ribs usually present as reluctance to move around with pain and swelling over the rib cage. Sometimes you will detect a clicking when feeling gently over the ribs. Occasionally when ribs are broken in a number of places a section can be seen to move in the opposite direction to the phase of breathing. This is a condition known as 'flail chest' and requires immediate veterinary attention

Action in the field

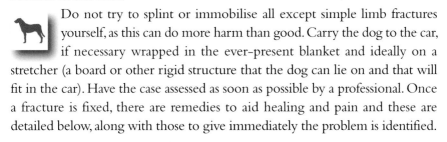

Do not try to splint or immobilise all except simple limb fractures yourself, as this can do more harm than good. Carry the dog to the car, if necessary wrapped in the ever-present blanket and ideally on a stretcher (a board or other rigid structure that the dog can lie on and that will fit in the car). Have the case assessed as soon as possible by a professional. Once a fracture is fixed, there are remedies to aid healing and pain and these are detailed below, along with those to give immediately the problem is identified.

Herbs

Comfrey (also known as 'knit bone') and horsetail are both reputed to aid faster healing of bones, and comfrey is also said to reduce pain as the bone heals. The leaves of either can be made into a tea and applied locally around a break unless it has been put in a plaster cast.

Comfrey root can be made into a decoction (different from a tea or infusion, this involves simmering for ten minutes and then straining off the healing liquid) and taken as a drink, one teaspoon three times daily, until the fracture is healed.

Homeopathy

Arnica 30c may be given initially for shock and bruising. It is often used by some consultant orthopaedic surgeons pre- and post-operatively to reduce swelling and bruising, making the operation easier.

Calc phos 30c is useful given daily to young pups that suffer fractures, to speed the healing. It is also indicated in all cases where a growth plate has been damaged, to try and restore its development potential.

Eupatorium perforatum 6c can be given twice daily where there is aching pain in bones. It is hard to assess this without speaking 'dog', but I tend to give it to those that grumble and cannot settle after surgery.

Hypericum 30c can be given as often as is needed if nerves have been damaged and the pain is severe. It is especially useful for crushed toes and for fractures of the upper arm.

Symphytum 6c is the homeopathic comfrey, and can be given daily whilst the fracture heals.

Bach flower remedies

Rescue Remedy should be given initially for the shock.

Walnut can be given three times daily to settle patients that find the immobility hard to deal with.

When to consult the vet

Always.

Gunshot wounds and Goring injuries

Fortunately I have only had to treat a couple of severe cases of these problems, but the latter especially is not uncommon in countries where boar are hunted routinely, and so this may become more of a concern in the UK with the increase in population of wild boar. Both muntjac and Chinese water deer can cause deep injuries with their tusks, and a dog that encounters the antlers of larger deer, especially the stabbing tines of roe or sika, can be really badly hurt.

Gunshot injuries vary enormously in severity. Accidental peppering by a shotgun at long range may just result in bruising, but if close, the damage is likely to be widespread through many tissues. X-rays will be needed to determine the extent and depth of the problem. Rifle bullets are extremely serious as most used for hunting are designed to expand on impact, and so the

Antlered fallow deer

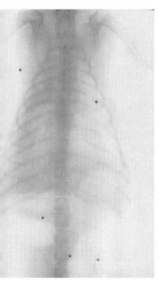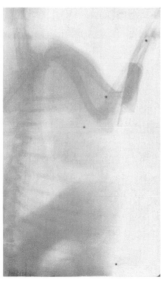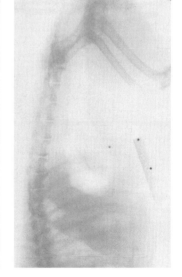

Gunshot wounds

223

exit wound will be greater than that of the entry, and tissue damage will be severe. Certain types of bullet also have a physical hydrostatic shocking effect that extends beyond the direct injury, and while this is unlikely to be obvious externally, there will be a lot of bleeding into surrounding tissues. All projectiles impacting into the body carry in contamination from hair and external dirt which makes immediate cleaning a priority once the patient has survived the initial impact.

Goring injuries can be a puncture type wound or a lacerating injury from the ripping tusks or antlers. They will be more localised but no less painful for that, but the problems of shock to tissues and exit wounds will not occur.

Action in the field

If the patient survives the initial accident then information on bleeding, bruising, bandaging and wound care is all useful to refer to. Get the dog to the vet as soon as possible as internal damage is rarely obvious and will need professional assessment. For all injuries, clean up the wounds as soon as possible with an antiseptic cleanser, even if that is just salt water. Do not apply homeopathic creams such as hypericum and calendula until the case has been assessed, as these can cause wounds to close over quickly and often small puncture wounds are best left to discharge any infection. Remove any hair from wounds using tweezers, and if near the surface, remove any obvious pellets.

If the injury has penetrated the chest, the lungs may be collapsed and you will need to try and reduce the effects of this by bandaging an occlusive dressing (bandage coated with cream or similar to prevent air flow through it) to the chest to cover and reduce airflow through the hole (do not do this too tightly, so as not to restrict breathing). If the patient will let you, it is worth blowing into the dog's nose to inflate the lung whilst a helper is covering the hole with the bandage. If nothing else, just holding your hand firmly over the sucking wound can help. Pink frothy blood around the wound or from the mouth should be noted for the vet as this can indicate bleeding into the airways. Some think this is a sign of terminal damage, but it may not be so, especially if the damage was due to pellets as opposed to expanding bullets, so don't condemn the dog on this symptom alone.

Homeopathy and other remedies

See remedies for anxiety and shock, bruising, bleeding, and wound care.

Of particular use is the remedy Staphysagria 200c, given frequently for the pain and shock of penetrating injuries.

Phosphorous 30c is used, given frequently, to help cases where there is oozing of fresh bright blood and would be worth considering if a ballistic type of bullet that causes hydrostatic shock was the culprit.

When to consult your vet

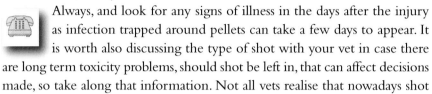

Always, and look for any signs of illness in the days after the injury as infection trapped around pellets can take a few days to appear. It is worth also discussing the type of shot with your vet in case there are long term toxicity problems, should shot be left in, that can affect decisions made, so take along that information. Not all vets realise that nowadays shot can be made of other metals than lead.

Heat stroke/Hyperthermia

Dogs being left in hot cars is the commonest cause of heat stroke, but do not forget this possibility if working your dog on a very hot day. Dogs cannot sweat over their bodies, and so they lose heat by panting and through the pads. When this simple system of heat control is overcome, then the dogs will rapidly heat up, become lethargic and may even collapse. Symptoms of this condition include an elevated body temperature (40°C/104°F+), persistent panting, sluggishness in response to command, bright brick-red gums, a rapid heart rate, weakness, muscle tremors and in some cases vomiting and diarrhoea. Severe cases can progress to developing collapse and convulsions. These cases can be confused with fever, but the circumstances of heat stroke (hot day, left in car, etc.) should be obvious as the differential.

Action in the field

First aid is to get the animal into shade, and either apply ice packs to the body, place the dog in a cool bath, or ideally run a cold hose over the dog.

Fans are really useful as circulating air carries away heat.

Cold water, given by mouth, with a teaspoon of honey and a pinch of salt added can help a lot if your dog will accept it.

Herbs

Chickweed, nettle and peppermint are a cooling combination and a cold infusion can be bathed over the patient as they recover (although there is rarely time to get this ready unless there are many hands available).

Homeopathy

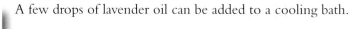

Aconite 30c is useful in mild cases showing signs of restlessness and delirium. Dose hourly for four doses.

Belladonna 30c given every five minutes for four doses, then every half hour for two hours is very useful. This is the primary homeopathic remedy for heatstroke.

Camphor 30c is said to help if there is dehydration and the gums are dry in appearance. These patients will be restless and anxious. Dose hourly as needed.

Aromatherapy

A few drops of lavender oil can be added to a cooling bath.

When to consult the vet

You will need to contact the vet as this can rapidly prove fatal, and intravenous fluids may be needed. Overheating, unless due to an obvious cause such as being left in a hot car, can be an indication that other problems exist in the patient and so ALL cases should be taken immediately to the vet for a check over and further treatment as required.

Hypothermia

Hypothermia (being too cold) can occur in dogs exposed to cold or wet weather, especially if it is very windy. A body temperature below 37°C/98.6°F is hypothermic, easily checked with a thermometer, and demands immediate attention.

Action in the field

Be prepared for this if you ask your dog to work in very cold and wet conditions. Wrap the dog in blankets or a space blanket, get the car heating going and head off as soon as possible to a warm environment. Human body heat can help warm up a cold dog too, so if you have help, one of you can drive and the other can hug the dog.

It is important not to panic in emergencies, and here the action to avoid is warming the dog up too quickly. Advice concerning rate of warming varies, but 1°C per hour until you reach a body temperature of 38°C/100.4°F is a useful guide.

Homeopathy

Initially, as soon as practical, give a dose of Camphor 30c every fifteen minutes. Once the temperature is coming up, then give Aconite 30c hourly for four to six doses. Then review the symptoms of the case. If the patient is restless and develops diarrhoea, give Arsenicum album 30c three times in 24 hours. If the eyes and nose are running clear fluid give Bellis perennis 30c, if coughing give Hepar sulph 6c, and if not eating the remedy Magnesium mur 6c is said to help.

Acupressure

Governor Vessel 26, combined with Kidney 1 (see Chapter 4) can be used to resuscitate collapsed patients.

When to consult your vet

An unexpected occurrence of hypothermia without obvious cause can indicate the presence of other underlying illness and so these cases merit veterinary attention.

Kennel Cough

A common problem each year, kennel cough is caused by a number of bacterial and viral infections that spread rapidly from dog to dog. It is usually self-limiting and will pass in a couple of weeks. There are vaccines that can be given for two of the causative organisms, but it seems these are never the ones involved in your dog's case, and some feel that dogs vaccinated against kennel cough get the other forms much more seriously. This is probably because any vaccine, although it may provide some specific protection, can also compromise the immune system.

Action in the field

Never ever work your dog with this problem, nor for a few weeks afterwards, as long-term chest problems can develop, and you risk spreading the infection to others. Dogs used in fast-running disciplines must be fully recovered before they are run again, otherwise permanent damage may result. Kennel cough is extremely contagious.

Simple home treatments

Natural cough syrups available from most health stores are fine to use for dogs; give a child's dose for most animals.

Honey and lemon juice has been used for years to soothe sore throats and coughs. Two tablespoons of honey mixed with a teaspoon of lemon juice in half a cup of water is a very palatable mix that can be given often throughout the day.

Vitamin C at 250 mg per day to a 15 kg dog (scale up or down to suit) can be given for its antiviral properties, but beware, it can cause diarrhoea in some dogs.

Herbs

Echinacea and goldenseal herbs have immune stimulating properties and both can be given to strengthen the immune system. In general the liquid extracts available commercially from health shops or your holistic vet are best.

Mullein is also often available and can be given, especially if the cough sounds congestive.

Old kennelmen swear by a string of raw onions hung in the dogs' sleeping area as a preventative, and some like to use cut raw onions there as well. Care should be taken to ensure that the dogs cannot reach the onions and possibly eat them, as they are toxic to dogs.

Homeopathy

Kennel Cough Nosode 30c can be obtained from a good homeopathic pharmacy and given twice daily to affected dogs with great success, and it may be combined with other remedies that may be indicated as well. The nosode is also a useful preventative and many kennels now give it routinely to all dogs in their care on a weekly basis to prevent the problem occurring. Give it to your dog if it has been in contact with the illness; every year my dogs come into contact with kennel cough from pet dogs being exercised after a spell in kennels while their owners were on holiday, and I have from personal experience found the nosodes invaluable as a preventative.

Bryonia 30c can be given three times daily to cases where the hard dry cough is set off by any movement.

Drosera 30c can be given to alleviate the spasmodic and incessant cough that has accompanying retching. Dose three times a day.

Use Veratrum alb 30c twice daily for the continuous violent barking cough.

Aromatherapy

 Eucalyptus and Cypress oils dropped into a glass of hot water will perfuse the room and help to alleviate the cough.

When to consult your vet

 Most dogs will suffer the cough with a degree of resignation, but if they become withdrawn, lethargic or develop a temperature then professional help should be sought.

Lacerations – See Barbed wire, Wounds, and Bleeding as needed

Lameness

Whilst arthritis has been covered in an earlier section – see Arthritis – and claws and cysts have also been mentioned, lameness can be caused by almost anything that stresses the locomotor system. Landing awkwardly, twisting the foot in a rabbit hole, getting caught up on fences, tearing a nail, cuts to the pad and so on are all possible causes. If the exact problem is not easily defined then some simple remedies can help speed recovery.

Action in the field

 In all undefined cases stop work to prevent more serious complications developing.

Simple home treatments

 Just as with humans, use heat and cold to alleviate the pain. Ice packs such as frozen peas, or similar, can be applied to inflamed joints and muscles in the early days after a lameness occurs to reduce swelling, but be careful not to over-use these as the dog cannot tell you when it has had enough. If problems last more than a couple of days, heat becomes more appropriate and wheat-filled bags that can be heated in the microwave are useful as they mould to the limb. Alternatively a hot water bottle wrapped in a towel can be applied as often as is needed for relief. It is important to understand that reducing the swelling and relieving the pain does not heal the injury: it merely makes it more comfortable for the patient. Pain-relieving drugs are not generally advisable here, as most dogs will run around as soon as the pain has lessened, perhaps injuring themselves further. Working dogs love their work so much that they will often do their best to continue with it, even when in an appreciable degree of pain.

Herbs

As with arthritis my favourite herbs here are the two Indian, or Ayurvedic, remedies, boswellia and turmeric (see Arthritis for doses).

Celery seed, meadowsweet and white willow are also herbs that can be combined in an infusion to drink which reduces pain and inflammation, as well as to eliminate toxins released from damaged tissue.

Devil's claw root can be made as a decoction and given as a drink. This is becoming a popular remedy for pain relief and so is often also available over the counter in a ready to use liquid or tablet form.

Homeopathy

Rhus tox, Ruta grav and Arnica 30c combined: this has proved a particularly useful combination of remedies for dogs suffering arthritis, tendon, ligament and muscle problems, including chronic back pain. Although homoeopathy traditionally adopts a 'one-remedy' approach, there are cases where exact definition of the symptoms is not possible, particularly as we cannot talk to our patients. From time to time good synergistic combinations of remedies are discovered and this is one. Dose twice daily.

Aromatherapy

Juniper or pine can be added to warm water and applied as a compress to inflamed areas.

Eucalyptus, lavender, marjoram and rosemary can be added to massage oils and rubbed into painful areas for relief.

When to consult your vet

Most lameness is temporary and should gradually get better. However, a lameness that persists beyond three days without improving generally merits attention.

Mange

Perhaps an odd inclusion for a first aid list, but this can be the scourge of working dogs in some areas, particularly if infection gets into a kennels as all incumbents will probably contract it. As foxhunting declines and fox populations increase so the risk of sarcoptic mange increases too. Homeopathy cannot itself kill mites, and herbal products sold as repellents are only that and do not stop infestation. In some instances the reaction to the mites can be intense and although you will need modern topical medications (which are thankfully now extremely effective and of low toxicity) to kill the mites, homeopathy has a history of treating the acute skin reactions, helping to prevent secondary problems arising. The remedies used are Arsenicum album 30c and Sulphur 30c, both given three times daily until symptoms subside.

Sarcoptic mange is different from demodectic mange, and the latter is mostly a result of other underlying health concerns so onset is more insidious and it is not generally infectious. It is therefore important for the type of mange to be correctly diagnosed from a skin scrape before treatment commences.

Aromatherapy

 Lavender oil is extremely effective at treating symptoms of either variety of mange. It is best used in a vegetable gel available from good suppliers of aromatherapy products, and then spread liberally on affected areas. Used twice over a three-day period, it will improve most cases of mange quite dramatically. In the case of demodectic mange, the stresses that triggered it must be changed as well.

Owners

The commonest cause of disaster is panic: remember ninety per cent of things we worry about never happen. If an accident or problem occurs, take a deep breath and help yourself to four drops of Rescue Remedy to calm the nerves. If feeling weak and shaky some homeopathic Aconite from the first aid kit will settle your fears and then you can make the decisions needed. You'll do your pet no favours if you cannot drive properly and have an accident, or you cannot deal rationally with the problem presented. If an emergency, do remember to call the vet before setting out as s/he may not be at the surgery ready to receive the patient otherwise, and on arrival remember s/he has been trained to treat problems and needs space to do so. The patient will come first in a life-threatening situation and the vet may not be able to attend to the owner's concerns until later.

Pads and Paws

Both the pads and the webs of the feet are prone to injury in the field. Although they bleed profusely, such injuries are rarely a medical emergency. Suturing is often optional and consideration should be given to the risk of sealing in infection. With proper bandaging (see Bandaging) and wound care (see Wounds) most injuries heal in a couple of weeks. Obviously such injuries prevent the dog working while healing, and if the pads are affected such that the protective thick layer has to grow back then care must be taken to prevent further damage until totally restored. Various boots and coverings are available, but in the end time is the greatest healer (an excuse to have more dogs in case one is laid up perhaps?)

Stopper Pads

At the back of your dog's front paws and level with the wrist joint is a large pad known as the 'stopper pad'. It is an exasperating piece of design as its purpose seems to be to add extra braking action and facilitate turning at speed, but it is prone to damage from those very actions. Not only is the stopper well furnished with blood vessels, it has a small bone (accessory carpal) connecting it to the wrist. Cut stoppers don't half bleed, and if that little bone breaks, the dog will be very lame until it heals. There is also a tendon (*flexor carpi ulnaris*)

Stopper pads aid turning at speed

that can be injured in connection with the same dramatic stop or turn that affects the pad and/or bone, though this can be identified by the resulting swelling. I have known stopper pads sliced almost off, where the only option was for the vet to continue the cut and remove the slice completely. Any obvious stopper pad injury that also involves lameness and swelling needs prompt treatment and rest. More trivial injuries that involve a lot of blood but only a graze of the pad generally heal quickly. It is difficult to protect a stopper pad without compromising the use of the wrist, though I have seen protective 'boots' used on whippet, where there is a gap cut out in front. I would not like to use these myself on a dog that needs to do a lot of running rather than the short sprints of the racing whippet because there is the risk of grit or a small stone getting inside the 'boot' and causing damage. A lot of stopper injury is aggravated by conformation or gait, and some dogs go their whole lives without injuring their stoppers, while some seem to carve them up at the slightest hint of rough ground. Flinty land is dreadful for causing stopper injuries, and faster dogs are best kept away from its dangers if possible.

... but sometimes get injured

Poisoning

Unfortunately a dog ingesting poison is an all too common event as they appear to love baited food left around for rats and squirrels, and they seem to crave slug bait which can prove fatal. If your dog does come into contact with these, or even eats a rat or mouse you suspect might have been poisoned, then veterinary attention is certainly needed, and if you have to use poisons, then make sure there is no way that your pet can access them. There are also many other items around the home that we would not commonly view as a poison risk, yet our canine companions are not so discerning. It is well worth considering how you store these, especially when you bring a new pup into the home, as these do love investigating their new world, sometimes a little too enthusiastically.

Some common poisons include:
Anti-freeze
Chocolate
Coconut mulch
Many Detergents and cleaning agents ★★
Fertilisers
Garden insecticides and slug baits★
Grapes, sultanas and raisins
Lead, including older style lead paints
Macadamia nuts
Onions and garlic
Paint, solvents and any petroleum based products ★★
Paracetamol (in excess or if used regularly) and many other human painkillers★
Many Prescription medicines★
Rat and mice baits★
Raw potatoes

Action in the field

If your dog ingests anything you suspect may be poisonous then you have to take whatever action you can to prevent or reduce the amount of poison absorbed into the system, as time is of the essence here. For some poisons this will mean inducing vomiting, while for others it will be diluting or absorbing the chemical. The list above is a very rough guide and those items marked ★ are where inducing vomiting can generally be beneficial, whilst for those marked ★★ it is not advised. Some poisons are best treated by absorbents such as activated charcoal dosed by mouth. Vets will keep this in stock in case of need. Always call the vet to discuss the best course of action in a suspected poisoning. He or she will have the most up to date information on products available, even if s/he has to call the professional poison information services.

When the poison has contaminated the dog by being poured onto it, you need to prevent licking and wash it off as soon as possible. Use large amounts of running water rather than a bath which rapidly becomes contaminated. Shampoos and detergents can be used then rinsed off thoroughly. Detergents are better if the product is petroleum based.

If the eyes have been contaminated, they should be flushed out with large amounts of warm water or saline solution.

Simple home treatments

 Your first aid kit (as designed above) will include some washing soda crystals (note that these are very different from caustic soda, which is poisonous and will kill a dog very painfully if administered). Washing soda cystals are an effective emetic, which means they will make your dog vomit if you place a few crystals on the very back of the tongue. As most poisons are rapidly absorbed from the gut, and certainly quicker than you could get to the vet, it is important to make your pet vomit immediately if it has eaten any of the poisons for which this is appropriate (see above). Remember always to keep some of the vomit, and take the packet of poison with you to the vet if you have it, as most poisons are colour-coded, and your vet will be able to identify the class of the drug from that.

If you don't have washing soda, a solution of mustard powder can also work in many cases. Salt water should not be used to induce vomiting in a dog.

Herbs

After the event, in cases showing nervous symptoms, skullcap and valerian can calm your pet without masking important signs for the vet.

Sylmarin, also known as milk thistle, can be a good liver cleansing and supporting remedy to give your dog once over the initial problem, but seek professional advice on doses for using this herb first. Dose for ten to fourteen days.

Homeopathy

Arsenicum album 30c is the major remedy for poisoning, and should be given three times daily for a few days to all cases, even if they seem all right afterwards.

When to consult your vet

Always, and if there are any chronic symptoms left over then seek the advice also of a holistic vet as there is much they can do to help. Supplements such as vitamin B12 can be useful in such cases.

Post traumatic stress – See section on Anxiety and Shock for useful remedies

Resuscitation – See Choking

Road Traffic Accidents – See Bleeding, Wounds, Fractures and Shock sections

Shooting accidents – See Gunshot wounds and Goring injuries, as well as Anxiety and Shock sections

Snakebites – see Bites

Spinal Injuries – see Fractures

Stings – see Allergies and Stings

Tails

Although tail docking markedly reduces the chances of trauma suffered by breeds such as spaniels, damage can still occur in any dog. Whilst the injuries caused by cuts and tears are obvious, what is often not realised is that muddy conditions and dampness can lead to dermatitis of the tail end. This weakens the skin and allows it to become damaged, often to the point of bleeding, from simple knocks and rubbing.

Once tails have become damaged they can be difficult to get to heal, not

Undocked spaniels at increased risk of tail injuries

least because they are always in use for communicating enthusiasm, and the resulting wound gets easily knocked and re-opened. It is very useful to know how to bandage a tail and this is covered in the detailed section on bandaging.

Action in the field

 If the tail is injured, clean and bandage any wound, carefully clipping away any hair around the wound that may become stuck to it (see Bandaging, Bruising and Wounds).

Homeopathy

 Other than the usual remedies for trauma, one remedy that has proven very useful for the tails that never seem to stop breaking open and bleeding is Erigeron 30c, given twice daily by mouth, whilst at the same time bathing the wound regularly in a lotion made from Arnica, Calendula and Urtica.

When to consult the vet

 Whenever the damaged area fails to heal, or if the tail is broken.

Cold water tail

Limber tail syndrome and 'cold water tail' while known to those who work with hunting dogs, may not be familiar to many vets. This condition is most often seen in working breeds such as English pointers, English setters, foxhounds, beagles, and labrador retrievers. Typically the presentation is a young adult dog with an acutely flaccid tail that hangs down from the tail base or is held horizontally for three to four inches and then drops down. The tail remains in this position even when the dog moves about. Some owners report that the dog seems uncomfortable and painful.

The cause of limber tail is not known although it is thought to be associated with hard workouts (especially in unfit dogs), heavy hunting, and swimming in water that is too cold or too warm. Tail conformation (high set or very active), gender (males more frequently affected), and nutritional factors have also been suggested as possible causes.

Action in the field

 Rest is recommended. Complete recovery is usually seen within two weeks and often within a few days, although the condition can recur in some cases. Warm packs at the base of the tail will help if there is pain and the dog will allow it.

Homeopathy

 Arnica 30c given three times daily seems to be very effective in relieving the problem and in dogs that have had a number of recurrences a course of Arnica for ten days seems to resolve that tendency.

When to consult the vet

 Only if you are worried that the tail might be broken, or if the dog is in pain.

Teeth

In general, dogs fed on a good diet will have healthy teeth and gums throughout most, if not all, of their lives. However, tartar, either from poor diets or caused by health problems, can form on teeth, leading to gum erosion and decay. This affects binding of teeth into the bony jaw and they may become loose. A dog's jaw action is very strong and so loose teeth can become dislodged and even fall out. A loose tooth can be painful and should be pulled out if possible, by grasping firmly and giving a quick tug. Unless the tooth is very loose this will be carried out by the vet under anaesthetic. Abscesses may also form, and these often present as swelling just in front of, and below, the eye (see Abscess section for remedies). As always, prevention of problems is better than cure, and teeth should always be part of the vet's annual health check, so problems can be headed off before they occur. It is always a good idea to get your pet to allow regular examination of the teeth from an early age, and even to allow brushing if you have elected to go for a processed diet. Do not use human toothpaste as these contain chemicals bad for dogs (and people!) if swallowed – special dog toothpaste can be bought from the pet shop.

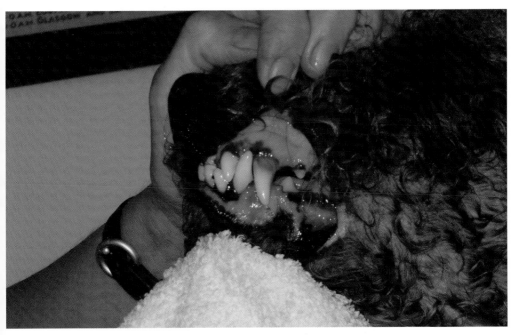

Tartare on canine tooth

Sometimes even healthy teeth can become damaged, and slices of enamel can shear off as a result of chewing stones and other hard objects. So long as only the enamel is affected a problem may not occur, but if you can see the underlying dentine then pain can be an issue and treatment is needed. Terriers are especially prone to losing their incisor teeth as they grip and pull away at tree roots when digging.

Herbs

Chamomile tea is a useful wash for sore or injured gums, and if drunk as well calms and soothes the distressed patient.

There are seaweed-based products which are useful for loosening or reducing the formation of tartar both in humans and dogs.

Homeopathy

Chamomilla 30c is useful for puppies with teething pain, especially if the pup has started chewing anything and everything. Dose twice daily.

Ulmus fulva 6c four times daily is said to ease gum pain and inflammation.

Fragaria 6c helps with problems created by tartar, given especially after dental work at the vet's. Dose daily for one week per month to prevent tartar in susceptible cases with gum recession.

Hepar sulph 30c is useful if abscess formation occurs around a tooth. Dose twice daily.

Merc viv 30c is useful for relieving gingivitis problems: dose twice daily for a few days as needed.

Aromatherapy

Oil of clove, diluted a few drops into a teaspoon of olive oil and then mixed with baking soda into a paste is a useful topical application for gum and tooth injuries. However, it is toxic in large doses and should be used very sparingly; other methods are preferable.

Bach flower remedies

Walnut and vervain are two remedies that can be given together and ease the distress of dental pain. Dose a few drops neat, three times daily.

Rescue Remedy, as ever, is a good standby if nothing else is available.

When to consult your vet

 This has been covered above.

Thorns

Unless these have penetrated the eyeball, try and remove them as soon as possible to prevent them burrowing deeper, setting up abscesses and in severe cases septicaemia. I regard thorns as potentially very serious due to quite a few cases seen at my clinic that have become very sick afterwards, including with joint infections and recurring pyrexia. In any case that shows symptoms of infection after work where a thorn has been seen, even if removed, tell the vet about this so appropriate antibiotics can be used. See also sections on Abscesses and Bite wounds for useful pointers. Thorns from blackthorn and briar can be particularly prone to causing infections, but any thorn penetration should be treated with respect.

Thunder, Lightning and Fireworks

Many dogs will suffer fear of these events, and a surprising number of them can be working dogs who are well used to the gun. Often fear may be specific to one noise type, but in most cases all will cause fright. Tranquillisers have commonly been used, but these do not allow adaptation to the fear and so can make matters worse, therefore being neither a long term solution, or even a desirable one.

Simple home treatments

 Closing the curtains and creating distracting noises such as having the radio or TV on, and playing with your pet, all help.

DAPs are useful in many cases, and can be switched on for stressful periods such as during November and New Year. Start this off a few days before events occur.

Herbs

 Skullcap and valerian can be given as a mild tranquilliser for minor cases. If a noise event can be predicted, such as a major firework display, start treatment several weeks beforehand.

Homeopathy

 The only solution I find reliable is the homeopathic remedy Phosphorous, usually in a 12c potency and given hourly at first, later as needed. The great thing about this remedy is that it seems to work almost instantly, and with time the dog will often adapt to the fears and learn to cope. Many will even eventually need no treatment, or just a single dose on the evening of fireworks, or as a storm approaches.

Bach flower remedies

 Walnut and Mimulus: a few drops given together, neat, is a really useful mix, especially for those cases that anticipate storms coming. It can be given three or four times daily, and can also be given alongside the phosphorous in particularly sensitive cases.

Rock Rose is helpful in severe cases as well.

When to consult your vet

 In severe cases tranquillisers are offered as the only solution, but should be viewed very much as a last resort. Sometimes, however inconvenient or distressing this may be to us, allowing the dog to express its fear is a healthier option, so long as it is in a safe environment.

Ticks

Originally more prevalent in spring and autumn, with the general warming that has occurred over the last few years and the rise in the deer population, ticks have become an almost year-round problem. Working dogs especially are exposed by their task of ferreting around in the undergrowth. Ticks can carry a number of infectious diseases, including the most well known, which is called Lyme disease. Increasingly there is the possibility of overseas diseases appearing in the UK due to the odd notion of pets travelling on holiday, and there have been a number of cases now where dogs have died as a result of infections caught overseas, resulting in many articles in the veterinary press on these 'emerging' diseases in the UK. The strongest insecticides do not seem to prevent this problem entirely, and many of us worry about potential side effects of these. Your vet will be able to advise on the risks of tick-borne diseases in your area and will help you with any preventative topical products you might choose to use.

Action in the field

After each day's work it is well worth checking your dog over for the presence of ticks. Commonly they will be found on the head and chest as these are the areas that get close to the vegetation in which the ticks are hiding, but they can be found almost anywhere including on you. As their saliva anaesthetises the skin where they attach themselves, they do not cause irritation until a bite becomes infected. Ticks feed by sucking blood from the victim into their bodies and so they become more obvious with time as they swell up. If any are found, make sure you check your dog over daily for a few days to pick up the ones you have missed. Any ticks found should be removed and this is done by grasping them firmly, with tweezers, specially designed tools or your fingers, and twisting them anticlockwise until they let go. Once removed clean the wound with either an antiseptic, strong salt water, lavender or tea tree oil or similar, and apply Calendula cream.

The advice for treatment of wounds is worth following if the wound appears raised and red, which can indicate infection (see also Chapter 2).

Homeopathy

Many owners like to give Lyme Disease Nosode 30c once weekly if working a lot in areas where Lyme disease is a risk. A nosode is the remedy made from the disease-causing organism, and the idea is that this primes the immune system to deal with the problem effectively. However, whilst the use of nosodes in illness is established, there is inadequate evidence of their effectiveness in preventing diseases of this type. Perhaps it is better than nothing as conventional medicine has only insecticides to offer. Probably the best idea is to combine conventional and homeopathic approaches.

When to consult your vet

If the wound does appear angry, and you are in a Lyme disease prevalent area, it is worth consulting your vet for antibiotics, as once the illness has a hold it is much harder to treat successfully.

Any dog that shows signs of fever two to three days after a tick bite may have one of the tick-borne diseases and will need professional treatment.

Legal snare

Traps

Traps for vermin can occasionally be found by dogs. They can be just unlucky, or have been attracted by bait used to lure the quarry. Many types of trap are banned in the UK, and there are strict controls on snaring, but with the best will in the world accidents can happen. Few gamekeepers will have traps and snares down when it is known there will be dogs working, but with the right to roam laws having been interpreted by many, incorrectly, as a right to go where they want when they want, it is difficult to prepare for all eventualities.

Action in the field

The key first move must be to release the patient from the trap without you getting injured. It is worth muzzling a dog first as the pain of release can be as bad as being trapped in the first place, and the dog will probably be panicking. Covering the dog's head in a blanket or coat can help calm it. Most traps are based on spring systems, so look for these and press them to release the patient, being careful not to accidentally release the strong springs too soon and cause further damage. Keep your fingers away from the trap mouth and use a stick to hold it open. If there is help to hand, one person should restrain the dog while the other releases the trap.

Snares are typically pegged, and the best way to release the dog is to pull the peg out or cut the wire rather than trying to work at the caught area first as if the dog struggles this will only tighten the noose. Once released the snare will usually loosen on its own as self-locking snares are banned in the UK.

Injuries from snares, if released quickly, will mostly include bruising and wounds (see these sections for treatment advice) but the dog can also be quite severely traumatised, which can affect its working ability (see Anxiety and Shock sections for treatment). All the joints in the affected leg should be checked as a struggling dog can do a fair bit of damage to itself.

Traps can occasionally break bones, and if noses are caught the damage can be quite severe.

When to consult your vet

 I would suggest in all cases, unless snared and released very quickly without much of a struggle.

Travel Sickness

Not all dogs will travel happily in cars, and although for some the problem may be sensitivity to movement or to static electricity, more usually it is a result of fear created by early experiences. Often a puppy's first trip will be to leave its home, or to go to the vet, where it is prodded, poked and injected. This fear and insecurity can last for life, and so it is a good idea to ensure that the breeder has introduced the litter to cars and short journeys as soon as possible in a pup's life; they can then experience the fun of travelling with their littermates and with their mother, thus never developing the problem. If this has not happened then playing with the pup in the car, feeding there, and making lots of short journeys to fun destinations will soon help most dogs adapt. It is worth experimenting by changing the driver, as some people drive more smoothly than others, and trying another car, as a harder or more wallowing suspension can make quite a difference, while some dogs are more sensitive either to petrol or diesel. For those left with a problem the remedies described below can help.

Simple home treatments

 Antistatic strips attached to the bumper of your car will often resolve the problem of the static sensitive pup.

Herbs

Ginger tablets from the health store are a great stabiliser of nausea, and when given fifteen minutes before a journey will help mild cases get over the problem.

Meadowsweet and peppermint tea is useful if your dog will drink it prior to travelling, and it can be taken in the car to give before the journey back to avoid vomiting then.

Homeopathy

All the remedies listed are given fifteen minutes before, and then just before each journey, stopping after a few successful trips.

Argentum nit 30c, for the dog with fear of being shut in, or which gets diarrhoea with the vomiting.

Gelsemium 30c for fear that is anticipatory – the case that won't even get in the car.

Pulsatilla 30c for the case that is better for fresh air, i.e. all right if the windows are down.

Tabacum 30c for the dog that seems collapsed as soon as the car moves, and is even wobbly for a while after stopping the journey.

Cocculus 30c for the dog that vomits if it can see out of the window but is all right if kept on the floor.

Petroleum 30c for dogs that need to keep their head up or else they are sick, and for dogs that are fine in one car, but not another, often worse for diesel engines.

Cocculus and Petroleum 30c in combination is a good place to start if you are unsure.

Aromatherapy

Fennel, ginger and peppermint oils can all be dropped onto some tissue and put in the car with the dog to perfuse the car, calming anxiety and nausea.

When to consult your vet

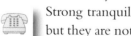

Strong tranquillisers are possible for severe cases for long journeys, but they are not a cure. Some vets will also recommend human anti-seasickness tablets, but generally there is little medically that can be done without side effects leaving the dog unable to work at the end of the journey. Many dogs will grow out of travel sickness at about a year old.

Urticaria – See Allergies and Stings

Vomiting

Though unpleasant to us, it is a perfectly normal part of a dog's system adjusting to minor digestive challenges, so isolated acts of vomiting are not usually anything to worry about, but if blood is seen, if the dog vomits a few times in a day, develops related diarrhoea, or vomits after each meal and after drinking, then attention is needed.

Action in the field

As continual vomiting depletes the body of essential electrolytes, and this is worsened by working, abandon work until the dog is better, and treat the problem.

Simple home treatments

All cases should be starved for 24 hours and then given a bland diet (see Diarrhoea). As before, don't feed an infection.

Pectin, used in jam making, binds to irritant surfaces in the gut and can ease vomiting problems. Give one teaspoon to a labrador and scale up or down accordingly.

Honey is a very good stomach-settler, and if the dog will not lick it off a spoon, is normally readily taken in a sandwich.

Herbs

Aloe vera juice, one teaspoon three times daily for a labrador (scale up or down), reduces nausea and pain. Make sure you use the drinking version only.

Liquorice extract, available from health stores or holistic vets, is a favourite for calming inflammation and promoting healing of the stomach walls.

Chamomile, balm and meadowsweet herbs combined and made into a tea are also extremely useful, and quite palatable to most dogs that will be thirsty after the loss of fluids. Peppermint tea is also a good anti-nausea therapy.

Slippery elm tablets, or powder, made into a paste is a useful therapy for sore stomachs, and can be spooned into the dog's mouth if it won't lick it off a spoon.

Homeopathy

Nux vom 30c is probably the most indicated homeopathic remedy for vomiting dogs. Dose hourly for four doses then three times daily.

Arsenicum alb 30c is indicated if diarrhoea develops as well (see Diarrhoea).

Phosphorous 30c is indicated to help cases that are extremely thirsty, but vomit back water shortly after drinking. Dose hourly for four doses.

Aethusa 30c can be used for puppies upset by a change of milk, such as when offered cows' milk for the first time.

Aromatherapy

Basil, peppermint, melissa and chamomile are all useful remedies here. Add a few drops to a massage oil or gel base and rub gently into the hairless skin of the abdomen to give relief.

When to consult your vet

If blood is seen, if the dog vomits several times in a day, develops a related diarrhoea, or vomits after each meal and after drinking, then attention is needed fairly quickly.

Bloating of the abdomen indicates a medical emergency. All puppies that vomit should also be checked for worms as this is a major cause of problems in young dogs.

Wounds

Whilst a huge subject that could make up a chapter on its own, simple guidance can go a long way to prevention of problems and to ensure good wound healing.

When skin is broken, bacteria and other organisms that inhabit our surroundings can get into the system and cause infection. Creation of wound environments that promote healing, whilst at the same time preventing infection, is the key to this subject and hence the treatments below, some of which are for the wound itself, and others to support and promote the immune system.

Action in the field

Once bleeding has been controlled or stopped (see Bleeding and Bandaging) then cleaning of the wound is the first priority. Simple solutions of salt water (two teaspoons to a pint of water) can be used to flush away dirt. It is often a good idea to trim fur away from the wound edges, but dip the scissors in some olive oil first so the hair sticks to the scissors rather than getting into the wound. If the wound is dirty then a poultice to draw away infection is indicated. An advantage of poultices is that they keep the wound moist, which keeps the skin edges supple and supports their healing across the injury, and they reduce pain by relaxing tension of the underlying tissues.

Bandages can be used to stem bleeding in severe cases, and are also useful to hold on poultices (see Bandaging).

Simple home treatments

POULTICES

Poultices are made by treating the source as detailed below, and then wrapping the result in some linen cloth, before holding onto the wound for ten to fifteen minutes three times daily. If linen cloth is not available, cotton is a good substitute, but it is important to use a natural fibre.

Linseed meal poultice: take ground linseed and sprinkle into boiling water until a thin smooth dough is formed. Allow cooling to bearable warmth before applying.

Bread poultice: A very effective non–irritating poultice made by pouring boiling water onto a few slices of bread. Pour off the water after a few minutes and repeat twice, then mash the bread with a fork into a paste. Note: fresh wholemeal bread made with flour that does not contain soya is the only sort that should be used. Be advised that most shop bread does contain soya unless specifically stated otherwise (as in '100% wholewheat flour').

Carrot poultice: boil organic carrots until they are soft, drain, and mash. Allow cooling to bearable warmth before applying.

In between poultices cover the wound with some ACU ointment, and keep larger wounds covered with dressings/bandages.

Honey is another useful traditional treatment for infected open wounds, and many owners swear by its healing properties. Honey has been shown in some studies (both human and veterinary) to suppress bacterial growth in open wounds, and so yet again Grandmother's wisdom is proven by modern research. Honey can be applied directly to the wound twice daily and covered. If the honey is smeared onto a piece of folded kitchen paper, or even a sanitary towel, it can be bandaged over more easily. Some swear by its ability to stop the bleeding of torn claws and ears. However, its downside is that the stickiness makes cleaning the wound an issue, especially with hairy dogs. If the dog can reach the wound, it will usually lick the honey off afterwards, which will clean the hair as well as giving it some honey internally.

Herbs

 Echinacea may be given to support the immune system. I prefer the liquid extract obtainable from health shops, given at the human dose, but scaled according to your dog's bodyweight. Note that for most calculations a human dose is based on a 70 kg female adult, as they spend more on health supplements than men.

Garlic ointment can be used to cover dirty wounds, being antiseptic and antibacterial. As a general rule ointments are better than creams for open wounds as they maintain a moist environment suitable for encouraging healing.

Comfrey, marigold and marshmallow made as a tea and then applied in a compress three times daily are soothing and healing to painful wounds.

Astragalus root, taken internally, stimulates the immune system, and can be of use in chronically infected wounds. This is obtained from Chinese herbal medicine shops.

Homeopathy

ACU lotion, added one teaspoon to a pint of water, can be used to cleanse a wound initially, and also as a general cleanser for long term management of dirty injuries, as well as other wounds between dressings and treatments. It is better than salt water for the latter as the salt can be too drying with repeated use.

Calendula and Hypericum ointment applied twice a day once a wound is clean rapidly promotes healing over of the wound, and has the added advantage of reducing the pain and itching of healing. Never apply this to a dirty wound as it works so fast that infection can be sealed in.

Arnica 30c should be given to all cases to reduce swelling and bruising. Dose two or three times daily.

Phosphorous 30c is good for stopping oozing of fresh blood from fresh wounds. Give twice in one hour.

Staphysagria 200c is excellent for the pain and distress of stitched wounds, where the dog becomes focused on removing the sutures. Dose twice in one day.

Hypericum 30c will relieve the pain of crushing injuries, and is useful in wounds affecting any area, but especially the toes. Dose twice daily.

Hepar sulph 6c can be given three times daily if the area is very painful to touch and the wound is dirty, with infection that needs to be encouraged to discharge.

Hepar sulph 30c is useful once the pus has discharged in assisting with clearing up any infection, given three times daily.

Silica 6c helps clear up wounds where there is infection, and also foreign bodies, such as road grit. Often given with the Hepar sulph.

Aromatherapy

 Eucalyptus, frankincense and lavender are all useful oils and can be dropped into a little water, then soaked into a flannel or gamgee, and applied frequently for ten to fifteen minutes a time as a compress.

Tea tree oil can be diluted in water and used as a wash to cleanse wounds.

Bach flower remedies

 Star of Bethlehem will calm a dog that refuses to allow wounds to be treated. Give a few drops before attending to the wound.

Other treatments

 Large wounds do seem to respond well to magnetic therapy. This is now more commonly used by people for their own health, and so a suitable soft flat magnet may be bought from health shops and similar outlets. If placed over a wound, often bound into the dressing, healing seems to be quicker and less painful.

Lasers are also extremely good at getting non-healing ulcers and extensive wounds to heal, and you may know someone who has one available. For wounds one uses an adaptation of the acupuncture method known as 'circling the dragon'. The laser light is slowly scanned around the edges of the wound twice daily to encourage the skin cells to grow across the gap and form new skin. Obviously protective eyewear should be worn, and you must avoid shining the laser towards the dog's eyes.

When to consult your vet

 Major wounds will need veterinary attention and possibly stitching or bandaging. Minor injuries are often treatable at home. However, if you have any doubts over which course of action to take, the answer is that you should be contacting your vet. He or she is the professional trained to deal with whatever problems have arisen, so do not delay in seeking advice. Above all, never leave an animal in distress.

USEFUL WEBSITES AND ADDRESSES

Please note that addresses and telephone numbers may change

Mark and Jackie's website www.working-dog.co.uk
Mark's practice website www.homeopathicvet.co.uk

Ainsworth's Homeopathic Pharmacy
36 New Cavendish Street
London W1M 7LH
Tel. 0207 935 5330
www.ainsworths.com

Association of British Veterinary
Acupuncturists
www.abva.co.uk

British Association of Homeopathic
Veterinary Surgeons
Faringdon
Oxon
Tel. 01367 710234
http://www.bahvs.com/vetmfhom.htm

Canine Health Concern
Box 6943
Forfar
Angus DD8 3WG

Canine Natural Cures (for Thornit)
49 Beaumont Road
Surrey CR8 2EJ
Tel. 020 8668 8011

Dorwest Herbs Ltd
Shipton Gorge
Bridport
Dorset DT6 4LP
Tel. 01308 897272
info@dorwest.co.uk

Fragrant Earth (for aromatherapy oils etc.)
Glastonbury
Somerset BA6 9EW
Tel. 01458 831216
www.fragrant-earth.co.uk

Freemans Homeopathic Pharmacy
18-20 Main Street
Busby
Glasgow
G76 8DU
Tel. 0845 22 55155
www.freemans.uk.com

Global Herbs Ltd.
Tamarisk House
12 Kingsham Ave
Chichester
West Susssex PO19 2AN
Tel. 01243 773363
herbsvet@aol.com
globalherbs.co.uk

Helios Homeopathy
89-97 Camden Road
Tunbridge Wells
Kent
TN1 2QR
Tel. 01308 897272
www.helios.co.uk

Natural Touch Aromatherapy
Holton House
Mayles Lane
Wickham
Hants PO17 5ND
Tel. 01329 835550
sales@aromatherapyonline.uk.com

Pet Nutrition Concepts Ltd
22a East Street
Westbourne
Emsworth
West Sussex
Tel. 01243 370123
www.petnutrition.co.uk

FURTHER READING

Billinghurst, Ian

Give your Dog a Bone
Grow your Pups with Bones

Available in the UK from Canine Natural Cures
(see Useful Addresses).

Elliot, Mark and Pinkus, Tony

Dogs and Homeopathy, The Owner's Companion

Available from homeopathicvet.co.uk
www.working-dog.co.uk (as above)

Lawless, Julia

The Encyclopaedia of Essential Oils
Published 1992 by Element Books Ltd
Longmead, Shaftesbury, Dorset

Levi, Juliette de Bairacli

The Illustrated Herbal Handbook
Published 1974 by Faber and Faber Ltd
3 Queen Square
London WC1

The Complete Herbal Handbook for the Dog and Cat
Published 1955 as above

INDEX